IN SEARCH OF YOUR ROOTS

ANGUS BAXTER

IN SEARCH OF YOUR ROOTS

A GUIDE FOR CANADIANS SEEKING THEIR ANCESTORS

REVISED AND UPDATED

MACMILLAN OF CANADA
A DIVISION OF CANADA PUBLISHING CORPORATION
TORONTO, ONTARIO, CANADA

Canadian Cataloguing in Publication Data

Baxter, Angus, 1912 –
    In search of your roots

Includes index.
Bibliography: p.
ISBN 0-7715-9866-1

1. Genealogy. 2. Canada—Genealogy. I. Title.

CS16.B39 1983   929′.371   C83-098966-8

Originally published 1978 in hardcover by The Macmillan
    Company of Canada under ISBN 0-7705-1577-0
First paperback edition 1980

Reprinted 1981 by Macmillan of Canada, A Division of
    Gage Publishing Limited
Revised and reprinted 1984
Reprinted 1986

Printed in Canada

FOR NAN
My life, my love, my wife

CONTENTS

ACKNOWLEDGEMENTS

A great many people across Canada have helped me with information for this book – several hundred, holding no official position, wrote to me as the result of a letter of mine in most daily newspapers. There are too many to list – but this does not mean I do not appreciate their kindness and help. It is good to know there is such widespread interest in our personal and national history.

I have been helped, too, by many people in official positions – in many cases over and above what could be expected:

First, the Archivists of all the provinces and, in particular, Leonard DeLozier (British Columbia), Richard Ramsay (New Brunswick), Burnham Gill (Newfoundland), and the late Bruce Fergusson (Nova Scotia).

Second, the Archivists of the various Churches, and these include Marion Beyca (Anglican), Joan Oliphant and David Drake (Baptist), D'Arcy Hande (Lutheran), Lawrence Klippenstein and Samuel Steiner (Mennonite), Kip Sperry (Mormon), Glen Lucas (United), and Rabbi Malcolm Stern and Stephen Speisman (Jewish).

Third, the various librarians across the country, including several particularly helpful ones – Shelagh Jameson (Glenbow–Alberta Institute), Ronald LeBlanc (Université de Moncton), Elizabeth Spicer (London, Ontario), Ruth Vukadinov (Windsor, Ontario), and Daniel Olivier (Salle Gagnon, Montréal).

Fourth, the various custodians of the Vital Statistics of all the provinces, and in particular, J. F. MacAleer (Prince Edward Island).

Fifth, the various officials of some forty foreign governments who supplied me with detailed information about their records.

Sixth, I must acknowledge my deep gratitude to Quebec's leading genealogist, Raymond Gingras, for supplying me with a wealth of information about genealogical records in his province.

Seventh, I must say "Thank you" to Robert Gordon, Director, Manuscripts, Public Archives of Canada, for his kind cooperation in providing me with full information about the holdings of the PAC and, over and above this, the details of the fabulous Likacheff-Ragosine-Mathers collection, described on page 6 and set out for the first time in any book on genealogy.

To all of the above, my gratitude and my hope they will find this book useful.

Finally, my thanks to my wife, who read each chapter as it came off the typewriter, and helped immeasurably with wise comments and sound advice.

When a society or civilization perishes,
one condition can always be found.
They forgot where they came from.
CARL SANDBURG

IN SEARCH OF YOUR ROOTS

1. AN INTRODUCTION TO ANCESTOR-HUNTING

We are a nation of immigrants. We – and our forebears – came to Canada to build a new life for our families. First came the French, bringing civilization to the wilderness, then the British settlers and soldiers, the Irish fleeing the potato famines of the early 1800s, the Ukrainians searching for the freedom denied them in Czarist Russia, the Scandinavian and Icelandic settlers farming the Prairies, the Finns logging the northern forests, the Chinese building the railroads, the Jews fleeing the pogroms and ghettoes and persecution of Europe – these men and women and others from a dozen different countries built the Canada we know today. Since the Second World War waves of immigrants have come from Europe, Asia, Africa, the Caribbean, and South America.

Now we are all Canadians, but we still have family and sociological ties with the countries from which we came. We have learned it is possible to be loyal Canadians without forgetting the history and culture of our own people. That is why more and more Canadians want to find out about their forebears – to learn about their past, their family history, without losing a moment of the exciting present and the unlimited future.

Of course, there are other reasons for this interest – the hope of finding a title in the family, the belief there is a vast sum of unclaimed money waiting to be collected. If these are your reasons, forget them. The odds against finding you are descended from a duke are so great they are not worth considering. As to the family fortune – nearly every family can produce one of these vague and mysterious tales but I have never known of a case where this particular dream came true.

Canada is still a new country and most of us have been too busy making a living to bother about what is often regarded as a frill. But now our children are looking for roots. It is not enough for us to say "Your grandfather came from Scotland (or from Italy, or from France)." We need to know from exactly where in these countries. We need to know the house he lived in, the clothes he wore, the work he did – a knowledge of all these things is possible as we start to grow our family tree.

"A family tree" – what exactly is it? It is a chart which you gradually extend as your ancestor-hunt continues. It starts at the bottom of the sheet with *you* and it goes back through your parents, your grandparents, and far beyond, until you can go no further. You will find examples of family trees in this book.

Before we start talking about what you do to grow the tree, let us speak for a few minutes about what you do *not* do:

1) You do not take the name of a famous person of two or three hundred years ago, a name the same as yours, and try and trace his or her descendants down to you. This is just not possible. Maybe, by some faint chance, he or she is an ancestor of yours, but the only way you will find out for certain is by tracing back from *you*.

2) Do not assume that everyone with the same surname as yours must be a relative. No one had surnames before about 1200. When a growing population made it necessary to distinguish between one person and another, the surname created was either occupational, geographical, or personal.

> i.e. John the baker became John Baker
> John, who lived in the green wood,
>   became John Greenwood
> John, the son of Harry,
>   became John Harry's son, or Harrison

There were many Johns whose father was named Harry, and many Johns who lived in a green wood, and many Johns who were bakers. Their surnames were duplicated ten thousand times and they were not related in any way.

3) Do not fall for advertisements which promise you a family tree and a coat-of-arms if you mail in $5 or $10. What you will get for your money will be a few paragraphs telling you about the origin of your name, a list of a few well-known people in history with the same surname (suggesting in some vague way you are descended from them), and a drawing of a coat-of-arms granted hundreds of years ago to someone with the same name and to which you have no right whatever.

4) Do not think that by writing to the National Archives in Ottawa, or to St. Catherine's House in London, or to Archivio Centrale della Stato in Rome, or to the Central Bureau voor Genealogie in the Hague, some magician is going to produce a family tree for you. No one can provide you with a family tree except *you* (or someone working for you).

5) Do not accept without question any story within your family about its place of origin. Many of these stories are true and can be a great help, but just as many have no basis in fact. So you must believe nothing until you can prove it is true.

6) Do not try and trace more than one side of your family at one time. If you try to trace your father's family (on both sides) and your mother's family (on both sides) at the same time you will find yourself floundering about in four different families and getting thoroughly confused. If you stick with one branch you will eventually memorize names and dates and places, and the people you find will become real persons to you. When you have finished one side, or come to a dead-end, then by all means start on a second side.

7) The cost of certificates of birth (or baptism), marriage, or death vary from province to province and from country to country. Unfortunately, too, world-wide inflation means that any specific information I give will be out of date very quickly. Generally speaking, you may assume that a certificate will cost between $5 and $10 in this country, and between $10 and $25 overseas.

8) Although it is much more rewarding to search for your genealogical roots yourself, there is a commercial organization which undertakes research in Canada and overseas for a reasonable charge. The Genealogical Research Library, 520 Wellington Street, London, Ontario N6A 3P9, is particularly strong in its records of Polish and Hungarian genealogy. You may want to use this organization as a supplement to your own research.

Is it easy to trace your ancestors? Is it a difficult and time-consuming job? Will you get back very far? There is no real answer to these questions. Availability of records will vary from country to country, and from one town to another. The answers also depend on how much information you have about your family when you start. It is not easy, but it is rarely impossible. You may only get back a hundred years, or you may go back five hundred – you won't know how far until you try.

So, if you have patience and determination this book will tell you how to start your search – in Canada, the United States, the United Kingdom, all European countries, and several others. Now turn the page to start growing your family tree.

2. THE PUBLIC ARCHIVES OF CANADA

This vast repository, known familiarly as PAC, is located at 395 Wellington Street, Ottawa, and its holdings grow almost hourly. No one with Canadian roots can go far without using this great source of information. What's more, ancestor-hunters are *welcomed* at the Public Archives!

In addition to its collection of public records, it holds private correspondence, family trees, histories, family Bibles and albums, diaries, recorded family histories, passports, and birth, marriage, and death certificates. You will find it fascinating to skim through the family records of the famous and the unknown – politicians and pioneers, writers and farmers, parsons and felons, sailors and steelworkers – the people who made us and made this nation.

It is not possible to list all available records at the PAC, but I give below a brief list of those I consider most important to the ancestor-hunter at the *start* of his or her search. If you eventually do more detailed research, you will want to explore the Public Archives more thoroughly.

Parish Registers: These are shown in the section of the book dealing with church records. You will find Wills and Censuses and Land Grants mentioned in other places.

Marriage Bonds: These exist for Quebec for 1779 and 1818-67, and for Ontario from 1803 to 1845. They are indexed.

Prison Records: People often "did time" for very trivial offences, and these records are covered for Quebec from 1800 to 1867, and for Ontario from 1823 to 1861.

Cemetery Lists: The PAC has some lists for scattered locations in Ontario and Quebec dated about the middle of the last century. These are indexed.

Passenger Lists: The *Quebec Gazette*, indexed from 1764 to 1825, shows lists of arrivals, but, unfortunately, steerage passengers were not detailed, and many immigrants came to Canada in this way. Lists of assisted emigrants from the U.K. between 1817 and 1831 are on microfilm and are indexed. There are some other nominal passenger lists on record, but they are few and far between.

Port of Entry Records: There are lists of these for Quebec from 1865 to 1900 and for Halifax from 1881 to 1899, with unfortunate gaps. You will need to know the names of the passengers and the ports of entry.

Quarantine Records: Scattered records exist for the period of the early 1800s.

Naturalization Records: British subjects were automatically Canadian citizens on settlement. Immigrants from other countries had to be naturalized, and records exist for the years 1828-50 in the PAC. Those from 1865 are with the Citizenship Registration Branch of the Secretary of State, and are indexed. It is not known what happened to the records for the period 1850-65.

Passports: The first passports were issued by local mayors or reeves. In 1862 special local agents were appointed for this purpose, and from 1867 the passports were issued by the Secretary of State. From 1882 to 1895 the provinces took over the task, and then it went back again to the Secretary of State until 1909. After then passports were issued – as they still are – by the Department of External Affairs. Records exist from 1862 to 1882 and from 1894 to 1937 in the PAC. Some of the records between 1882 and 1894 may be in the various Provincial Archives.

Military Records: These cover the South African (Boer) War at the turn of the century, and later wars. Militia units of the period, which included the War of 1812, the Rebellion of 1837, and the Fenian invasions, did not keep their records of enlistment. However, there are some Muster Rolls and Pay Lists in the PAC. First and Second World War and Korean War service records are also in the PAC. They are not open to public search but individual queries will be answered if a relationship can be proved.

There is also a great deal of information in the PAC about military land grants, bounty awards, and pensions.

School Records: Many public school records from Quebec and Ontario are in the PAC. They go back as far as 1768 for Quebec and 1841 for Ontario, and continue up to the middle of the last century.

I have saved the most dramatic development at the Public Archives for the end. It is rare nowadays for a vast new source of genealogical information to be discovered, but thanks in the main to Robert Gordon, Director of the Manuscript Division, this has happened in North America.

For years there were rumours that a great hoard of genealogical material existed in Washington, consisting of the records of the Tsarist Russian Consuls in Montreal, Halifax, and Vancouver. It was known to have disappeared in 1917 – the year of the Russian Revolution – and was thought to have been sent to Russian consulates in the United States, which did not recognize the government of the U.S.S.R. until 1933.

In 1980 a PAC search team, headed by Robert Gordon and "acting on information received", found the records in an underground vault in Washington. The name and location of the particular repository cannot be revealed, because it contains other confidential records (not applicable to Canada). This is real cloak-and-dagger stuff!

The collection of documents covers the period 1900-22 and was compiled by Serge Likacheff, Consul in Montreal, Harry Mathers, Vice-Consul in Halifax, and Constantine Ragosine, Consul in Vancouver. It cannot be described as a collection of Russian consular records since from 1917 the three individuals kept the lists up to date in an unofficial capacity, and were immigration agents rather than consuls. After the Revolution the three men lost their jobs. In 1922 the Soviet government asked our own government to return all records from the three offices, but no trace could be found of them at the time. The LiRaMa Collection, as it is known, was only given to the PAC by the United States government after some persuading.

Although the official period covered by the documents is 1900-22, many records in the collection date back to the 1850s, and some of the information recorded dates back to the early 1800s.

The collection relates to people who came from the area covered by the old Russian Empire before 1917. In modern ethnic terms they include Jews, Ukrainians, Russians, Finns, Poles, Byelorussians, Lithuanians, Latvians, Estonians, Armenians, Doukhobors, Germans (Mennonites), Georgians, Cossacks, and several other minority groups.

Some idea of the extraordinary size and nature of the LiRaMa Collection can be got from a general list of its contents:

1) About one hundred thousand registration forms containing names, places and dates of birth, nationality, ethnic origin, religion, occupation, names and places of residence of next of kin, places and lengths of residence in Canada, signatures, and other related information.
2) About one hundred and fifty thousand photographs.
3) Cancelled passports and other travel documents.
4) Birth certificates, identity cards, war service records, affidavits, school records, estate records and wills, nationality certificates, work permits, and correspondence with the consular offices and relatives.

Because of the personal and confidential nature of the files, access will be restricted to persons who are related to the immigrants recorded in the collection. All the records will also be microfilmed to protect the originals. If you are descended from any of the immigrants included in the records, you may find a rich source of information about your ancestors.

One small story will illustrate what could result from this valuable genealogical find. One of the staff at the PAC who was helping to sort the collection, knowing of his family's East European background, asked permission to search for a file in the family name. He found it, and opened the file to see family photographs showing his great-grandfather, his grandfather, and their brothers and sisters, as well as other important documents and certificates. All of a sudden his family history was before him.

3. STARTING THE FAMILY TREE

So, what *do* you do? You take a large sheet of paper and, in pencil, near the bottom, you write down *your* name and those of your brothers and sisters, if any. These should be in order of age, from left to right, starting with the eldest. I am going to use as an example an entirely imaginary JOHN SMITH whose family came from England, but he could just as well be Jean Leduc from France, or Otto Schmidt from Germany, or Nils Larsen from Norway.

When you have your name and those of your brothers and sisters down, add the dates and places of birth:

JOHN	WILLIAM	MARY
Born: 8 June 1920	Born: 13 January 1922	Born: 2 February 1924
Toronto	Toronto	Toronto

Now you join the three of you together:

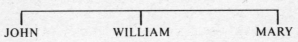

JOHN	WILLIAM	MARY

Next, you write in the same information about your father and mother (i.e., date and place of birth and also of marriage and death). Your family tree now begins to grow:

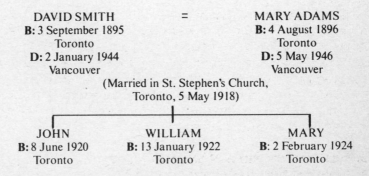

DAVID SMITH	=	MARY ADAMS
B: 3 September 1895		B: 4 August 1896
Toronto		Toronto
D: 2 January 1944		D: 5 May 1946
Vancouver		Vancouver

(Married in St. Stephen's Church, Toronto, 5 May 1918)

JOHN	WILLIAM	MARY
B: 8 June 1920	B: 13 January 1922	B: 2 February 1924
Toronto	Toronto	Toronto

You are now going to have to find out about your grandparents and other relatives. You also want to know where the family came from. Don't keep the project to yourself; talk to your brothers and sisters, talk to aunts and uncles, talk to old family friends; look up any old family papers, or photographs lying around in desk drawers or old trunks. At this point try and get information from three possible sources within your family.

FAMILY STORIES

As I have mentioned, these can be invaluable but must be treated with caution until they are proved; otherwise you may start off in the wrong direction.

Let me give you an example. Thirty years ago, in England, as a beginner in genealogy (the fancy name for ancestor-hunting), I started to trace my Baxter ancestors. I had no information to go on, except for the dates of birth and death of my father and the name of my grandfather. However, I found a very distant woman relative who told me the Baxters originally came from a place called TARBERT. She seemed quite definite about this and I accepted it without question.

So I went there and searched the church registers and read local histories in the library and enquired about wills. I could find no mention anywhere of anyone called Baxter – not for two hundred years. After several months of searching and of writing to various people, I decided the information was not true and all I had done was to waste time and money.

I then started off again in a more methodical way and after a couple of years was able to trace my family back in Lancashire and Westmorland – two counties in the north of England – as far as 1362. In the course of doing this I found that some hundred years ago they had owned a farm in Westmorland called TALBERT. So you see, the story had a very slight basis of truth, but also enough error to put me on the wrong path. So, with family stories be sure you check – and re-check.

OLD RELATIVES

If you do not know much about your family, try and find your oldest relative – it may be like finding a water-course in the middle of the Sahara. Hopefully, it will be a woman, because women are more interested in families than men. If you can visit this relative, so much the better. Take along a notebook, or a tape recorder, and a prepared set of questions – something on the following lines:
 1. Where was my grandfather born?
 2. When?
 3. What were the names of his parents?
 4. When and where did they get married?
 5. Did my grandfather have any brothers and sisters?
 6. Were they older or younger than he?
 7. What else do you know about them?

8. Did they have children?

9. Do you know where they are?

10. What was my grandfather's religion? (Remember that people change their religion, often as a result of marriage.)

11. Do you know if he left a will when he died?

12. What else can you tell me about the family?

13. Is there a family Bible anywhere?

14. Do you have any old family papers I can see?

There are other questions which may occur to you – depending on the size of your family and your knowledge of it.

When you are asking questions of your relatives you must be prepared for a mixed reception – not everyone is interested in finding out about their family. Some people may actively object to your searches. Sometimes people are afraid of what they may discover – perhaps an illegitimate child or someone with a criminal record. It seems incredible to me that anyone should be bothered by this. I could not care less whether my grandfather was a bastard who served time for theft.

In actual fact, you will rarely discover very much about the character of your ancestors. You will find out when they were born, got married, had children, and died, but – unless there was a story in the local newspaper, or in a local history book – you will never know whether they were angels or rogues.

You may also meet with suspicion – someone may think you have found a vast sum of unclaimed money and are trying to get your hot little hands on it! So be prepared to be patient and tactful.

Sometimes a will gives you some insight into an ancestor's thoughts at the time – like a forebear of my wife's back in 1685 who left a long will detailing quite large sums of money, and estates, and possessions, to be given to his sons and "my dear daughter, Elizabeth, wife of William Talentire, Esquire", and then ended the long list with the words "to my daughter Jane, wife of John Sharp, the sum of five shillings."

I wonder what family unhappiness and feuding is hidden behind those words?

FAMILY BIBLES

Up until about 1850 in most countries, one of the wedding presents was a Bible, and the new husband, and potential father, would start his own family record – either on the inside front cover, the flyleaf, or on a blank page between the Old and New Testaments. He would start out with his own marriage and the date and place and then add his children as they were born.

If you have one of these Bibles, first check the date of publication. If you find the first entry is dated very shortly after this you will know the entries were made as the events happened. If there are family dates which are *before* the date of publication you will know they were entered from memory at a later date, and therefore may be hearsay.

Now let us revert to the questions I listed above, and let us assume you have an old aunt who is the widow of your father's elder brother, William. You go and see her and she gives you the following answers to your questions: ·

1. *Where was my grandfather born?*
   I never knew much about him. He never got on with my husband. I know his name was John and he was a farmer near Lakefield. He died in 1925.
2. *When was he born?*
   I don't know but he must have been about fifty-five or fifty-six when he died.
3. *What were the names of his parents?*
   I never knew that.
4. *Do you know where his parents got married?*
   No.
5. *Did my grandfather have any brothers or sisters?*
   He must have had a brother, because I heard my husband talk about an Uncle Bill, who farmed in Alberta. Maybe, though, it was an uncle on his mother's side. I never heard of anyone else.
6. *Was this Uncle Bill older or younger than my grandfather?*
   Don't know.
7. *What else do you know about him?*
   Oh, I remember now. Bill, in Alberta, was a brother of your grandfather's, because in 1925, when he died, Bill came east for the funeral.
8. *Did he have any children?*
   I never heard of any.
9. *If there were any, where in Alberta would they be?*
   I don't know.
10. *What was my grandfather's religion?* _
    He was an Anglican; they all were.
11. *Do you know if he left a will when he died?*
    No, he didn't. His wife died before him, and there were just the two boys, my husband and your father. Some lawyer in Peterborough sold the farm and the money was divided between the two of them.
12. *What else can you tell me about the family?*
    Well, they were all hard-working, I can tell you that. Farmers from way back. My husband always said they came from England to Canada, but I don't know how far back.
13. *Is there a family Bible anywhere?*
    There used to be one around but it's gone now.
14. *Do you have any old family papers I can see?*
    No, I threw everything out a few years ago when I sold the

house and moved into this apartment. There didn't seem to be anything worth keeping.

Be sure you take clear notes as you search for your ancestors. You may have a wonderful memory but you are going to collect a mass of names and places and dates and you will need to write it all down.

As the result of your meeting with your old aunt you now have some information about your grandfather and can add to the family tree.

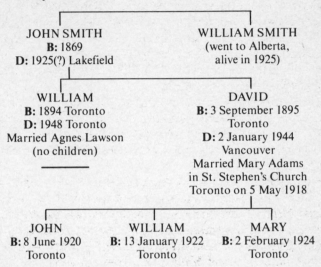

At this point, you are concentrating on your grandfather. You know that, *according to your aunt*, he died in 1925 in Lakefield and was aged fifty-six. That means he was born in about 1869. You must confirm this information – it may not be right. You then write or visit the office of the Registrar General of Ontario, at the Parliament Buildings in Toronto.

This is as good a time as any to talk about this man and his office. He is a civil servant appointed by the provincial government to keep the *Vital Statistics* as they are called (i.e., records of births, marriages, and deaths). Each province in Canada has such a civil servant and the same records, but sometimes he is called a *Registrar*, or a *Director*, or a *Recorder*.

The date on which these records start varies from province to province and you will find full information about these dates in the chapters on the various provinces. In Ontario, for example, the records started on 1 July 1869, and have been kept continuously since then. In Nova Scotia, however, they started in 1865 but, for some quite extraordinary reason, were discontinued until 1908 (except for records of marriages). Before these records were kept by the government the various churches maintained registers of baptism, marriage, and burial. There will be more about these later.

At the office of the Registrar General you will fill out application forms for the information you need – or, if you are unable to go there, you write for the forms. You will need two forms for the information you want about your grandfather, and you will have to explain why you want it. The reason you give is, of course, "tracing my ancestors" or "genealogical research" – whichever you prefer.

One form is for you to find out about his exact date of birth. So you tick the space marked "Birth" and write in the name of your grandfather – JOHN SMITH – stating he is believed to have been born in 1869. The other form is for you to find out his exact date of death. So you tick the space marked "Death" and state he died in Lakefield in 1925. You will receive an extract of the original certificate.

I have already mentioned that registration started on different dates in the different provinces. Remember, the starting date in Ontario was 1 July 1869, and that was the year of your grandfather's birth, you think. So you must hope he was born after that date.

Let us assume, then, you have mailed off the forms. In about a month you will hear back. In this case, let us pretend you have had both good news and bad news. The good news is that you get your grandfather's death extract, and you now know he died in Lakefield on 18 January 1925. It should also give date and place of birth and names of parents (if this information was known by the person who gave the original information about his death). However, the bad news is that there is no trace of his birth in 1869 (from 1 July onwards when registration started). In fact, there is no trace of him during the next four years. If the office cannot trace an entry in the year you give they will automatically search two years before and two years after – in this case four years after as registration only started in 1869.

This means one of three things: he was born before registration started, or his birth was not registered, or your aunt's information was not correct.

You can have a search made for the event in the next five years, or you can move into the area of church records. Before civil registration started our only records of birth, marriage, and death are in the registers of the churches – Anglican, Catholic, and to a lesser degree the various nonconformist sects. The latter were restricted for many years as to the functions at which their clergy could officiate. The records, of course, referred to baptisms, marriages, and burials. Baptismal records sometimes also show the actual date of birth in brackets, but not always. By and large a child was baptized on the first Sunday after its birth – although if a child was ill this did not always apply. Burials usually occurred within a few days of death and the burial records usually show the date of death, and very often the cause.

The further back we go in time in Canada the more difficult the tracing of these records becomes, and the records themselves become more and more unreliable. If we are trying to trace the registers of a particular church we may find them in the church itself; in the Public Archives in Ottawa; in the Provincial Archives; in the local library; or in private hands.

In England and Wales it is now compulsory for parish churches to deposit registers which are over one hundred years old with the County Record Office or some other approved archive, such as the Borthwick Institute in York, the Bodleian Library in Oxford, or the National Library of Wales in Aberystwyth. Also, more and more registers in the County Record Offices are being microfilmed and indexed. In Scotland, all the parish registers up to 1855 are in the New Register House in Edinburgh. In Canada, we still have to learn to store this information safely and efficiently.

Another invaluable record is that of tombstones. It is not always easy to decipher the earlier ones – depending on what local stone was used and how much care has been taken of the burial ground. In pioneer days it was often customary for several farming families to bury their dead in their own graveyard, located where several farm boundaries met. These graveyards are scattered throughout the various provinces and are usually in very bad condition – the exceptions are in places where descendants of the dead settlers are still living in the area, or where a local church group has assumed responsibility for the upkeep.

A recent trend has been for local branches of the provincial Genealogical Society to copy the wording on the tombstones, index and map the location of graves, and deposit the information in either the Society library or the local public library. All over Canada today a few historically-minded men and women are doing this thankless and unpaid work in their spare time.

In older countries overseas tombstones can be found dating back to the sixteenth century and earlier, and you will often find a surprising amount of information – not only the name of the ancestor in whom you are interested but also, in many cases, his date and place of birth, the maiden name of his wife, and the names of brothers and sisters and children. In those days families stayed together even in the grave.

In public interdenominational cemeteries it is also wise to check the record books in the cemetery office. Often you will find additional information – such as the name of the person authorizing the burial or paying for the tombstone. This can often give you a lead to an unknown child or brother or sister. Sometimes you will find an address, and this information can be of great value.

I remember, on one occasion, when I was tracing ancestors for a client in Toronto, I found an address in the records of the Necropolis Burial Ground on Parliament Street. From there I went to the public library and looked up the city directory of that year. Then I worked back, year by year (the earliest directory was 1818), and got a clear picture of where the particular man lived and what his occupation was. His earliest address was near a church on King Street. I took a chance that he might have been associated with that church and searched the tombstones and the church records. This filled in gaps in the family history, provided me with the names of his brothers and sisters, and — most valuable of all — gave me the place of birth of his father, in Ireland.

With all this knowledge about the importance of church records in mind you write to the rector of the Anglican Church in Lakefield and ask him if he can find the following information for you:

1. John Smith's baptism or birth between 1 January and 1 July 1869 (you are assuming here that he was born in Lakefield, but he may very well not have been).
2. Any information about his marriage in the period from 1892 to 1894 (you know his eldest son was born in 1894).

There is no set scale of fees for a search of church records, but a donation to church funds of two or three dollars for a short search is always welcome.

In this particular case, let us pretend you are in luck. You hear that JOHN SMITH was born in Lakefield on 4 April 1869, the son of WILLIAM SMITH and ANN SMITH (maiden name TODD). You also hear that he was married on 22 June 1892, in Lakefield, to JANE ADAMSON, of the same parish. His age is given as twenty-three and hers as twenty. His address at the time of his birth and his marriage was given as Lake Farm, Lakefield. Now you know the Smiths occupied that farm at least from 1869 to 1892.

What do you do now? You know all you need to know about your grandfather, so you concentrate on your great-grandfather William. You now know he was WILLIAM SMITH, married to ANN TODD some time before 1869.

At this stage a visit to Lakefield and a personal search of the registers and the graveyard seem worth while. Of course, if you can't get there this can be done by correspondence with the rector.

You search the registers and you find several very interesting items:

1. WILLIAM SMITH married ANN TODD on 10 August 1867. His age was twenty-two and so was hers. His parents are shown as DAVID and ELIZABETH SMITH of Keynsham, England!
2. Their first child was DAVID and he was born on 6 June 1868.
3. The second child was your grandfather, JOHN.
4. There were four other children – MARGARET (1871), ANN (1872), ANN (1873), and WILLIAM (1874).

Don't be confused by the fact you have found two children named Ann. This often happened when the first child with the name died. A hundred years ago infant mortality was very high. Whenever you find a birth, always check for the death of the child – usually within weeks, months, or three or four years.

In the church graveyard you find a number of old graves – some of them impossible to decipher because the soft stone has been worn away by weather over the last hundred years.

However, you are in luck again, and you find a tombstone with the following names on it:

WILLIAM SMITH

died 16 August 1897, aged 52 years

ANN SMITH, his wife

died 10 September 1897, aged 52 years

and their son DAVID

died 10 July 1872, aged 4 years

and their daughter ANN

died 18 September 1872, aged 4 months

and their daughter MARGARET

died 4 January 1873, aged 2 years

Now the Smith family tree is really sprouting and looks like the chart on the facing page.

This is the point where you move out into the wide, wide world and explore new territory, because your sources now are overseas. The main object of all your thoughts is now your great-great-grandfather, DAVID SMITH of Keynsham, England.

What do you know about him? A little. His wife was named ELIZABETH and they were alive in 1845 when your great-grandfather WILLIAM was born.

What do you not know? You have never heard of Keynsham, and do not know where it is in England. You also do not know the exact date in 1845 when your great-grandfather was born, or whether he had brothers and sisters. You do not know when your great-great-grandparents were married (except that it was before 1845).

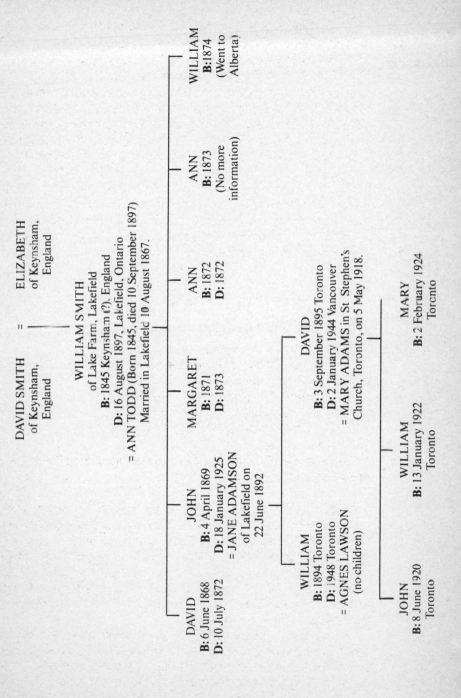

DAVID SMITH
of Keynsham,
England

= ELIZABETH
of Keynsham,
England

WILLIAM SMITH
of Lake Farm, Lakefield
B: 1845 Keynsham (?), England
D: 16 August 1897, Lakefield, Ontario
= ANN TODD (Born 1845, died 10 September 1897)
Married in Lakefield 10 August 1867.

DAVID
B: 6 June 1868
D: 10 July 1872

JOHN
B: 4 April 1869
D: 18 January 1925
= JANE ADAMSON
of Lakefield on
22 June 1892

MARGARET
B: 1871
D: 1873

ANN
B: 1872
D: 1872

ANN
B: 1873
(No more
information)

WILLIAM
B: 1874
(Went to
Alberta)

WILLIAM
B: 1894 Toronto
D: 1948 Toronto
= AGNES LAWSON
(no children)

DAVID
B: 3 September 1895 Toronto
D: 2 January 1944 Vancouver
= MARY ADAMS in St Stephen's
Church, Toronto, on 5 May 1918.

JOHN
B: 8 June 1920
Toronto

WILLIAM
B: 13 January 1922
Toronto

MARY
B: 2 February 1924
Toronto

Of course, you also have a couple of loose ends in the family tree so far. You do not know what happened to your grandfather's sister ANN (born 1873) or his brother WILLIAM (born 1874) — you remember? — the one who went to Alberta. However, don't worry too much about them because they are not direct ancestors of yours and can be left until you have some spare time. Don't be diverted from David Smith of Keynsham, England. The following chapters will show you sources of information in Canada, in England, and in most other countries.

What would have happened if you had not found your great-grandfather's birth in the church registers in Lakefield? What could you have done?

You could have searched the registers of neighbouring parish churches — such as Douro. If you had an idea he came from England, you could have written to St. Catherine's House in London, England, since the indexed records there started in 1837 (see the chapter on English sources and records for more information about this office). There is also information to be obtained from wills and land records (see under Ontario in the chapters on Canadian sources).

The imaginary Smith family we have discussed was located in Ontario — it could just as easily have been in Manitoba or Alberta and the same patient procedure could have been followed.

The Smith family was traced back to England, but it could very well have been a family originating in another country (see under the country concerned in the chapter on European sources).

4. CANADIAN CHURCH RECORDS

The location of individual church registers of births or baptisms, marriages, and deaths or burials is given under each province in Chapters Five to Eight inclusive.

Details of the present organization of the Churches – of all major denominations – in Canada are given in the following pages. If you know the religion of your ancestors in Canada I suggest you read the information about the particular denomination first – before you turn to the particular province.

Denominations have merged, or separated, or disappeared, and the history of the various Churches has a direct bearing on the records and their locations. For example, when the Methodist, Congregational, and Presbyterian churches merged in 1925 to form the United Church of Canada, some forty per cent of the Presbyterian churches rejected the merger. So, you will find Presbyterian registers in as many as five different places:

1. the United Church Archives
2. the Public Archives of Canada
3. the Provincial Archives
4. the Presbyterian Archives
5. the individual United Church or Presbyterian churches.

This does not make life easy for the Presbyterian ancestor-hunter, but it is hoped this book will solve some of the problems.

However, I have not attempted to list the location of every church register in Canada – this is a monumental task and does not come within the scope of this particular book. Perhaps, some time in the future, it will be possible for a book to be written which will do just this.

In many cases, the Archives of the various denominations now include microfilms of some early church registers in addition to the original registers of many of the churches. There has been no concerted *national* effort on the part of the various denominations to persuade individual churches either to hand over their early registers for safe-keeping, or even to permit them to be microfilmed. The many local archives of the various Churches across the country are, in some cases, now doing this – as are the various Provincial Archives – but this only accounts for a small percentage of the registers.

In Chapters Five to Eight, under the various provinces, you will find listed all the church registers, or microfilms, held by the various archives – governmental, ecclesiastical, university, library, and museum. These lists are as complete as it has been possible for me to make them – based on information supplied by the various organizations concerned. This has been a long and difficult job because, in a number of cases, the particular authority – for reasons not easy to understand – has been reluctant to release any information about its holdings.

I have not differentiated between original registers and microfilmed copies because, in my opinion, the important thing is to provide accurate information as to where records may be inspected in a central and convenient location – irrespective of whether they are originals or copies. In several cases there are microfilm copies of a church register in two or three different archives – for example, in the Public Archives of Canada in Ottawa; in the Provincial Archives in the capital city of a particular province; or in the central or local Archives of the particular Church denomination. Often, the period covered by the microfilm copy varies from archive to archive. In this case I have only listed the archive whose microfilms cover the longest period.

So far as the Catholic Church is concerned, it is Church policy to leave the original registers in the individual church – unless it no longer exists. In that case the registers will be found in the church with which it merged – if it did merge – or in the archives of the particular diocese, if the church simply ceased to exist because of fire or any other cause.

The other churches do not have a national policy – or if they do, it is not enforced on a national scale.

THE ANGLICAN CHURCH

The *Anglican Year Book* is published by the General Synod of the Anglican Church of Canada, 600 Jarvis Street, Toronto. It gives details of the existing parishes, and the dioceses to which they belong.

There are four Provincial Synods. They were formed as follows:

British Columbia (1914) This covers British Columbia and the Yukon Territory. Archivist is the Rev. Cyril Williams, Vancouver School of Theology, 6050 Chancellor Blvd., Vancouver.

Canada (1860) This covers Quebec and the Atlantic Provinces. The Archivist is Rev. J. B. Hibbitts, MA, King's College, Halifax.

Ontario (1912) The Archives are located in the Synod Office, 135 Adelaide St. East, Toronto M5C 1L8.

Rupert's Land (1875) This covers Alberta, Manitoba, Saskatchewan, and the Arctic. Archives are lodged in the Manitoba Provincial Archives and the Provincial Archivist is also Honorary Archivist for the ecclesiastical Province of Rupert's Land.

Details of the various dioceses, their date of foundation, and the Anglican Province to which they belong, are given below:

British Columbia		Canada	
British Columbia	1859	Fredericton	1845
Caledonia	1879	Montreal	1850
Cariboo	1914	Newfoundland	1839
Kootenay	1899	Nova Scotia	1787
New Westminster	1879	Quebec	1793
Yukon	1891		
(previously Selkirk)			

Ontario		Rupert's Land	
Algoma	1873	Arctic	1933
Huron	1857	Athabasca	1874
Moosonee	1872	Brandon	1913
Niagara	1875	Calgary	1888
Ontario	1862	Edmonton	1914
Ottawa	1896	Keewatin	1902
Toronto	1839	Qu'Appelle	1884
		Rupert's Land	1849
		Saskatchewan	1874
		Saskatoon	1874

Addresses of the Anglican dioceses:

Algoma: Box 1168, Sault Ste. Marie, Ontario P6A 5N7
Arctic: 1055 Avenue Road, Toronto, Ontario M5N 2C8
Athabasca: Box 279, Peace River, Alberta T0H 0X0
Brandon: 341–13th Street, Brandon, Manitoba R7A 4P8
British Columbia: 912 Vancouver Street, Victoria, B.C. V8V 3V7
Caledonia: 208–4th Avenue W., Prince Rupert, B.C. V8J 1P3
Calgary: 3015 Glencoe Road, S.W., Calgary, Alberta T2S 2L9
Cariboo: 360 Nicola Street, Kamloops, B.C. V2C 2P5
Edmonton: 10033–84th Avenue, Edmonton, Alberta T6E 2G6

Fredericton: 116 Princess Street, Saint John, N.B. E2L 1K4
Huron: Box 308, London, Ontario N6A 4W3
Keewatin: Box 118, Kenora, Ontario P9N 3X1
Kootenay: Box 549, Kelowna, B.C. V1Y 7P2
Montreal: 1444 Union Avenue, Montreal, P.Q. H3A 2B8
Moosonee: Box 841, Schumacher, Ontario P0N 1G0
New Westminster: 692 Burrard Street, Vancouver, B.C. V6C 2L1
Newfoundland: 68 Queen's Road, St. John's, Newfoundland
    A1C 2A8
Niagara: 67 Victoria Avenue S., Hamilton, Ontario L8N 2S8
Nova Scotia: 5732 College Street, Halifax, Nova Scotia B3H 1X3
Ontario: 90 Johnson Street, Kingston, Ontario K7L 1X7
Ottawa: 71 Bronson Avenue, Ottawa, Ontario K1R 6G6
Qu'Appelle: 1501 College Avenue, Regina, Saskatchewan S4P 1B8
Québec: 36 rue Desjardins, Québec, P.Q. G1R 4L5
Rupert's Land: 66 Cross Street, Winnipeg, Manitoba R2W 3X8
Saskatchewan: Box 1088, Prince Albert, Saskatchewan S6V 5S6
Saskatoon: Box 1965, Saskatoon, Saskatchewan S7K 3S5
Toronto: 135 Adelaide Street E., Toronto, Ontario M5C 1L8
Yukon: Box 4247, Whitehorse, Yukon Territory Y1A 3T3

Note: The Diocese of the Arctic includes the previous Diocese of Mackenzie River, and the previous name of the Diocese of the Yukon was the Diocese of Selkirk.

The following parishes of the Anglican Church were in existence in the various dioceses *before* civil registration of births, marriages, and deaths. The parishes are listed alphabetically under the name of each diocese, and the date of civil registration for the particular province is shown in brackets after the diocesan name:

Athabaska (1897)
Fort Chipewyan, Lesser Slave Lake, Smoky River, Vermilion, Wabiskaw, White Fish Lake.

British Columbia (1872)
Cadboro Bay, Cedar Hill, Chemainus, Comox, Cowichan, Craigflower, Esquimalt, Lake, Metlakahthla, Nanaimo, Port Simpson, Quamichan, Sandwick, Saanich, Saanichton, Salt Spray Island, Victoria.

Calgary (1897)
Banff, Blackfoot Reservation, Blood Reservation, Bowden, Calgary, Canmore, Fish Creek, Gleichen, Innisfail, Lacombe, Lamerton, Lethbridge, Macleod, Mitford, Piegan Reservation, Pincher Creek, Poplar Lake, South Edmonton, Wetaskiwin.

Fredericton (1888)

Andover, Burton, Baie des Vents, Cambridge, Carlton, Chatham, Dalhousie, Derby, Douglas, Fairville, Dorchester, Fredericton, Grand Falls, Greenwich, Hampton, Johnston, Kingston, Moncton, Musquash, Newcastle, New Denmark, New Maryland, Norton, Petitcodiac, Petersville, Portland, Queensbury, Richibucto, Richmond, Rothesay, Sackville, St. Andrew's, St. David, St. George, St. John, St. Mary's, St. Martin's, Shediac, Simonds, St. Stephen, Springfield, Stanley, Studholm, Sussex, Upham, Waterford, Westmorland, Woodstock, Wicklow.

Huron (1869)

Adelaide, Amherstburg, Auburn, Bayfield, Beachville, Belmont, Berlin, Bervie, Biddulph, Brantford, Brooke, Burford, Carlisle, Chatham, Clinton, Colchester, Crosshill, Delaware, Dungannon, Durham, Dresden, Eastwood, Edwardsburg, Exeter, Florence, Froomfield, Galt, Goderich, Greenock, Hanover, Harrietsville, Hillsboro, Holmes Hill, Howick, Ingersoll, Katesville, Kincardine, Kingsville, Lambeth, London, Meaford, Metcalfe, McGillivray, Mitchell, Mohawk, Moore, Morpeth, Mount Pleasant, Oneida Chapel, Otterville, Owen Sound, Parish, Pine River, Port Albert, Port Burwell, Port Dover, Port Stanley, Port Rowan, Proton, St. Thomas, Sandwich, Sarnia, Simcoe, Southampton, Stratford, Strathroy, Thorndale, Tyrconnell, Thamesford, Vienna, Vittoria, Walkerton, Walpole Island, Wardsville, Warwick, Westminster, Wilderness, Wilmot, Windsor, Wisbeach, Woodstock, Zorra.

Montreal (1926)

Abbotsford, Rougemont and West Farnham, Aylmer and Hull, Bedford, Berthier, Brome, Buckingham, Chambly, Christieville, Clarenceville and St. Thomas, Clarendon, Cowansville and Churchville, Coteau du Lac, Dunham and West Dunham, Edwardstown and St. Rémi, Frost Village, Gore, Granby and North Shefford, Grenville, Hemmingford, Huntingdon, Isle aux Noix, Lachine, Lacolle and Sherrington, Laprairie and Longueuil, Mascouche and Terrebonne, St. Martin, Ste. Thérèse, Milton, Montreal, New Glasgow, Ormstown, Onslow, Potton, Rawdon and Kildare and Ramsay, Russelltown, St. Andrew, St. Armand, St. John's, Sabrevois, Stanbridge East, Sorel, Sutton, St. Hyacinthe, Shefford and Waterloo, Vaudreuil.

New Westminster (1879)

Barkerville, Derby, Douglas, Hope, Lillooet, Lytton, New Westminster, Sapperton, and Yale.

Newfoundland (1891)

Battle Harbour, Bay de Verde, Bay of Islands, Bay Roberts,

Belleoram, Bonavista, Bonne Bay, Brigus, Brooklyn, Burgeo, Burin, Carbonear, Catalina, Channel, Exploits, Flowers Cove, Fogo, Fox Trap, Green Bay, Greenspond, Harbour Briton, Harbour Buffett, Harbour Grace, Heart's Content, Hermitage, Herring Neck, King's Cove, Lamaline, New Harbour, Port de Grave, Portugal Cove, Random, Rose Blanche, Salmon Cove, Salvage, Sandwich Bay, Spaniards Bays, St. George's Bay, St. John's, St. Pierre, Topsail, Trinity, Twillingate, Upper Island Cove, White Bay.

Nova Scotia (1865)
Albion Mines, Amherst, Antigonish, Aylesford, Arichat, Barrington, Beaver Harbour, Bridgetown, Dartmouth, Halifax, Horton, Hubbard's Cove, Kentville, Liverpool, Lunenburg, Maitland, Manchester, Melford, New Dublin, Newport, New Ross, Pictou, Pugwash, Rawdon, River John, Shelburne, Ship Harbour, St. Margaret's Bay, Stewiacke, Sydney, Sydney Mines, Tusket, Weymouth, Wallace, Yarmouth.

Ontario (1869)
Adolphustown and Fredericksburgh, Amherst Island, Arnprior, Ashton, Almonte, Barriefield, Bath, Belleville, Brockville, Beachburg, Cornwall, Carleton Place, Clark's Mills, Carrying Place, Cumberland, Douglas, Fitzroy, Franktown, Finch, Gananoque, Huntley, Hawkesbury, Hillier, Horton, Kingston, Kemptville, Killery, Lanark, Leeds, Loughborough, Lyn, Madoc, March, Matilda, Merrickville, Marysburgh, Mountain, Maitland, North Augusta, Napanee, Newboro, North Gower, Nepean, New Edinburgh, Ottawa, Osgoode, Osnabruck, Perth, Picton, Prescott, Pembroke, Portsmouth, Richmond, Roslyn, Smith's Falls, Stirling, Shannonville, Trenton, Tyendinaga, Tamworth, Wolfe Island, Williamsburg, Waterloo.

Qu'Appelle (1889)
Cannington, Churchbridge, Fort Qu'Appelle, Grenfell, Medicine Hat, Moose Jaw, Moosomin, Qu'Appelle Station, Regina, Souris, Sumner, Whitewood.

Quebec (1926)
Bury, Cape Cove and Percé, Compton and Waterville, Danville and Trout Brook, Drummondville and Lower Durham, Dudswell and South Ham, Durham Upper, Eaton, Frampton and Cranbourne and Standon, Gaspé Basin and Little Gaspé, Hatley and Coaticook, Hopetown, Ireland and Inverness, Kingsey and Spooner's Pond, Leeds and Lamby's Mill, Lennoxville, Lake Beauport and Stoneham, Magdalen Islands, Nicolet, New Carlisle and Paspebiac, Point Lévis and New Liverpool, Portneuf and Bourg Louis, Quebec, Richmond and Melbourne and Ely, Rivière

du Loup, Sandy Beach and Malbaic, Sherbrooke, St. Sylvester and Cumberland Mills, Stanstead, Trois-Rivières, Valcartier.

Rupert's Land (1882)

Assiniboia, Birtle, Brandon, Chafyn-Grove, Devon, Dynevor, Emerson, Fairford, Fort Alexander, Fort Frances, Griswold, Headingly, High Bluff, Islington, Lac Seul, Lisgar, Mapleton, Minnedosa, Morris, Nelson, Pembina, Portage la Prairie, Pultney, Rapid City, Rounthwaite, Russell, St. Andrew's, Stonewall, Touchwood Hills, Turtle Mountain, Westbourne, Winnipeg.

Saskatchewan (1889)

Battleford, Bresaylor, Cumberland, Holy Trinity, Onion Lake, La Corne, St. Alban's, St. Augustine, St. Cyprian's, St. David's, St. Mary's, St. Paul and St. Catherine, Sandy Lake, Saskatoon, Stanley.

Toronto (1869)

Amherst Island, Ancaster and Dundas, Arthur, Barrie and Shanty Bay, Barriefield, Bath, Barton and Glandford, Belleville, Berkeley and Chester, Brockville, Brampton, Bowmanville, Brock, Cavan, Cobourg, Carleton Place, Credit and Sydenham, Collingwood, Charlestown, Chippawa and Stamford, Cartwright and Manvers, Clarke, Cornwall, Carrying Place, Camden and Sheffield, Darlington, Douro, Dunnville, Etobicoke, Elora and Fergus, Emily, Franktown, Fitzroy and Pakenham, Fredericksburg and Adolphustown, Fenelon Falls, Fort Erie, Georgina, Glenallan, Goulbourn and Huntley, Gananoque, Garden River, Grimsby, Georgetown and Norval, Grantham, Guelph, Grafton and Colborne, Hamilton, Kingston, Kemptville, Lakefield, Lindsay, Lamb's Point, Louth, Lloydtown and Albion, Mono and Orangeville, Merrickville, Manetoahning, Markham, Minto, Mountain, March, Metcalfe and Osgoode, Milton and Hornby, Morrisburg, Newborough and Leeds, Napanee, Niagara, Newmarket, Northport and Sophiasburg, Ottawa, Oakville and Palermo, Orillia, Osnabruck, Otonabee, Oak Ridges, Perrytown, Pembroke, Peterborough, Picton, Pickering, Prescott and Maitland, Penetanguishene, Perth, Port Hope, Portsmouth, Richmond, Rockton and Beverley, Rice Lake, Reach, Rockwood, Saltfleet and Binbrook, St. Catharines, Scarborough, Sydenham and Frontenac, Stirling, Seymour, Smith's Falls, Streetsville, Stewart-town, Toronto, Thornhill and Vaughan, Thorold and Port Robinson, Tecumseth, Port Trent, Tyendinaga, Weston, Welland and Marshville, Walpole, Wellington Square, Woodbridge, Watertown, West Gwillimbury, Whitby, Wellington, West Hawkesbury, Wolfe Island, York, York Mills.

Yukon (1896)

Conrad, Dawson, Fort Selkirk, Moosehide, Whitehorse.

THE BAPTIST CHURCH

The Baptist Church in Canada – like the other dissenting or Nonconformist denominations – has been split and re-split a number of times by schisms within the church. Probably the very qualities of character, determination, and general "awkwardness" which led people to leave the original established church also led to the internal strife which over the years has fragmented the various denominations.

A book published in 1967 by the Fellowship of Evangelical Baptist Churches listed 1812 Baptist congregations in Canada, split into 10 different sects:

Baptist Federation	1181
Evangelical Baptists	335
North American Baptist Conference	91
Baptist General Conference	58
Southern Baptists	24
Ukrainian Baptists	40
Fundamental Baptists	16
Primitive Baptists	20
Regular Baptists	8
Others	39

It is not within the scope of this book to examine theological differences, but if your ancestors were Baptist it is important for you to realize the divisions within the Church. If your ancestor came from a place where splits occurred you may have to search Church records in three or more different locations. Also remember a split could take two forms:

1. The pastor and his entire congregation could move *en bloc* from one sect of the Baptist Church to another. In this case the original church and its records would remain in the same place, but some slight change might be made in the name of the church to reflect its changed beliefs. In other cases, no change of name would be made because the congregation believed it had not changed its beliefs – but everybody else had!

2. If the congregation itself split, then the minority would stop attending that particular church and hold meetings in a barn or a private house until such time as it could build a new meeting-place. If the pastor himself left with the minority, he might take the church records with him to the new congregation – believing he was preserving the continuity of the true believers.

Baptist records list marriages and burials in the registers, but not births. The church practises baptism of *believers*, not babies, and so you may find records of people being baptized at any age from nine to ninety!

Churches are "encouraged" to lodge their records in the Baptist Archives. No attempt has been made to microfilm registers. In addition to the registers, you will find other church records in the Archives which may tell you more about an ancestor if he was active in his church. These include minutes, membership rolls, legal documents, Sunday School attendance lists, accounts, pew rents, press clippings, and church histories.

The Baptist Archives are in two places:

McMaster Divinity College, Hamilton (for Quebec to British Columbia, inclusive);

Acadia University, Wolfville, Nova Scotia (for the Atlantic Provinces).

Books about the Baptist Church in Canada include the following:

E. R. Fitch, *The Baptists of Canada* (Toronto, 1911).

Stuart Ivison and Fred Rosser, *The Baptists in Upper and Lower Canada before 1820* (Toronto, 1956).

Dr. T. T. Shields, *The Plot That Failed* (Toronto, 1937).

Leslie K. Tarr, *This Dominion, His Dominion* (Willowdale, Ontario, 1968).

One more fact to bear in mind is that before the Marriage Act of 1831 (11th Provincial Parliament, William IV), Baptist ministers were not permitted by law to perform marriages. The previous Marriage Act of 1798 in Upper Canada (Ontario) allowed marriages to be performed by other denominations in addition to Anglicans and Roman Catholics. However, it specified these other denominations as Church of Scotland, Presbyterians, Calvinists, and Lutherans. The Baptists were not mentioned, and this led to a lot of complications for them.

Some Baptist ministers were able to persuade local authorities they were Calvinists within the meaning of the Act, and obtained permission to officiate at marriages. Others could not succeed in doing this, and still others were not prepared to forswear their religion even to the extent of claiming to be Calvinists. The first marriage by a Baptist minister I have been able to trace took place in London, Ontario, in 1807. The number increased over the years, and the Act of 1831 simply legalized a position which already existed.

If your ancestors were Baptists you must bear these legal questions in mind. If you cannot trace the Baptist marriage of a particular person before 1831 you should search the registers of the nearest Calvinist, Lutheran, Presbyterian, or Church of Scotland church – because this is probably where the marriage took place. If you still get no results then try the Anglicans, or even the Methodist circuit records – all things are possible.

The Baptist Archives at McMaster Divinity College contain some registers of early Baptist churches in Quebec and Ontario, and these are listed in Chapters Six and Seven. There are also copies of early Baptist periodicals and yearbooks dating back to 1837. The former often contained obituaries. The Archivist, Miss Joan Oliphant, is extremely knowledgeable about Baptist history and records and is anxious to be as helpful as possible to ancestor-hunters. However, due to lack of staff and lack of funds, the time she can give to genealogical research is limited. If you have a specific date and place she will search for you, but if you want an extended search over a longer period you will be referred to the Hamilton Branch of the Ontario Genealogical Society. A member will make a search for a fee.

So far as the Province of Quebec is concerned the legal position regarding church records is different from other provinces (see Chapter Six). Since 1851 all churches there have been compelled by law to lodge copies of their registers of births, marriages, and deaths in the district office of the Prothonotary of the Supreme Court. Please notice I mentioned *births* since, as I mentioned earlier, infant baptism does not take place in the Baptist Church.

The best collection of Baptist records is undoubtedly that located in the Library of Acadia University, Wolfville, Nova Scotia, and called the Maritime Baptist Historical Collection. The area covered is, of course, confined to New Brunswick, Nova Scotia, and Prince Edward Island. The Baptist churches in the three provinces were very numerous at one time – particularly in the last half of the nineteenth century – and a great many of the records have been given to the collection. The holdings include – besides the church records – many books about Baptist history in the three provinces.

The Librarian and his staff will do their best to assist ancestor-hunters, but as at McMaster, if you require a protracted search you may be referred to a local researcher. In both the Baptist Archives I am sure a small donation to their funds would not be refused, and would be a kindly gesture on your part.

The churches whose records are preserved at Acadia University are listed in Chapter Five (The Atlantic Provinces). You will find the records of the Baptist churches – unlike the registers of the Roman Catholic and Anglican churches – include other matters of church interest, such as membership rolls, Sunday School registers, land and financial transactions, and so on. Do not ignore these other items – they will not tell you when an ancestor was married or died, but if he was at all active in the congregation you will certainly be able to build up a picture of what he did and thought about church matters.

THE LUTHERAN CHURCH

The Lutheran Council in Canada is the co-ordinating body of the Church and it has three member churches:
The Evangelical Lutheran Church of Canada
The Lutheran Church in America – Canada Section
The Lutheran Church – Canada (Missouri Synod)
There are also some other branches of the Church which are small in number – these include the Danish Lutheran Church Abroad, the Wisconsin Evangelical Lutheran Synod, the Lutheran Brethren, and the Church of the Lutheran Reformation.

All branches of the Church are working toward the joining together of the various branches and this is likely to take place within a year or so. Speaking generally, the differences between the various branches are not theological and this makes union easier than in other denominations. The divisions are those of national origin – German, Swedish, and Icelandic – and started during the mass immigrations of the last century when the settlers massed in a particular district, brought with them their own pastors, and set up churches which used the language of the old country.

The details of the three main churches are:

The Evangelical Lutheran Church of Canada
212 Wiggins Avenue, Saskatoon, Saskatchewan S7N 1K4.
The oldest congregation of the present E.L.C.C. was organized in 1890 and the Archives of the Church hold no registers which pre-date civil registration in the various provinces. Generally, the registers remain in the individual churches. Most of the congregations of the E.L.C.C. are in the four western provinces. Should you need help about the Archives I suggest you contact Dr. G. O. Evenson, Mount Olivet Lutheran Church, 205 Fir Street, Sherwood Park, Alberta T8A 2G6.

The Lutheran Church in America – Canada Section
600 Jarvis Street, Toronto, Ontario M4Y 2J6
This section is organized in three synods:
Eastern: 3rd Floor, Commerce House, 50 Queen St. N., Kitchener, Ont. N2H 6P4
(Rev. E. Schultz)
Central: Room 211, 2281 Portage Avenue, Winnipeg
(Mr. D'Arcy Hande)

Western: 9901–107th Street, Edmonton, Alberta.

The names in brackets are those of the synod archivists. The central synod's archives are lodged in the Lutheran Theological Seminary, University of Saskatchewan, Saskatoon, Saskatchewan S7N 0W0, but the earliest registers there do not date before 1910. There are also minutes of synodical conventions dating back to 1861, and other church records, in the library of Wilfrid Laurier University, Waterloo, Ont. N2L 3C5.

The Lutheran Church – Canada (Missouri Synod)
3500 Askin Avenue, Windsor, Ontario N9E 3J9
There are three district offices of the Church:
Alberta–British Columbia
205–10645 Jasper Avenue, Edmonton, Alberta T5J 1Z8
Manitoba–Saskatchewan
1927 Grant Drive, Regina, Saskatchewan S4S 4V6
Ontario
Box 481, Kitchener, Ontario N2G 1W2

Generally speaking, it seems clear from the information given to me by the three sections of the Church that no early Lutheran records exist in the various offices and archives, and that few of the registers in the various individual churches pre-date civil registration.

THE MENNONITES

The Mennonite Church was founded in Switzerland in 1525. As a result of persecution the members moved to the Rhine Palatinate of Germany. A similar group formed in Holland in 1536 led by Menno Simons, and it was also persecuted. They fled to England and later emigrated to Pennsylvania in 1683 and founded Germantown. Immigration to Canada commenced in 1794 from the United States.

Various splits and schisms occurred over the years – mainly in 1849 when Daniel Hoch led a group out of the Church. Another took place in 1872. In 1875 the Reformed Mennonites and New Mennonites joined to form the United Mennonites; and they were joined in 1879 by the Evangelical Mennonites, and in 1883 by the Brethren of Christ (The Tunkers). Further schisms took place in 1889 and 1917. The Amish Mennonites formed their Church in Ontario in 1882. The Mennonite numbers increased with immigration from Russia in 1873 and from Germany in 1923.

The co-ordinating body for most Canadian Mennonites today is the Conference of Mennonites in Canada, 600 Shaftesbury Blvd., Winnipeg, Manitoba R3P 0M4. Mennonite congregations are to be found in the four western provinces and in Ontario, and the number of congregations in each province is: Alberta 23, British Columbia 21, Manitoba 47, Ontario 16, Saskatchewan 27.

Good books to read for information about the Church are L. J. Burkholder, *A Brief History of the Mennonite Church in Ontario* (Toronto, 1935), and Frank H. Epp, *Mennonites in Canada, 1786-1920* (Toronto, 1974), and *Mennonites in Canada, 1920-1940* (Toronto, 1982).

The individual congregations are being encouraged either to lodge their early records in the various Mennonite archives or to allow them to be microfilmed. However, all congregations are autonomous and there is considerable resistance to the idea.

The Historian Archivist for Canada is Mr. Lawrence Klippenstein, History-Archives Committee, 600 Shaftesbury Blvd., Winnipeg. The various Archives are as follows:

Conrad Grebel College, University of Waterloo, Waterloo, Ontario (Mr. Samuel Steiner, Archivist). These Archives have a very large amount of material about the church but unfortunately very few records of baptism, marriage, and death. They have a large number of MS histories of Mennonite families in Ontario and if your ancestor is Mennonite you may well find family information here.

Unfortunately, there are many sects in Ontario which do not deposit their records at Conrad Grebel College. These include Old Order Mennonite (retain within the group); Old Order Amish (retain within the group, but many genealogical records at the Amish Historical Library, R.R. #4, Aylmer, Ontario N5H 2R3); Beachy Amish Mennonite; Old Colony Mennonite (retain within the group); Conservative Mennonite (retain within the group); Reformed Mennonite (retain within the group); Church of God in Christ, Mennonite (retain within the group); Evangelical Mennonite Mission (retain within the group, but some records in Manitoba); Mennonite Brethren (see below). These groups comprise some five thousand members in Ontario – the last group having many more members in the western provinces.

The Mennonite Conference of Ontario and the Western Ontario Mennonite Conference deposit their records at Conrad Grebel College (the first group was formed by the original migration from Pennsylvania, and the latter by the Amish migration from Europe). The United Mennonite Conference has some records at the College and some in Winnipeg. These three groups total about twelve thousand members in Ontario. The background is Russian-German.

The Canadian Mennonite Brethren Archives, The Bible College, 77

Henderson Highway, Winnipeg, Manitoba R2L 1L1.

The Conference of Mennonites in Canada, 600 Shaftesbury Blvd., Winnipeg.

The Mennonite Genealogical Institute, Steinbach, Manitoba.

The Mennonite Library and Archives, Newton, Kansas, U.S.A.

Note: The Conference of Mennonites has recently acquired the duplicates of church registers kept in Russia by one group which migrated to Canada in 1874-80 from the Bergthal Colony. The dates run from 1843 until migration to Canada.

THE PRESBYTERIAN CHURCH

As mentioned elsewhere in this book, the present Presbyterian Church consists of the section of the original Church which dissented from the union with the United Church in 1925.

The Church is organized into eight *Synods* and these, in turn, are divided into *Presbyteries*. Within each Presbytery there are a number of individual churches.

The Archives of the Church are located at Knox College, 59 St. George Street, Toronto, but additional material can probably be found in the individual Synod offices, or the Presbyteries, or the original churches. In addition, there are Presbyterian records in the Public Archives, the various Provincial Archives, and the United Church Archives. In other words, they are very widely scattered and badly organized because the Church has, apparently, neither the people nor the money to organize proper archives in a central location, or to, at least, microfilm the scattered records.

The information which I have obtained from the Synods and Presbyteries is included in the listings for each province. If a particular church in which you are interested is not mentioned, you should write to the Presbytery for the district. To obtain the name and address of the Clerk of the Presbytery, write first to The Clerk of the General Assembly, The Presbyterian Church in Canada, 50 Wynford Drive, Don Mills, Ontario M3C 1J7. Be sure you enclose a stamped, self-addressed envelope for your reply.

Synods	Presbyteries
Atlantic Provinces	Cape Breton, Newfoundland, Pictou, Halifax and Lunenburg, Saint John, Miramichi, Prince Edward Island.
Quebec and Eastern Ontario	Quebec, Montreal, Glengarry, Ottawa, Lanark and Renfrew, Brockville.

Synods	Presbyteries
Toronto and Kingston	Kingston, Lindsay and Peter-borough, East Toronto, West Toronto, Brampton, Barrie, Temiskaming, Algoma and North Bay, Waterloo and Wellington.
Hamilton and London	Hamilton, Niagara, Paris, London, Chatham, Sarnia, Stratford-Huron, Bruce-Maitland
Manitoba and N.W. Ontario	Superior, Lake of the Woods, Winnipeg, Brandon.
Saskatchewan	Assiniboia, Northern Saskatchewan.
Alberta	Peace River, Edmonton, Red Deer, Calgary-Macleod.
British Columbia	Kootenay, Kamloops, Westminster, Vancouver Island.

When ancestor-hunting among Presbyterian records it should be remembered that — apart from the obvious registers of births, marriages, and deaths – some information can also be found in such records as communion rolls and Sunday School books. These are much more plentiful in the Archives than the registers themselves. They will not give you information about vital dates, but they may help you in filling some gaps.

Once you have found the particular church or churches in which you are interested, you may find it worth while to buy one of the series of booklets published by the United Church Archives called "Church Historic Sites". (See p. 42.)

THE ROMAN CATHOLIC CHURCH

The Catholic Directory of Canada (Le Canada Ecclésiastique) is published annually by Librairie Beauchemin, Montreal. It gives details of the existing parishes, their date of formation, and the diocese to which they belong. It is written in French, but even if you do not speak or understand the language, there is no problem with the basic facts. Dates, names, and addresses are basically the same.

So far as the Church is concerned, there are seventeen provinces, divided into sixty-three dioceses.

The names and addresses of the Catholic dioceses are:

Alexandria: Box 340, Alexandria, Ont.

Amos: 450 rue Principale N., Amos, Abitibi East, Québec.

Antigonish: Box 1060, Antigonish, N.S.

Bathurst: 123 St. Andrew's Street, Bathurst, N.B.

Calgary: 219–18th Ave. S.W., Calgary, Alta.

Charlottetown: Box 637, Charlottetown, P.E.I.

Chicoutimi: C.P. 336, Chicoutimi, Québec.

Churchill: Box 10, Churchill, Man.

Edmonton: 10044–113th St., Edmonton, Alta.

Edmundston: Box 370, Edmundston, N.B.

Gaspé: Box 440, Gaspé, Quebec.

Grand Falls: Grand Falls, Nfld.

Gravelbourg: Box 690, Gravelbourg, Sask.

Grouard-McLennan: Box 388, McLennan, Alta.

Halifax: 1508 Barrington Street, Halifax, N.S.

Hamilton: 714 King Street West, Hamilton, Ont.

Hauterive: 639 rue de Bretagne, Hauterive, Québec.

Hearst: Box 817, Hearst, Ont.

Hull: 5 rue de la Salle, Hull, Québec

Joliette: 2 rue St. Charles Borromée N., Joliette, Québec

Kamloops: 255 Nicola Street, Kamloops, B.C.

Keewatin–The Pas: Box 270, The Pas, Man.

Kingston: 279 Johnson Street, Kingston, Ont.

Labrador–Schefferville: Box 700, Schefferville, Quebec

London: 196 Dufferin Avenue, London, Ont.

Mackenzie–Fort Smith: Fort Smith, N.W.T.

Moncton: 226 St. George Street, Moncton, N.B.

Mont-Laurier: 435 rue de la Madone, Mont-Laurier, Québec

Montréal: 1085 rue de la Cathédrale, Montréal, Québec.

Moosonee: Box 40, Moosonee, Ont.

Nelson: 813 Ward Street, Nelson, B.C.

Nicolet: C.P. 820, Nicolet, Québec.

Ottawa: 60 Avenue Guigues, Ottawa, Ont.

Pembroke: Pembroke, Ont.

Peterborough: Box 175, Peterborough, Ont.

Prince Albert: 1401–4th Avenue West, Prince Albert, Sask.

Prince George: 887 Patricia Boulevard, Prince George, B.C.

Québec: 16 rue Buade, Québec, Québec.

Regina: 2140 Cameron Street, Regina, Sask.

Rimouski: 11 rue St. Germain O., Rimouski, Québec.

Ste. Anne-Pocatière: Comté Kamouraska, Québec.

St. Boniface: 190 avenue de la Cathédrale, St. Boniface, Man.

St. Catharines: 3 Lyman Street, St. Catharines, Ont.

St. George's: Corner Brook, Nfld.

St. Hyacinthe: 1900 rue Girouard, St. Hyacinthe, Québec.

St. Jean: 215 rue Longueuil, St. Jean, Québec.

St. Jérôme: 355 rue St. Georges, St. Jérôme, Québec.

Saint John: 91 Waterloo Street, Saint John, N.B.

St. John's: Cathedral Square, St. John's, Nfld.
St. Paul: 4625–50th Avenue, St. Paul, Alta.
Saskatoon: 720 Spadina Crescent East, Saskatoon, Sask.
Sault Ste. Marie: 480 McIntyre St. W., North Bay, Ont.
Sherbrooke: 130 rue de la Cathédrale, Sherbrooke, Québec.
Thunder Bay: 213 Archibald Street South, Thunder Bay, Ont.
Timmins: Box 965, Timmins, Ont.
Toronto: 55 Gould Street, Toronto, Ont.
Trois-Rivières: C.P. 879, Trois-Rivières, Québec.
Valleyfield: 31 rue de la Fabrique, Valleyfield, Québec.
Vancouver: 646 Richards Street, Vancouver, B.C.
Victoria: Blanshard Street, Victoria, B.C.
Whitehorse: Box 940, Whitehorse, Y.T.
Winnipeg: 353 St. Mary Avenue, Winnipeg, Man.
Yarmouth: 43 Albert Street, Yarmouth, N.S.

UKRAINIAN CATHOLIC DIOCESES

Edmonton: 10825–97th Street, Edmonton, Alta.
Saskatoon: 214 Avenue M. South, Saskatoon, Sask.
Toronto: 143 Franklin Avenue, Toronto, Ont.
Winnipeg: 115 McGregor Street, Winnipeg, Man

The following parishes of the Catholic Church were in existence in the various dioceses *before* civil registration of births, marriages, and deaths. The parishes are listed alphabetically under the name of each diocese, and the date of civil registration for the particular province is shown in brackets after the diocesan name:

Alexandria (1869)
Alexandria, Cornwall, Lancaster, St. Andrew's West, Williamstown.

Antigonish (1908)
Antigonish, Arichat, Arisaig, Boisdale, Bras d'Or, Bridgeport, Broad Cove, Brook Village, Cheticamp, Christmas Island, D'Escousse, East Bay, Guysborough, Havre Boucher, Ingonish, Johnston, Judique, L'Ardoise, Main-Dieu, Mulgrave, North Sydney, Pictou, Pomquet, Port Felix, St. Andrew's, St. Margaret's, South West Marg, Sydney, Tracadie, West Arichat.

Bathurst (1888)
Bathurst Cathedral, Bathurst Ste. Famille, Balmoral, Belledune, Campbellton, Caraquet, Charlo, Grande-Anse, Inkerman, Jacquet River, Lamèque, Miscou, Néguac, Paquetville, Petite Rivière, Petit Rocher, Pokemouche, St. Isidore, Shippegan, Tracadie.

Calgary (1897)
Banff, Canmore, Coalhurst, Cochrane, Fort Macleod, Lethbridge, Pincher Creek.

Charlottetown (1906)
Cathedral, Alberton, Bloomfield, Brac, Cardegan Bridge, Corran-Ban, Cove Head, East Point, Egmont Bay, Fort Augustus, Georgetown, Grand River, Hope River, Indian River, Kelly's Cross, Kinkora, Lennox Island, Lot 7, Lot 11, Miscouche, Morell, Mt. Carmel, Palmer Road, Rollo Bay, Rustico, St. Andrew's, St. Charles, St. George, St. Margaret, St. Peter, St. Theresa, Seven Mile Bay, Souris, Sturgeon, Summerfield, Summerside, Tignish, Trassade, Tyrone, Vernon River, Wellington.

Chicoutimi (1926)
Cathedral, Bagotville, Hébertville, Jonquière, L'Anse-St-Jean, Laterrière, Roberval.

Edmonton (1897)
Beaumont, Hobbema, Lac Ste. Anne, Lamoureux, Leduc, St. Albert, Stony Plain, Wetaskiwin.

Edmundston (1888)
Cathedral, Grand Sault, Lac Baker, Red Rapids, Ste. Anne de Padoue, St. Basile, St. François, St. Hilaire, St. Jacques.

Gaspé (1926)
Nearly all parishes in this diocese pre-date civil registration.

Grand Falls (1891)
Baie de Verde, Brigue, Harbour Grace, Harbour Main, Tilting.

Halifax (1908)
No information obtainable.

Hamilton (1869)
Hamilton (St. Mary), Acton, Arthur, Brantford, Burlington, Carlsruhe, Dundas, Formosa, Guelph, Hespeler, Macton, Maryhill, Mt. Forest, New Hamburg, Oakville, Owen Sound, Paris, Riversdale, St. Agatha, St. Clement's, Teeswater.

Hauterive (1926)
Betsiamites, Les Escoumins, Tadoussac.

Hull (1926)
Aylmer Est, Buckingham, Farrelton, Lac Ste. Marie, Montebello, Old Chelsea, Pointe Gatineau, St. André Avellin, Ste. Cécile de Masham.

Joliette

Nearly all parishes in this diocese pre-date civil registration. For exact dates of individual parishes write to the Diocesan Office or consult the Catholic Directory in your library.

Keewatin–The Pas (1882) Manitoba and (1905) Saskatchewan, Brochet, Man., and Pelican Narrows, Sask.

Kingston (1869)
Cathedral, Belleville, Brockville, Centreville, Erinsville, Kemptville, Marysville, Morrisburg, Napanee, Perth, Picton, Prescott, Read, Smith's Falls, Stanleyville, Stoco, Toledo, Westport, Wolfe Island.

London (1869)
Cathedral, Ashfield, Belle River, Chatham, Corunna, Goderich, Ingersoll, Kinkora, La Salette, Lucan, Maidstone, Merlin, Mount Carmel, Pain Court, Petrolia, Perth, River Canard, St. Columban (Dublin), St. Joseph (Zurich), St. Peter's (Kent), St. Thomas (Elgin), Sarnia, Stoney Point, Stratford, Tecumseh, Thamesville, Tilbury, Windsor (Assumption, St. Alphonsus).

Mackenzie–Fort Smith (1897)
Arctic Red River, Fort du Lac, Fort Chipewyan, Fort Good Hope, Fort Liard, Fort McMurray, Fort Norman, Fort Providence, Fort Rae, Fort Resolution.

Moncton (1888)
St. Bernards, Barachois, Cap Pelé, Cocagne, Grande-Digue, Memramcook, Port Elgin, Richibuctou Village, Ste. Anne, St. Anselme, St. Charles, St. Ignace, St. Louis, Ste. Marie, St. Paul, Shediac.

Mont Laurier (1926)
Maniwaki

Montreal (1926)
No information. See note under Joliette above.

Nelson (1872)
Kelowna

Nicolet (1926)
Cathedral, Arthabaska, Bécancour, Blandford, Drummondville, Gentilly, Kingsey, La Baie, Odanak, Pierreville, Princeville, St. Bonaventure (Upton), St. Célestin, St. David, St. Eulalie, St. François du Lac, St. Germain de Grantham, Ste. Gertrude, St. Grégoire, St. Guillaume (Upton), St. Léonard, St. Louis, Ste.

Monique, St. Norbert, St. Pierre les Becquets, St. Wenceslas, Tingwick, Yamaska.

Ottawa (1869)
Cathedral, St. Joseph, St. Patrick, Almonte, Corkery, Curran, Embrun, Fallowfield, Fitzroy Harbour, L'Orignal, Orléans, Pakenham, Richmond, St. Eugène, South Gloucester, South March.

Pembroke (1869)
Cathedral, Arnprior, Brudenell, Chapeau, Ile de Grand-Calumet, La Passe, Mattawa, Mount St. Patrick, Portage du Fort, Quyon, Renfrew.

(*Note*: This Diocese includes part of Quebec as well as Ontario.)

Peterborough (1869)
Bowmanville, Cobourg, Douro, Downeyville, Hastings, Lindsay, Port Hope.

Prince Albert (1889)
Cathedral, Aldma, Batoche, Battleford, Delmas, Duck Lake, Green Lake, Onion Lake, St. Laurent.

Quebec (1926)
See note under Joliette.

Regina (1889)
St. Mary's

Rimouski (1926)
Bic, Cacouna, Ile Verte, St. Arsène, St. Eloi, St. Fabian, Ste. Flavie, Ste. Luce, St. Matthieu, St. Modeste, St. Octave.

Ste-Anne-de-la Pocatière (1926)
See note under Joliette.

St. Boniface (1882)
Cathedral, Letellier, Lorette, Ste. Agathe, Ste. Anne, St. Jean-Baptiste, St. Joseph, St. Labre, St. Norbert.

St. Catharines (1869)
Cathedral, St. Mary, Caledonia, Fort Erie, Grimsby, Niagara Falls, Niagara-on-the-Lake, Port Colborne, Thorold.

St. George (1891)
Harbour Breton, Port-au-Port West, St. Bernard's, St. George's, Searston, Stephenville.

St. Hyacinthe (1926)
Cathedral, Acton Vale, Ange-Gardien, Beloeil, Bromont, Dunham, Granby, Henryville, Iberville, La Présentation, Marieville, Milton, Mont St. Grégoire, Mont St. Hilaire, Notre Dame de Stanbridge, Roxton Falls, Roxton Pond, St. Aimé, St. Alexandre, St. Antoine, St. Barnabé, Ste. Brigide, St. Césaire, St. Charles, St. Damase, St. Denis, St. Dominique, Ste. Hélène, St. Hugues, St. Jean, St. Joachim, St. Joseph, St. Jude, St. Liboire, St. Marc, St. Marcel, St. Mathias, St. Ours, St. Paul, St. Robert, St. Roch, Ste. Rosalie, St. Simon, St. Théodore, St. Valérien, Ste. Victoire, Sorel, Sorel St. Pierre, Upton.

St. Jean (1926)
See note under Joliette.

St. Jérôme (1926)
See note under Joliette.

Saint John (1888)
Cathedral, Blessed Virgin, Bartibogue Bridge, Blackville, Boiestown, Chatham, Douglastown, Fredericton, Johnville, Loggieville, Milltown, Newcastle, Oromocto, Red Bank, Renous, St. Andrews, St. George, St. Margaret's, South Nelson, Sussex, Woodstock.

St. John's (1891)
Cathedral, Bay Bulls, Bell Island, Burin, Freshwater, Lamaline, Placentia, Renews, St. Joseph, St. Kyrans, St. Lawrence, St. Mary's, Trepassey, Witless Bay.

St. Paul (1897)
La Biche, Le Goff, Morinville, Saddle Lake.

North Bay (1869)
Garden River

Sherbrooke (1926)
Richmond, Stanstead, Stratford, Wotton.

Thunder Bay (1869)
Holy Family, Gull Bay, Lake Head.

Toronto (1869)
Cathedral, St. Basil, St. Joseph (Highland Creek), St. Mary, St. Patrick, St. Paul, Beaverton, Bradford, Colgan, Collingwood, Lafontaine, Markham, Mississauga, Newmarket, Orillia, Oshawa, Penetanguishene, Phelston, Pickering, Richmond Hill, Stayner, Thornhill, Uptergrove, Whitby, Wildfield.

Trois-Rivières (1926)
See note under Joliette.

Valleyfield (1926)
See note under Joliette.

Winnipeg (1882)
St. Charles, St. Eustache, St. François-Xavier, St. Laurent, St. Lazare.

Yarmouth (1908)
Cathedral, Annapolis Royal, Buttes Amirault, Butte Comeau, Digby, Kentville, Meteghan, Plympton, Pointe-de-l'Eglise, Pubnico, Quinan, Rivière-aux-Saumons, Ste-Anne-de-Ruisseau, St. Bernard, Wedgeport.

THE SOCIETY OF FRIENDS (QUAKERS)

The Society of Friends first held meetings in Canada in the latter part of the eighteenth century in the Atlantic Provinces, and a little later in Ontario. Since then there have been Meetings or Settlements of the Friends all across Canada from time to time, but not many are now in existence. Archives of the Society of Friends are located at the Friends Meeting House, 60 Lowther Avenue, Toronto, Ontario, but are very few in number. A great deal of information about the Society of Friends in Canada can be found in the following books:

Arthur G. Dorland, *The Quakers in Canada* (Toronto, 1927).

Genealogical Publishing Company, *Encyclopedia of American Quaker Genealogy* (Baltimore, 1969).

The following registers are in the Quaker Archives – all from Meetings in Ontario:

Pelham	BMD	1790-1856
Pickering	BMD	1845-74
West Lake	MD	1829-66
Yarmouth	M	1859-1974
Yonge Street	BD	1803-66
	M	1804-40, 1859-97

Note: It should be noted that the Archives also contain a number of other Meeting records – particularly minute books – and these may well contain information about births, marriages, and deaths not included in the registers. If you are of Quaker stock and know the particular district where your ancestors lived in Ontario, a thorough check of the minutes may be worth while.

Meetings of the Society of Friends are being held in the present day in the following places in Canada:

Argenta, B.C.	Newmarket, Ont.	Thousand Islands, Ont.
Brandon, Man.	Niagara Falls, Ont.	Toronto, Ont.
Calgary, Alta.	Norwich, Ont.	Vancouver, B.C.
Edmonton, Alta.	Ottawa, Ont.	Vernon, B.C.
Halifax, N.S.	Pelham, Ont.	Victoria, B.C.
Hamilton, Ont.	Peterborough, Ont.	Welland, Ont.
Kitchener, Ont.	Raymond, Alta.	Wellington, Ont.
Lobo (Coldstream),	Regina, Sask.	West Lake, Ont.
Ont.	Saskatoon, Sask.	White Rock, B.C.
London, Ont.	Simcoe, Ont.	Winnipeg, Man.
Montreal, Que.	Sparta, Ont.	Wooler, Ont.

There have been two major splits or schisms among the Society of Friends in the past, and this should be remembered, because it means that in certain places two or three separate meetings were held, and burials took place in two separate burial-grounds.

A sect called the Hicks-ites split off from the Orthodox Quakers in 1828 and a further schism occurred in 1880 when the Fast Friends set off on their own. Basically, these splits were caused by disputes between ultra-conservatives and liberals – ecclesiastically speaking! The three sections were eventually reconciled, and today there is only one Society of Friends.

I have not listed any addresses for the various Meetings in Canada because there are frequent changes. Up-to-date information can be obtained from Mrs. Dorothy Muma, The Society of Friends, 60 Lowther Avenue, Toronto, or from the Archivist at the same address, Miss Grace Pincoe.

THE UNITED CHURCH OF CANADA

The Church was formed in 1925 by the merger of the Methodist, Congregational, and Presbyterian churches (except that a large segment of the latter Church, and a very small segment of the other two churches, elected to remain outside the new United Church).

The Presbyterian Church (in 1917) started to collect all possible historical material about the Church and this was deposited in the libraries of the eight Presbyterian theological colleges. The Methodist Church was collecting similar material and this was left in the custody of the various Methodist colleges. The collection was not at all systematic. In 1922 the

Methodist Church appointed a Chief Archivist and a concerted effort was made to collect early historical material at the Methodist colleges in Sackville, N.B.; Montreal, Quebec; Toronto, Ontario; Winnipeg, Manitoba; Regina, Saskatchewan; Edmonton, Alberta; and New Westminster, B.C. The Congregational Union did not even have a central Church office until 1919, and very few early records of this Church have survived.

When the United Church came into existence in 1925, an attempt was made to bring the various records of the three churches into one central Archive. There were problems with the dissenting Presbyterian Church and it was not until 1946 that the United Church was awarded possession of their records. As you can imagine, there was bad feeling about this, and even today members of the Presbyterian Church claim "our records were stolen by the United Church."

During the period from the merger in 1925 until 1953 very little work was done on the United Church Archives and – during this period – many early records were destroyed or disappeared. Now, the Archives are an example to all other churches both in their wide scope and in their general organization. The Central Archives of the Church are located at Victoria University, Toronto, which is federated with the University of Toronto. There are also archives located at various centres across Canada.

There are seven of these locations, but only the following have records of interest to the ancestor-hunter. The records are listed with other church records in the various provinces in Chapters Five to Eight, and the addresses of these local archives are as follows:

St. Stephen's College, Edmonton, Alberta.

St. Andrew's College, Saskatoon, Sask.

The Central Archives at Victoria College also contain complete sets of early church newspapers – the *Christian Guardian*, the *Canada Christian Advocate*, the *Presbyterian Witness*, the *Westminster*, the *Home and Foreign Record*, etc. Some of these contain obituary notices, and also births, marriages, and deaths.

The Archives have published an interesting series of small booklets (25¢ each). The series is called "Church Historic Sites" and the booklets list and describe historic churches of the United, Presbyterian, Methodist, Congregational, and Evangelical United Brethren in all parts of Canada. There are four booklets – Atlantic Provinces, Ontario, Quebec, and Western Canada.

INTRODUCTORY NOTE TO CHAPTERS 5 TO 8

The following chapters cover the main sources of records in
the various provinces – divided into the Atlantic Provinces,
Ontario, Quebec, and the Western Provinces. In each chapter
I list the church registers of births or baptisms, marriages, and
deaths for that particular province in cases where they have
been separated from the original church, or where copies exist
in various archives, libraries, or museums. No attempt has
been made to list such records since the date of civil registration in each province. There are many thousands of registers
of various denominations for the years since civil registration
was introduced and perhaps, one day, a complete list of these
registers may be published. Meanwhile, the registers you will
find listed will help you to trace your ancestors prior to civil
registration – it is comparatively easy to trace them in the
period since that date.

The earliest date in the registers is shown. This does not
always apply to births, marriages, *and* deaths, but where it has
been found possible to obtain this information it is shown, e.g.

Adolphustown: **B** 1823 **M** 1873 **D** 1847

The registers are not always complete from the first date
shown – particularly in the early years. The *concluding* date,
if not given, may be assumed to be later than the start of civil
registration in the province concerned.

The following abbreviations are used:

B	Births or Baptisms
M	Marriage
D	Deaths or Burials
A	Anglican
B	Baptist
BWM	British Wesleyan Methodist
C	Congregational
CS	Church of Scotland
DR	Dutch Reformed
EL	Evangelical Lutheran
EUB	Evangelical United Brethren

FP	Free Presbyterian
L	Lutheran
MEN	Mennonite
M	Methodist
ME	Methodist Episcopalian
MNC	Methodist (New Connection)
MO	Moravian
P	Presbyterian
PM	Primitive Methodist
PR	Protestant
RC	Roman Catholic
RE	Reformed Episcopalian
SF	Society of Friends (Quaker)
U	Unitarian
UC	United Church (may include C, M, and P)
WM	Wesleyan Methodist
WMNC	Wesleyan Methodist (New Connection)

The various church registers listed in each chapter show the location of the records in a particular archive, library, museum, university, or private collection. The abbreviations for these are listed below, and the addresses can be found in the chapter concerned:

PAC	Public Archives of Canada
AA	Archives of Alberta
ABC	Archives of British Columbia
AM	Archives of Manitoba
ANB	Archives of New Brunswick
ANF	Archives of Newfoundland
ANS	Archives of Nova Scotia
AO	Archives of Ontario
APEI	Archives of Prince Edward Island
AQM	Archives of Quebec (Montreal)
AQQ	Archives of Quebec (Quebec)
ASR	Archives of Saskatchewan (Regina)
ASS	Archives of Saskatchewan (Saskatoon)
ADQ	Archives of the Archdiocese of Quebec (Roman Catholic)
ANG(C)	Anglican Diocese of Calgary
ANG(Cal)	Anglican Diocese of Caledonia
ANG(K)	Anglican Diocese of Keewatin
ANG(M)	Anglican Diocese of Montreal
ANG(O)	Anglican Diocese of Ontario
ANG(Ot)	Anglican Diocese of Ottawa
ANG(Q)	Anglican Diocese of Quebec
ANG(T)	Anglican Diocese of Toronto

AAM	Archives Acadiennes
ACO	Archives des Châtelets
BAP	Baptist Archives (McMaster University)
CBA	Cape Bretonia Archives (St. Francis-Xavier University)
GA	Glenbow-Alberta Institute
HWM	Hiram Walker Museum
KKC	Knox Crescent and Kensington Church
LMH	London and Middlesex County Historical Society
MA	Mennonite Archives (Waterloo)
MBA	Baptist Archives (Acadia University)
NBM	New Brunswick Provincial Museum
PAK	Presbyterian Archives (Knox College)
PCM	Presbyterian College (Montreal)
PTE	Private collections
QU	Queen's University
UCA	United Church Archives (Victoria University)
UCE	United Church Archives (University of Alberta)
UCM	United Church Centre, Montreal
UM	Université de Montréal (Département de Démographie)
UNB	University of New Brunswick
UWO	University of Western Ontario

Explanatory Notes

The two following notes apply to all provinces in Chapters Five to Eight. They are listed here for convenience and you will be referred back to these pages at the appropriate time.

1. CHURCH REGISTERS: Before referring to the church registers of the various denominations listed for any province, please make sure you understand the following explanatory notes:

1. The church registers are listed alphabetically by name of city, town, or village *under each denomination* — starting with the Anglican Church.

2. The registers listed are either originals which are no longer in the particular church *or* microfilm copies.

3. The locations shown are the archives in which the registers or copies have been lodged for safe-keeping. The list is complete according to information given to me by the various archives at this time. *However, new additions are being made from time to time.*

4. Very many original registers are still in the original church, and if the church in which you are interested is not listed *it does not mean the register does not exist*. It simply means that the original or a copy has not been lodged in the archives. In that case, you must check with the church authorities to find out if the register is still in the church or whether it has been lost or destroyed. (The policy of the Roman Catholic Church is to leave the registers in the local church, so you will not find too many of them listed – except in the Province of Quebec.)

5. The registers listed cover the period *up* to the date of civil registration. There are many registers or copies *after* this date which I have not listed because, once civil registration started, a search of church registers is not so vital.

6. The letters **B**, **M**, and **D** refer to Births or Baptisms, Marriages, and Deaths. The letters in the right-hand column are an abbreviation of the name of the particular archive. Details of them appear at the beginning of each list of registers.

7. Dates shown are the *starting* date of the registers. For example **B**1845- means the entries start in 1845 and continue up to the date of civil registration at least. **B** 1845-50 means the entries cover that period only. "**B** 1845 only" means only that year is available. The same explanation applies to **M** and **D**.

2. CENSUSES: These started on a Canada-wide basis in 1851 – covering Upper and Lower Canada and gradually extending across the country as other areas became settled and entered Confederation. They are held every ten years and those for 1851, 1861, 1871, and 1881 are in the custody of the Public Archives of Canada, Ottawa. They are on microfilm and copies can be inspected by arrangement with your local library or at your Provincial Archives. In some cases the library itself may have its own microfilm copies for its particular area.

Although Canada has no automatic "hundred years rule" as in many other countries, in actual fact census returns are not available for public inspection until approximately this period has elapsed. The 1881 census has recently been microfilmed and can be borrowed from the Public Archives through any library that has a microfilm viewer. It can also be inspected in the Provincial Archives.

5. THE ATLANTIC PROVINCES

NEW BRUNSWICK

CIVIL REGISTRATION
New Brunswick became a province in 1784 – before that it was known as Sunbury County, Nova Scotia. The history of civil registration of births, marriages, and deaths in New Brunswick is more than a little complicated. In 1888 a law came into force which compelled ministers of all churches to report baptisms, marriages, and burials. Unfortunately, this meant that Baptists, for example, who do not baptize *infants*, had their births unrecorded. This also applied to others who, for various reasons, did not approve of baptism. In addition, the law was not enforced properly until after 1900. This rather loosely organized period means you may have problems in establishing a date of birth. From 1 January 1920, compulsory registration has been in force, and entries are complete and in the custody of the Registrar General, Department of Health (Vital Statistics), P.O. Box 6000, Fredericton, New Brunswick E3B 5H1. He also has custody of the records from 1888 to 1920. Searches will be made by the staff for a small fee per three-year period.

PROVINCIAL ARCHIVES
These are located on the University of New Brunswick campus. Mailing address: Provincial Archives, P.O. Box 6000, Fredericton, New Brunswick E3B 5H1. The staff are particularly helpful to genealogists, and the records are extremely well organized and documented. The most useful records there include land, marriage, church, census, and probate. There is also a large and growing genealogical library, a very good microfilm collection, many individual genealogies and family histories, and an outstanding collection of early directories and newspapers.

In many ways, the Archives of New Brunswick are the best organized in Canada and, above all, the ancestor-hunter is not regarded as a nuisance to be got rid of as quickly and quietly as possible. New Brunswick, of course, is one of the oldest provinces and the inhabitants generally have a deep sense of history.

Many of the records in the Archives are on a county basis. If you do not know the county from which your ancestors came it may be worth while to check the land records (1784-1850), which may give you the link you need – provided one of them applied for or received a grant of land.

I mentioned earlier that the Registrar General has the baptism, marriage, and death records for the period 1888-1920, when civil registration in its modern form commenced. The years *before* 1888 are covered by records in the provincial archives – again, on a county basis, and for *marriages* only. Details are as follows:

*Albert	1846-88 (indexed)
†Carleton	1832-88 (unindexed)
Charlotte	1806-80, 1882-4 (indexed)
‡Gloucester	1832-60 (indexed), 1873-87 (unindexed)
§Kent	1844-87 (unindexed)
Kings	1812-89 (indexed)
Northumberland	1792-1887 (indexed)
Queens	1812-87 (indexed)
St. John	1810-87 (indexed)
Westmorland	1790-1875 (indexed), 1875-85 (unindexed) 1885-7 (indexed)
York	1812-32 (indexed), 1832-6 (unindexed) 1837-88 (indexed)

Note: The index shows only the name of the groom.

Most important of all, the records listed above are on microfilm and can be borrowed through your local library by arrangement with the regional library system.

Before we leave the provincial archives I should repeat that records are on a county basis. The archives will supply you with details of their genealogical records for whichever county you want. There is no charge for this. Since you may not know the exact county from which your ancestor came, it will be helpful if I describe the location of each county and its parishes. This information was supplied by the Provincial Archivist:

Albert
This county is located in the southeastern corner of New

*Albert County – for pre-1846 marriages see Westmorland
†Carleton County – for pre-1832 marriages see York
‡Gloucester County – for pre-1826 marriages see Northumberland
§Kent County – for pre-1826 marriages see Northumberland

Brunswick and to its north and east is Westmorland County, from which Albert was created in 1845. To the west are the counties of St. John and Kings. Two of the six parishes, Hillsborough and Hopewell, were erected as part of Westmorland County in 1786; Coverdale was set off from the former in 1828, and Harvey from the latter in 1838. Elgin was part of Salisbury, in Westmorland, until 1847. Alma was separated from Harvey in 1855.

Carleton

This county is located in the western part of the province, next to the state of Maine. To the north lies Victoria County, and to the south and east York County, from which Carleton was created in 1831. Five parishes, Woodstock, Northampton, Wakefield, Kent, and Brighton, were created as parishes in York County in 1786, 1786, 1803, 1821, and 1830 respectively. Carleton County was separated from York County in 1831, and Wicklow Parish was created in 1833 from part of Kent Parish. Simonds Parish was separated from Wakefield in 1842, and Richmond from Woodstock in 1853. In 1859 Peel was separated from Brighton, and in 1863 Aberdeen from Kent. Wilmot was set up from Simonds in 1867. Two parishes, Perth and Andover, were part of Carleton County until 1833 when Victoria County was created.

Charlotte

This is located in the southern corner of New Brunswick, east of the state of Maine. Its northern and eastern boundaries adjoin the counties of York, Sunbury, Queens, Kings, and St. John. Seven parishes were set up in 1786 – a year after the creation of Charlotte County – Pennfield, St. Andrews, St. David, St. George, St. Patrick, St. Stephen, and West Isles. Campobello and Grand Manan were set off from West Isles in 1803 and 1816 respectively. St. James was created in 1823 from part of St. Stephen. A portion of St. Patrick became Dumbarton in 1856 and Lepreau was created from Pennfield in 1859. In 1869 Clarendon was established, and in 1873 Dufferin was set off from St. Stephen, and in 1874 St. Croix was established.

Gloucester

This is located in the northeastern corner of the province. To the west is Restigouche County and to the south is Northumberland, from which Gloucester was created in 1826. The parishes of Saumarez and Beresford were set up in 1814 as parishes of Northumberland County. New Bandon and Caraquet were set up from Saumarez in 1831 as parishes of Gloucester County. Shippegan, Inkerman, and Saint Isidore were created from parts of Saumarez in 1851, 1855, and 1881 respectively. Paquetville was created from Inkerman in 1897.

Kent

This is on the eastern coast of New Brunswick. To the south are the counties of Queens and Westmorland. To the north and west is Northumberland, from which Kent was created in 1826. The parishes of Wellington and Carleton were created as parishes in Northumberland in 1814. Liverpool (re-named Richibucto in 1832), Dundas, Huskison, and Harcourt were set up in 1826 when the County of Kent was established. Weldford was created from part of Richibucto in 1835, and the parishes of St. Louis, St. Mary, Acadieville, and St. Paul were erected in 1855, 1867, 1876, and 1883 respectively.

Kings

This is one of the original counties established in 1785. To the north is Queens County and to the south St. John. Charlotte is to the west and Albert and Westmorland to the east. The four parishes of Westfield, Sussex, Springfield, and Kingston were created in 1786. Norton and Greenwich and Hampton were set up in 1785. Upham was separated from Hampton in 1835 and Studholm from Sussex in 1840. Havelock, Hammond, and Kars were created in 1858, 1858, and 1859 respectively. In 1870 Rothesay was created a parish, and in 1874 Cardwell and Waterford were set up.

Madawaska

This county is located in the northwestern part of New Brunswick. To the north is Restigouche county and to the south the state of Maine. On the west is the Province of Quebec and on the east Victoria County, from which Madawaska was created in 1873. The parish of Madawaska was set up in Carleton County in 1833, and St. Leonard and St. Basil in 1850. St. Francis, St. Jacques, St. Hilaire, and St. Ann's were all established as parishes in 1877.

Northumberland

This county was created in 1785 and is in the centre of the province. To the north are Gloucester and Restigouche counties and to the south York and Sunbury. On the west is Victoria, and to the east Kent County. The parishes of Alnwick and Newcastle were created in 1786. In 1814 Glenelg, Chatham, Nelson, Ludlow, and Northesk were set up. Blissfield and Blackville were established in 1830; Hardwicke in 1851; Derby in 1859; Southesk in 1879; and Rogersville in 1881.

Queens

This county was established in 1785. To the north is Kent and to the south Charlotte. To the east is Kings and to the west is Sunbury. In 1786 the parishes of Wickham, Waterborough, Hampstead, and Gagetown were created. Brunswick, Canning, and Chipman were set up in 1816, 1827, and 1835 respectively. Petersville was established in 1838, Johnston in 1839, and Cambridge in 1852.

Restigouche

This is in the northern part of the province. To the north and west lies the Province of Quebec. To the south are the counties of Madawaska, Victoria, and Northumberland. On the east is Gloucester County, from which Restigouche was created in 1837. Addington and Eldon parishes were set up in 1826 as parts of Gloucester County. In 1839 Durham, Colborne, and Dalhousie were set up. Balmoral was created from part of Dalhousie in 1876.

St. John

This county was created in 1785. To the north is Kings County, and on the west is Charlotte. The city of Saint John was chartered in 1785. The parishes of Portland, St. Martins, and Lancaster were created in 1786. Simonds was established in 1839 and Musquash in 1877.

Sunbury

This was created in 1785. To the north is Northumberland, and to the south Charlotte. To the east is Queens and to the west York. The four parishes of Burton, Lincoln, Sheffield, and Maugerville were created in 1786. Blissfield, Northfield, and Gladstone were established in 1834, 1857, and 1874 respectively.

Westmorland

This county was created in 1785 and until 1845 also included Albert County. It is in the southeastern part of New Brunswick. To the north is Kent and to the south lies Albert. On the west are Queens and Kings, and to the east, the province of Nova Scotia. The parishes of Westmorland, Sackville, and Moncton were set up in 1786. Dorchester and Salisbury were created in 1787. Botsford and Shediac were established in 1805 and 1827 respectively.

York

This county was established in 1785 and is in the centre of the province. To the north is Northumberland, and to the south Charlotte County and the state of Maine. East is Sunbury and west is Carleton. The town of Fredericton came into existence in 1786. In that year the parishes of Kingsclear, Prince William, St. Mary's, and Queensbury were created. Douglas was set up in 1824; Dumfries and South-hampton in 1833; Stanley and New Maryland in 1846; Manners, Sutton, and Canterbury in 1855; Bright in 1869; North Lake in 1879, and McAdam, in 1894.

LIBRARIES
The Harriet Irving Library, P.O. Box 7500, Fredericton, New Brunswick E3B 5H5, has a certain amount of genealogical material, particularly in manuscript form, including histories of such families as the Glasiers, Chipmans, Closes, and others. It will be worth checking there for any mention of your family.

The New Brunswick Museum (established 1842), 277 Douglas Avenue, Saint John, New Brunswick E2K 1E5, also has a number of genealogical items and records worth investigating.

CEMETERIES
Do not overlook the value of cemeteries in cases where, as in New Brunswick, there are gaps in early records. There are very many burial-grounds of various kinds in the province – too many to list. However, let me cite one or two examples of the value of them:

1. There were several early cemeteries in Saint John. The first burial place was in Germain Street, and it was in use until 1819. The bodies were later removed to other burial-grounds. The Anglican Cemetery on Thorne Avenue is associated with Trinity Church, although it now has its own management. The first burial took place in 1839. At first its use was confined to Anglicans, but by 1871 Methodists and Presbyterians were being buried there. The records of the burial-ground are kept by Teed and Teed, Barristers, Harbour Building, Saint John.

2. There is also a Wesleyan burial-ground on Thorne Avenue in Saint John. This was in use between 1838 and 1959 and is administered by Queen Square and Portland United churches. It has been badly neglected over the years, but efforts are now being made to restore it. The stones are being reset and the inscriptions copied.

GENEALOGICAL SOCIETY
The address is P.O. Box 3235, Station B, Fredericton, N.B. E3A 2W0. There is also a New Brunswick Historical Society (P.O. Box 575, Saint John).

WILLS
Most of the early wills are now in the Provincial Archives, and

those which are still in the custody of the local registrars are in the process of transfer to the Archives. The wills at present included come from the following counties:

Albert	1846-85	Restigouche	1839-95	**53** OTHER SOURCES
Carleton	1833-85	St. John	1785-1888	
Charlotte	1785-1885	Sunbury	1786-1896	
Gloucester	1806-85	Victoria	1850-85	
Kings	1788-97	Westmorland	1787-1885	
Northumberland	1872-1950	York	1794-1887	
Queens	1785-1885			

All of the above are on microfilm and may be borrowed through your local library. See the librarian and explain they may be borrowed through the Inter-Library Loan system, quoting the particular county in which you are interested. Be sure, of course, that your library has a microfilm viewer available. All the above records are indexed and the staff of the archives will search for a particular entry for you without charge.

LAND TITLES
Copies of the early land records are in the Archives – that is, the petitions for land. Copies of the actual grants may be obtained from the Department of Natural Resources, Lands Branch, Centennial Building, Fredericton. A charge is made for these copies. The records in the Archives cover the period 1784-1850 and often contain genealogical information. These are indexed and in two sections – Petitions and Grants.

CENSUSES
These are available for 1851, 1861, 1871, and 1881 (see Note 2 on p. 46).

The Provincial Archives are at present indexing and printing the 1851 returns on a county basis, and the following are now available:

    Carleton County $7

    Charlotte County $5 (Volume I) (covers the parishes of Campobello, Grand Manan, Pennfield, St. Andrews, St. Davids, and West Isles)

    Sunbury County $5.50

    There is also *The Fredericton Census of 1871* ($4).

Remember the returns are by county, so be sure you find out first where your ancestor lived in 1851, 1861, 1871, and 1881. If you are interested in Madawaska County, remember it was not created until 1873, and before that was part of Victoria County.

OTHER SOURCES

These include tax assessment records; elections records; gravestone lists; local histories; school returns; poll books; mortgages and deeds; voters lists; Surrogate Court minutes, etc.

The availability of these records varies from county to county, but you can obtain details from the Provincial Archives. Most of these records have been microfilmed. There is also an excellent book published by the Archives called *New Brunswick History: Checklist of Secondary Sources* by Hugh A. Taylor. This consists of two volumes and costs $8.

There are also a number of county historical societies which, I am sure, will be helpful to you if you write a short letter, ask simple questions, and enclose a reply-paid envelope:

Albert County Historical Society, Box 39, Hopewell Cape.
Carleton County Historical Society, Box 768, Upper Woodstock.
Grand Manan Historical Society, Grand Harbour, Grand Manan (Charlotte County).
Kings County Historical Society, Hampton.
Miramichi Historical Society, Newcastle (Northumberland County).
Gagetown-Hampstead Historical Society, Gagetown (Queens County).
York-Sunbury Historical Society, Queen St., Fredericton (Sunbury and York counties).
Southern Victoria Historical Society, Andover (Victoria County).
New Denmark Historical Society, R.R. #2, New Denmark (Victoria County).
Westmorland Historical Society, Box 1187, Sackville.

So far as Restigouche County is concerned, you may be able to get useful information from the Chaleur Area History Museum, Box 1717, Dalhousie.

CHURCH RECORDS

The Provincial Archives have microfilmed the *records* of very many churches in the province – mostly Anglican, but also including other denominations. These *records*, as listed by the Archives, may or may not contain registers of births, marriages, and deaths. Details of the churches concerned are contained in the various county leaflets issued by the Archives. I suggest the following:

1. Get the leaflet for the county in which you are interested. If the church you want is listed, ask the Archives if the records for that church contain registers.

2. If so, then apply for the microfilm through your local library, but be prepared to find some very dull minutes, accounts, etc., before you reach the registers.

CHURCH REGISTERS

In addition to the church records listed by the Archives of New Brunswick, the following church registers exist in various archives – either in the originals or in microfilm copies. So before referring to any of the church registers listed below please reread Note 1 on pp. 45-6.

Anglican

ANB   Provincial Archives, P.O. Box 6000, Fredericton, New Brunswick E3B 5H1.

PAC   Public Archives of Canada, 395 Wellington Street, Ottawa, Ont.

UNB   University of New Brunswick, Fredericton, N.B.

ANS   Provincial Archives of Nova Scotia, Coburg Rd., Halifax, N.S.

Church	Dates	Archives
Andover	BMD 1845-	ANB
Bathurst	BMD 1864-	ANB
Cambridge	B 1833- M 1885- D 1883-	ANB
Cambridge and Waterloo	BMD 1823-	ANB
Campobello	BMD 1830-	ANB
Canning and Chipman	BD 1846- M 1858-	ANB
Chatham	B 1822- M 1835- D 1833-	ANB
Douglas and Bright	B 1845 M 1843- D 1856-	ANB
Fredericton (Christchurch)	B 1816- M 1874- D 1859-	UNB
Fredericton (St. Marys)	B 1843- MD 1846-	ANB
Grand Falls	B 1882- M 1887- D 1883 only	ANB
Grand Manan	BMD 1832-	ANB
Greenwich and Westfield	BM 1801- D 1822-	ANB
Hampton	BMD 1819-	ANB
Kingsclear	B 1816-	ANB
Kingston	BMD 1816-	ANB
Lancaster	BMD 1874-	ANB
Lepreau	BMD 1861-	ANB
Maugerville	BM 1787- D 1788-	ANB
Moncton	BMD 1843-	ANB
Newcastle	BMD 1843-	ANB
New Maryland	B 1836- M 1867- D 1860-	ANB
Pennfield	BMD 1822-	ANB
Prince William (and Queensbury)	B 1823- M 1826- D 1848-	ANB
Richibucto	B 1815- MD 1825-	ANB
Rothesay	BMD 1870-	ANB
Sackville	M 1863-80	ANB
St. Andrews	BMD 1787-	ANB
Saint John (St. Johns)	BMD 1852-	ANB
Saint John (Trinity)	B 1835- MD 1836-	ANB
St. Stephen (Christ Church)	BMD 1812-	ANB
St. Stephen (Trinity)	BMD 1870-	ANB
Shediac (St. Andrew)	BM 1825- D 1830-	ANB
Shediac (St. Martin) (including Richibucto and Buctouche 1833-5)	BMD 1822-35	PAC

Church	Dates	Archives
Simmonds	BM 1846- D 1859-	ANB
Sussex and Norton	BMD 1817-	ANB
Welford	BM 1848- D 1884-	ANB
Wellington and Buctouche	BMD 1868-	PAC
Woodstock	B 1812- MD 1816-	ANB
Westmorland County (St. Mark)	BMD 1790-	ANS

Note: The diocese of Fredericton holds a number of registers which pre-date civil registration, but unfortunately it has not been possible to obtain a list of them for publication. I suggest you write for information about a particular parish to the Diocesan Archives, 808 Brunswick Street, Fredericton. If you will refer to Chapter Four (Canadian Church Records) you will find listed the parishes of the diocese which existed prior to civil registration in 1888.

Baptist

All the Baptist Church registers listed below are in the Maritime Baptist Archives, Acadia University, Wolfville, Nova Scotia. It must be remembered that Baptists do not practise infant baptism, and that, generally speaking, the registers are not always separated from the general records of business of the particular church. In some cases marriages are recorded for a period but not deaths – and vice versa. For that reason, it is too complicated to list all the dates under each heading. The date shown below is the starting date of the registers and may apply to either adult baptisms, marriages, or deaths – or to all three.

Church	Dates	Church	Dates
Avondale	1871-	Lower Cambridge	1839-59
Bayside	1838-	Lower Queensbury	1841-
Belleisle Bay	1855-	McDonald's Corner	1839-
Belleisle Creek	1888-	Nashwaak	1833-70
Burtt's Corner	1812-	Point de Bute	1850-
Cambridge	1855-88	Prince William	
Canning	1800-73		1800-20, 1852-
Cape Tormentine	1892-	Sackville	1808-83
Cookville	1896-	St. Andrews	1865-
Fredericton		St. Francis	1888-
(Brunswick)	1814-	Saint John	1904-
Fredericton (George St.)		Scotchtown	1856-
	1845-77, 1879-	Tennant's Cove*	1866-
The Glades	1877-	Upper Queensbury	1873-
Hatfield's Point	1809-67	Victoria (Carleton)	1895-
Jacksontown	1843-	Wakefield	1804-10
Jemseg	1854-85	Wakefield (Rosedale)	1877-
Keirstead Mountain	1838-	Whitneyville	1819-
Little South West	1845-81	Woodstock*	1857-

*Free Baptist

Roman Catholic

AAM   Archives Acadiennes, Université de Moncton, New Brunswick

ANB   Provincial Archives, P.O. Box 6000, Fredericton, New Brunswick E3B 5H1.

PAC   Public Archives of Canada, 395 Wellington Street, Ottawa.

UM   Université de Montréal (Dépt. de Démographie).

Church	Dates	Archives
Baie-Ste-Anne	BMD 1801-	PAC
Baie-des-Vents	BMD 1801-	PAC
Barachois	BD 1812-70 M 1820-70	PAC
Bartibogue	BMD 1801-21	AAM
Bathurst	BMD 1798-	AAM
Botsford	See Cap Tourmentin	PAC
Bouctouche	BMD 1800-70	PAC
Cap-Pelé	BMD 1813-	AAM
Cap Tourmentin	B 1839-53 M 1846-7 D 1839-48	PAC
Caraquet	BMD 1768-99	PAC
Charlo	BMD 1853-	AAM
Cocagne	BMD 1800-70	PAC
Dalhousie	BMD 1843-	PAC
Ekoupag	BMD 1767-68	PAC
Fredericton	BMD 1806-59	PAC
Grande-Digue	BM 1800-75 D 1802-75	PAC
Haute-Aboujagane	See Barachois	PAC
Hillsborough	See Acadie and Gaspésie, Nova Scotia	PAC
Hopewell	See Acadie and Gaspésie, Nova Scotia	PAC
Inkerman	BMD 1818-	AAM
Lamèque	BMD 1841-	AAM
Madawaska	BMD 1792-	PAC
Memramcook	BM 1806-70 D 1807-70	PAC
Moncton	BMD 1873-	AAM
Naboiyagan	See Barachois	PAC
Nash Creek	BMD 1867-	AAM
Neguac	BMD 1796-1848	PAC
Paquetville	BMD 1874-	AAM
Petitcodiac	See Acadie and Gaspésie, Nova Scotia	PAC
Petit-Rocher	BMD 1824-	AAM
Pointe-Sapin	BMD 1821-69	PAC
Pokemouche	BMD 1843-	AAM
Richibouctou	BD 1796-1871 M 1800-71	PAC
Robertville	BMD 1885-	AAM
Rogersville	BMD 1877-87	AAM
St. Anselme	BMD 1832-75	PAC
St-Basile-de-Madawaska	BMD 1792-1850	PAC
St-Charles-de-Kent	BMD 1800-70	PAC
Ste-Anne-de-Kingsclear	BMD 1767-	AAM
St-Ignace-de-Kent	BMD 1887-	AAM
St. Isidore	BMD 1876-	AAM

Church	Dates	Archives
St-Louis-de-Kent	**BMD** 1800-70	PAC
St. Martins	**BD** 1876- **M** 1877-	ANB
St-Paul-de-Kent	**BMD** 1883-	AAM
Scoudouc	**B** 1850-70 **M** 1852-70 **D** 1855-70	PAC
Shediac	**BMD** 1863-	AAM
Shemogue (and Chimogoui)	**BD** 1813-99 **M** 1818-99	PAC
Shippegan	**BMD** 1824-	AAM
Tracadie (St. Jean)	**BMD** 1798-	AAM
Tracadie (St. Pierre)	**BMD** 1811-	AAM
New Brunswick Registers	**BMD** 1753-57	UM

United Church (including Methodist and Presbyterian)

ANB   Provincial Archives, P.O. Box 6000, Fredericton, New Brunswick E3B 5H1.

NBM   New Brunswick Provincial Museum, 277 Douglas Avenue, Saint John, New Brunswick E2K 1E5.

Church	Dates	Archives
Campbelltown (UC)	**BMD** 1874-	ANB
Fredericton (UC)	**BM** 1794-	NBM
Newcastle (P)	**B** 1831- **M** 1830- **D** 1891-	ANB
Newcastle (M)	**B** 1882- **M** 1884- **D** 1893-	ANB
Sussex (UC)	**BMD** 1857-	ANB
New Brunswick Registers (P)	**BMD** 1817-	NBM

M Methodist **P** Presbyterian **UC** United Church

Non-Denominational (town and civil registers)

Place	Dates	Archives
Chipoudy (and Petitcodiac)	**B** 1755 and 1756 **M** 1756	PAC
Jemsek (Rivière-St-Jean)	**B** 1681 only	PAC
Missions-de-N-Brunswick	**B** 1755-7	PAC
Petitcodiac (Hopewell)	**BMD** 1753-5	PAC
Sackville*	**M** 1748-1822	NBM
Sheffield	**B** 1750-1829 **MD** 1766-1845	PAC
Westmorland County	**M** 1790-1835	PAC

*In addition to the above, the Provincial Archives of Nova Scotia, Coburg Road, Halifax, Nova Scotia, have the township records of Sackville between 1760 and 1871. Sackville was originally part of that province. These records include land transactions, cattle marks, births, marriages, and deaths. Often children are listed who were born before the parents came to the township.

NEWFOUNDLAND

Newfoundland became Canada's tenth province in 1949 — before that, it was a British colony and, for a time, a self-governing Dominion.

CIVIL REGISTRATION
This started in 1891. Before that year the the various clergy maintained records of baptisms, marriages, and deaths. These latter records are in the Provincial Archives (see below). Since 1891 the records have been held by the Registrar of Vital Statistics, Department of Health, St. John's. A fee is charged for each certificate issued.

PROVINCIAL ARCHIVES
These are a branch of the Department of Tourism and are located in the Confederation Building, St. John's. They have very extensive holdings of early Newfoundland records. Apart from the usual government documents, the Archives contain early court records; deeds of sale; probates of wills; and registers of deeds – all going back to the early 1800s but not necessarily covering the whole province. There are also very many early newspapers and magazines – some of them dating back to 1837.

In addition, the Archives contain a number of papers from Newfoundland families – Andrews, Calvert, Currie, Holdsworth, Oke, Pinsent, etc. There is also the Devine Collection – originally put together by P. K. Devine, of St. John's, and containing a mass of early papers, documents, records, books, magazines, and newspapers.

Finally, the Archives has on file practically all parish records of the various religious denominations before 1891. Details of these will be found under Parish Registers later in this section.

LIBRARIES
The Newfoundland Public Libraries Board, Arts and Culture Centre (Library Administration), has a number of aids to ancestor-hunting:
1. Newfoundland Directories 1864-7, 1871, and 1898.
2. Colonial records and journals of the House of Assembly in which names of early settlers often appear. The journals date from 1833, and the colonial records from 1780.
3. Keith Matthews, *Who Was Who in the Fishing Industry, 1660-1840* (St. John's, 1971).
4. An early census of 1675 for St. John's and nearby areas such as Torbay, Petty Harbour, etc.
5. Some early education reports listing teachers and pupils.
6. Early court records.
7. An index file of personal names appearing in early Newfoundland newspapers and magazines.

LAND TITLES
The original Crown title records are in the custody of the

Registry of Crown Grants, Confederation Building, St. John's. Later records are in the Registry of Deeds in the same building.

WILLS

All wills probated in Newfoundland are recorded in the Registry Office of the Supreme Court, St. John's. The earliest will on file dates from 1832. The cost of searching the records, provided the exact date is known, is quite small.

CENSUSES
Early censuses in Newfoundland are listed below (N means each member of the family is listed, HF only the head of the family):

Plaisance	1671 N		Plaisance	1698 HF
Plaisance	1673 N		General	1704 HF
General	1691 N		Plaisance	1706 HF
General	1693 N		Plaisance	1711 HF

Note: These census records are available on microfilm in the Public Archives, Ottawa, and may be inspected by arrangement with your local library. Copies are also in the Provincial Archives in St. John's.

Province-wide censuses were held in 1921, 1935, and 1945. There are also partial records for 1911, and these records are in the Department of Social Services, St. John's. No charge is made at present for a search. There is no public access to the records, but people making enquiries in person may be shown specific entries. The information requested for these modern censuses included name, address, age, and occupation. (The exact date of birth was not required.)

PARISH REGISTERS
The majority of these are in the Provincial Archives, with a few in the Public Archives in Ottawa. Those which pre-date civil registration (1891) are listed below. There are, of course, many more *after* that date in the Provincial Archives:

ANF   Provincial Archives, Confederation Building, St. John's.

PAC   Public Archives of Canada, 395 Wellington Street, Ottawa.

Church	Denomination	Dates	Archives
Argentia	RC	BM 1835 only	ANF
Bay Roberts	A	B 1837- M 1840- D 1838-	ANF
Bay St. George	UC	BM 1883- D 1875-	ANF
Bonavista	A	BM 1786-	ANF

Church	Denomination	Dates	Archives
Brigus	UC	B 1822- M 1804- D 1824-	ANF
Bryants Cove	A	*See* Harbour Grace (A)	ANF
Burin	RC	BM 1833-	ANF
Burnt Island	UC	B 1860-	ANF
Carbonear	A	B 1834- M 1859-	ANF
Carbonear	RC	B 1850- M 1859-	ANF
Carbonear	UC	B 1817-34 M 1794-1848 D 1820-88	ANF
Catalina	A	B 1834-79 M 1833-79	ANF
Change Islands	A	B 1841-79 D 1829-	ANF
Cupids	UC	B 1877-88 M 1837	ANF
Ferryland	RC	BM 1870-	ANF
Fogo	UC	B 1863- M 1890- D 1890-	ANF
Fogo	A	M 1841- D 1879-	ANF
Greenspond Circuit	UC	M 1871-86 D 1889-	ANF
Harbour Grace	WM	B 1820-99	ANF
Harbour Grace	A	BD 1775- M 1776-	ANF
Harbour Grace	RC	B 1806- M 1811	ANF
Harbour Grace South	A	B 1872-	ANF
Harbour Main	RC	BM 1857-	ANF
Heart's Content	A	B 1879- M 1815- D 1886-	ANF
King's Cove	RC	BM 1815-	ANF
Lower Island Cove	UC	B 1816-52	ANF
Northern Bay	RC	BM 1838-	ANF
Old Perlican	UC	B 1816-82 M 1816-66	ANF
Placentia	RC	B 1882- M 1822- D 1884-	ANF
Portugal Cove	A	D 1830-38	ANF
Random South Circuit	UC	B 1890-	ANF
Renews	RC	B 1857- M 1838-	ANF
St. John's	RC	B 1802- M 1793- D 1891-	ANF
St. John's (Cathedral)	A	BMD 1752-90, 1800 only	ANF
St. John's (District)	A	B 1786-1803, 1849 only M 1784-95 D 1795-1803	PAC
St. John's	C	B 1780- M 1802- D 1837 only	PAC
St. Mary's	RC	B 1843- M 1844- D 1891-	ANF
St. Thomas	A	B 1830-70 M 1830-79 D 1865-78	ANF
Tilting	RC	BM 1842-	ANF
Trepassey	RC	B 1843- M 1861- D 1856-	ANF
Trinity	A	B 1753-1867 MD 1757-1867	PAC
Twillingate	A	B 1816-24	ANF
Twillingate	UC	B 1853-78 M 1853-76	ANF
Western Bay	UC	B 1817-42, 1877-88	ANF
Whitbourne	RC	BM 1891-	ANF
Whitbourne	UC	B 1892 MD 1893 only	ANF

Denominational abbreviations:

    A Anglican
    C Congregational
    RC Roman Catholic
    UC United Church (may include Congregational, Methodist, and Presbyterian)
    WM Wesleyan Methodist

NOVA SCOTIA

CIVIL REGISTRATION
In the early days the civil registration of births, marriages, and deaths in the province was a mess. The official recording of births, marriages, and deaths started in 1864. Nova Scotia entered Confederation in 1867, and one of the terms of the agreement which led to this event was that civil registration would be taken over by the Dominion Bureau of Statistics in Ottawa, starting ten years later, in 1877. However, nothing happened, the job was never started, and finally Ottawa admitted it could not do it. So the province re-started its own civil registration of births and deaths in 1908. (Fortunately it had continued the registration of marriages during this thirty-one-year period.)

The records are in the custody of the Registrar General of Nova Scotia, P.O. Box 157, Halifax, Nova Scotia B3J 2M9. The office will not undertake extended searches based on little information. You are expected to supply the full name, the approximate date (within three years), and (for births) the name of the father or mother, or both. The Assistant Deputy Registrar General informs me "there is no way this office can assist you in preparing a genealogy because the information for a genealogy is that which we must have to be able to locate a record on file." Well, *you have been warned!*

PROVINCIAL ARCHIVES
In contrast, the Provincial Archives are an extremely helpful department – most anxious to be of all possible assistance to the ancestor-hunter. The Archives are located at Coburg Road, Halifax, Nova Scotia B3H 1Z9. The actual Archives building is on the Studley Campus of Dalhousie University. The holdings are extensive and include books on Nova Scotian history; a number of family histories and genealogies; county and town histories; provincial and city directories; and the publications of the Nova Scotia Historical Society.

A GENEALOGICAL GUIDE
Terrence Punch, the province's leading genealogist, has written *Genealogical Research in Nova Scotia*. This detailed and reliable book is essential reading for all those tracing their Nova Scotian ancestors.

PASSENGER LISTS
The Archives contain some information about immigrants arriving from the United Kingdom between 1749 and 1801. The passenger lists of a few ships arriving from the United Kingdom are available, but quite often the "list" merely says

"about four hundred emigrants from the Hebrides" or "fifty in the steerage from Liverpool".

Extensive searches in both Canada and Great Britain have failed to produce any comprehensive lists of immigrants arriving in Canada before 1865. There are a few scattered lists in connection with subsidized emigration schemes but that is all. These are in the Public Archives of Canada, in Ottawa, and are indexed.

ACADIAN RECORDS
See pp. 76-80.

LIBRARIES
The Halifax City Regional Library, 5381 Spring Garden Road, Halifax, has a large number of family histories, and many other genealogical aids.

WILLS
Wills are filed in the Court of Probate in the capital of the county where the deceased lived or owned property. The Probate Registrars are in Annapolis Royal, Antigonish, Sydney, Truro, Amherst, Digby, Guysborough, Sherbrooke, Halifax, Windsor, Port Hood, Kentville, Lunenburg, Pictou, Liverpool, Arichat, Shelburne, Barrington, Baddeck, and Yarmouth.

LAND TITLES
Original land grants are in the custody of the Crown Lands Office, Department of Lands and Forests, Halifax, and later transactions are recorded in the district registry offices, of which there are twenty-one. The Public Archives has an alphabetical file of the draft grants of the first time a piece of land was granted by the Crown, and also of petitions by settlers asking the Governor of the colony for a grant of land. Photocopies of the petitions and grants can be supplied by the Archives for a small fee.

Petitions sometimes give information about the settler's family and country of origin – but the latter is usually "North Britain" or "Ireland" or "Somerset". Of course, not all settlers petitioned for land, and not all settlers occupied the land when it had been granted. The Crown Lands Department, Halifax, has a series of maps showing the first grants in each district. Land Deeds are also available for inspection.

The Registrars of Deeds are located in the main centres of the province: Amherst, Antigonish, Arichat, Baddeck, Barrington, Bridgetown, Bridgewater, Chester, Guysborough, Halifax, Kentville, Liverpool, Pictou, Port Hood, Shelburne, Sherbrooke, Sydney, Truro, Weymouth, Windsor, and Yarmouth.

CENSUSES: Please see Note 2 on p. 46.

The earliest census in Nova Scotia was that of 1671 (under the French occupation), but the first one of any use to the ancestor-hunter is that of 1770, which gives the name of the head of the family, the number of people in the household, and the country of origin. This one covered the areas of Amherst, Annapolis, Barrington, Conway, Cumberland, Falmouth, Granville, Hillsborough (now in New Brunswick), Horton, Londonderry, New Dublin, Onslow, Pictou, Sackville (now in New Brunswick), and Truro. Microfilm copies are in the Provincial Archives. Later ones in 1811 (Cape Breton), 1817 (Sydney County), 1818 (Cape Breton), and 1827 (Annapolis, Bras d'Or Lake, Louisbourg, Cumberland, Digby, Halifax County – not the city – Liverpool, Shelburne, and Yarmouth) all give similar information.

It was not until 1861, 1871, and 1881 that the censuses were complete for the whole province, and only the latter censuses give the names of each member of the family.

GENEALOGICAL SOCIETY

There is no society as such. However, the Royal Nova Scotia Historical Society has a Genealogical Committee which publishes a quarterly newsletter. The subscriptions secretary is W. S. Murphy, 57 Primrose Street, Dartmouth, Nova Scotia B3A 4C6.

CHURCH REGISTERS

The following records are listed by the Provincial Archives as church *registers* but I believe, in some cases, they may be church *records*, which is a very different matter. They are, however, on microfilm and may be borrowed by your local library. The dates shown are starting dates and no information is available as to whether this applies to baptisms, marriages, and deaths or to only one or two of these events:

United Church (including Presbyterian, Congregational, and Methodist)

Church	Denomination	Dates
Amherst (St. Stephen)	P	1840-
Annapolis Royal	M	1875 and 1876
Annapolis (Circuit)	M	1793-
Antigonish (Dorchester)	P	1821-53
Barrington	M	1786-
Barrington	WM	1823-
Bridgewater (Grace) (inc. Grace (M) St. John (P))	UC	1877-
Canning	M	1865-

Church	Denomination	Dates
Canso	UC	1854-
Chebogue	C	1767-1857
Chester	C	1762-85
Coldstream	P	1833 and 1834
Cornwallis	M	1815-
Dartmouth (St. James)	P	1835-50
Dorchester	P	1821-53
Earltown	P	1782-
Elmsdale (and Nine Mile River)	P	1879-
Falmouth	C	1844-
Folly Village (Erskine Church)	P	1798-1833
Glenholme (Erskine Church)	P	1896-
Grand Pré (Horton)	UC	1819-
Granville	M	1816
Great Village	P	1852-72
Guysborough	M	1822-
Guysborough	UC	1845-
Halifax (Brunswick St.)	UC	1784-
Halifax (City Mission)	M	1855-68
Halifax (Fort Massey)	P	1875-
Halifax (Poplar Grove)	P	1843-91
Halifax (St. Andrew)	P	1818-
Halifax (St. Matthew)	P	1769-
Halifax (Salem)	C	1868-76
Ingonish	M	1874-
Kennetcook	P	1876-
Kings County	M	1819-
Kingsport	C	1819-
Liverpool	C	1843-
Liverpool (Zion)	M	1795-
Lochaber	P	1811-
Lunenburg	M	1815-37
Lunenburg	P	1770-
Middle Musquodoboit	P	1848-
Middle Musquodoboit	M	1860-
Milton (Queens County)	C	1854-
New Glasgow	P	1801-
New Harbour	UC	1854-
New Minas	M	1819-
Newport and Walton	UC	1824-
North Beaverbank	P	1886-
Northeast Harbour	UC	1878-
Oxford	M	1879-
Parrsboro (Circuit)	M	1824-37
Petite Rivière	UC	1847-
Pictou	P	1855-
Pictou	UC	1808-
Port Morien (St. John)	P	1868-
Port Mouton	UC	1849-
Pugwash	P	1857-
St. Croix and Ellershouse	P	1873-
St. Margarets Bay	UC	1820-
Sambro	P	1820-
Scotsburn	P	1840-
Shelburne County	M	1790-1821
Shubenacadie	P	1817-40

Church	Denomination	Dates
Stellarton	UC	1863-97
Sydney (St. Andrew)	UC	1865-
Tatamagouche	UC	1851-
Truro	P	1834-54
Upper Londonderry	UC	1859-
Valley Station	P	1871-
Wallace	M	1817-83
West Branch, East River	P	1827-
Windsor	UC	1876-
Yarmouth	M	1846-
Yarmouth	P	1848-

UC United Church C Congregational M Methodist
WM Wesleyan Methodist

Anglican

Church	Dates
Annapolis Royal (St. Luke)	1782-
Arichat (St. John)	1828-
Aylesford	1789-
Aylesford (St. Mary)	1791-
Baddeck (St. John)	1877-
Bear River (St. John)	no dates given
Blandford (St. Barnabas)	1859-
Bridgetown	1830-54
Bridgewater (Holy Trinity)	1854-96
Centre Rawdon	1793-
Chester (St. Stephen)	1762-1859
Clementsport (St. Edward)	1841-
Clements Township (St. Clement)	1841-
Conquerall Mills (St. James)	no dates given
Cornwallis Township (St. John)	1775-
Country Harbour (Holy Trinity)	1851-
Dartmouth (Christ Church)	1793-
Digby (Trinity)	1785-
Falmouth (St. George)	1793-
French Village	1834-
Granville	1790-
Green Harbour	1885-
Guysborough (Christ Church)	1786-
Halifax (St. George)	1783-
Halifax (St. John)	1839-
Halifax (St. Luke)	1858-
Halifax (St. Mark)	1861-
Halifax (St. Paul)	1749-
Halifax (St. Stephen)	1876-
Horton and Wolfville (St. John)	1775-1876
Hubbards (St. Luke)	1858-
Jeddore (St. James and St. John)	1863-
Kentville (St. James)	1893-
La Have (St. Matthew)	1884-
Lawrencetown (St. Andrew)	1846-
Liscomb (St. Luke)	1852-
Liverpool (Holy Trinity)	1819-70
Lockeport	1883-

Church	Dates
Londonderry	1873-89
Lower Stewiacke (Holy Trinity)	1849-
Lunenburg (St. John)	1752-
McPhee Corner (St. Thomas)	1860-
Mahone Bay (St. James)	1833-70
Maitland, Hants County	1855-
Milton, Yarmouth County	1890-
New Dublin	1821-
Newport and Walton (St. James)	1793-
New Ross (Christ Church)	1822-
Port Morien (St. Paul)	1865-
Rawdon (St. Paul)	1793-
Sackville (St. John)	1813-
Seaforth (St. James)	1865-
Shelburne (Christ Church)	1783-
Ship Harbour (St. Stephen)	1841-
Sydney (St. George)	1785-
Sydney Mines (Trinity)	1850-
Truro (St. John)	1824-
Upper Stewiacke	1872-
Westphal (St. John)	1889-
Weymouth (St. Peter)	1823-
Wilmot Township	1789-
Windsor (Christ Church)	1811-
Yarmouth (Trinity)	1813-

Roman Catholic

Church	Dates
Annapolis Royal (St. Jean Baptiste)	1702-55
Beaubassin	1712-48
Enfield (St. Bernard)	1857-85
Grand Pré (St. Charles)	1707-48
Halifax (St. Mary)	1800-
Ile Royale (Cape Breton) Lorembec	1715-21, 1726-45
Ile Royale (Cape Breton) Havre St. Esprit	1728-37
Ile Royale (Cape Breton) Port au Basque	1740-
Ile Royale (Cape Breton) Forchu	1741-9
Sheet Harbour (St. Peter)	1857-80

Other Denominations

Church	Denomination	Dates
Barrington	Free Will Baptist	1851-6
Cornwallis Township	Baptist	1804-22, 1855-74
Dartmouth	Society of Friends	1786-98
Halifax (Central)	Baptist	1848-
Halifax (Granville)	Baptist	1827-44
Liverpool	Baptist	1821-70
Lunenburg (N.W. Range)	Baptist	1795-1874
Lunenburg (N.W. Range)	Lutheran	1770-1884
Milton (Queens County)	Baptist	no dates given
Sackville	Baptist	1832-
Yarmouth (First)	Baptist	1784-98

Acadie and Gaspésie   1679-1758

68
NOVA SCOTIA

The following are definitely church registers of various denominations and are in the custody of the following archives:

AAM   Archives Acadiennes, Université de Moncton, N.-Brunswick.

ANS   Archives of Nova Scotia, Coburg Road, Halifax, N.S.

CBA   Cape Bretonia Archives, St. Francis-Xavier University, Sydney, N.S.

MBA   Maritime Baptist Archives, Acadia University, Wolfville, N.S.

PAC   Public Archives of Canada, 395 Wellington St., Ottawa.

Before referring to any of the church registers listed below, please reread Note 1 on pp. 45-6.

Church	Denomi-nation	Dates	Archives
Arichat (Notre Dame)	RC	BMD 1811 only	CBA
Arichat (L'Assomption)	RC	BMD 1839-	AAM
Arichat (St. John)	A	M 1828-	CBA
Annapolis (Circuit)	M	B 1835-54 M 1834-52	PAC
Annapolis (St. Luke) (inc. Clements, Granville, Dalhousie, M 1806, 1834)	A	B 1782-1817, 1833-88 M 1782-94, 1807-17 D 1808-17	PAC
Aylesford (St. Mary)	A	B 1792-1861	PAC
Aylesford (Trinity)	A	*See under* Wilmot	PAC
Baie-Ste-Marie (Ste. Marie)	RC	BMD 1799-1801	PAC
Beaubassin	RC	BMD 1679-86, 1712-48	PAC
Bridgetown (Trinity)	A	*See under* Wilmot	PAC
Chester (St. Stephen)	A	B 1762-1841	PAC
Cheticamp	RC	BMD 1811-	AAM
Chezzetcook	RC	BMD 1785-	AAM
Church Point	RC	*See under* Baie-Ste-Marie	PAC
Clements (St. Edward)	A	B 1841-74 M 1841-	PAC
Clements (St. Luke)	A	*See under* Annapolis (St. Luke)	PAC
Coldstream	P	M 1833 and 1834	PAC
Cornwallis	B	M 1801-22	PAC
Cornwallis	M	B 1814-27	PAC
Cornwallis (St. John)	A	BM 1783- D 1830-	PAC
Dalhousie	A	*See under* Annapolis	PAC
Digby (Trinity)	A	B 1786-1830 M 1786-1834 D 1786-1845	PAC
Douglas	A	*See under* Rawdon	PAC
Grand Pré	RC	B 1707-48 MD 1709-1848	PAC

Church	Denomi-nation	Dates	Archives
Horton (St. John)	A	B 1823-77	PAC
Ile Royale (Havre de St. Esprit)	RC	BMD 1726, 1745, 1749	PAC
Joggins	RC	BMD 1849-	AAM
Liverpool	M	B 1796- M 1816-	PAC
Liverpool (Trinity)	A	BMD 1819-69	PAC
Londonderry (St. Paul)	A	BMD 1873-	PAC
Louisbourg	RC	BMD 1722-58	AAM
Lunenburg	B	B 1793-1874 M 1819-56 D 1816-58	PAC
Lunenburg	DR	B 1770- M 1770-1855 D 1771-1854	PAC
Lunenburg	M	BM 1815-37	PAC
Lunenburg (St. John)	A	BMD 1852-69	PAC
Mahone Bay (St. James)	A	B 1845- MD 1844-	PAC
Margaree	RC	BMD 1806	AAM
Petit Nord	RC	BMD 1740-45	PAC
Pomquet	RC	BMD 1820-	AAM
Port-Royal	RC	BMD 1702-55	PAC
Rawdon (St. Paul)	A	B 1793- M 1814- D 1815-	PAC
Ste-Anne-de-Ruisseau	RC	BMD 1799-	AAM
Ste-Claire-de-Lorembec	RC	BMD 1714-45, 1750-7	PAC
St. James (Hants County)	A	See under Rawdon	PAC
Shelburne (Christ Church)	A	BMD 1783-1869	PAC
Sydney (inc. Cape Breton to 1817)	A	BMD 1785-1851	PAC
Wilmot (Trinity) (inc. Aylesford and Bridgetown)	A	BMD 1789-	PAC

Civil Registers

Church	Dates	Archives
Annapolis	BMD 1747, 1774-1874, 1884	PAC
Beaubassin	B 1680-6 M 1679-82	PAC
Chester	BMD 1762-1829	PAC
Cornwallis Township	BMD 1720-1885	PAC
Cumberland County	BMD 1757-1817	PAC
Falmouth	BMD 1747-1825	PAC
Fort Lawrence (inc. Town of Cumberland)	BMD 1766-1891	PAC
Granville	BMD 1720-1881	PAC
Horton	BMD 1823-95	PAC
Les Mines	B 1686 only	PAC
Newport	B 1752-1845 MD 1762-1858	PAC
Onslow	BMD 1761-1855	PAC
Rivière des Mines	B 1684 only	PAC
Truro	BMD 1761-1851	PAC
Wilmot Township	BMD 1749-	PAC

Baptist

The following records are in the Maritime Baptist Archives, Acadia University, Wolfville, Nova Scotia:

Church	Dates	Church	Dates
Advocate Harbour	1839-90	Indian Harbour	1843-85
Antigonish	1823-1900	Kentville	1876-1911
Avonport	1876-1909	Liverpool	See Milton
Barrington (Central)	1859-1912	Londonderry	1903-26
Barrington (Bethel)	1811-78	Lower Granville	1832-49
Barrington		Maitland and Noel	1891-1909
(Providence)	1907-28	Milton	1823-1913
Barrington (Temple)	1841,	New Tusket	1843-85
	1878-97	North Brookfield	1828-1917
Barrington West	1848-63	Onslow	1791-1869
Barss' Corners	1842-1913	Onslow West	1868-81
Bear Point	1866-1944	Paradise-Clarence	1827-1949
Bedford	1899-1947	Scotch Village	1799-1855,
Berwick	1829-58		1871-95
Bridgetown	1838-88	Smith's Cove	1842(B)
Bridgewater	1848-86	South Ohio	1859-1928
Canning	1882-1903	South Rawdon	1823-94
Canning (Free)	1850-1906	Springfield	1835-1921
Centreville (Digby)	1836-62	Springhill	1904-31
Centreville		Upper Canard	1847-77 (M)
(Shelburne)	1821-66	Summerville	1859-1903
Chegoggin	1892-1905	Upper Stewiacke	1839-68
Clementsvale	1825-1911	West Bay	1869-90
Cornwallis	1778-1806	Weymouth Bridge	1902-03
Falmouth	1843-1934	Weymouth North	1809-67
Gaspereaux	1857-86	Windsor	1879-81
Greenfield	1858-1949	Wine Harbour	1897-1907
Guysborough	1848-1919	Wolfville	1778-1819,
Halifax	1835-64(M)		1831-1909
Hebron	1837-1915	Yarmouth*	1767-71
Horton	1778-1816	Yarmouth West	1863-1928

*Congregational

PRINCE EDWARD ISLAND

CIVIL REGISTRATION

The registration of births and deaths in the province started in 1906. The marriage records date back to 1787 but are missing between 1813 and 1824. The custodian is the Director, Division of Vital Statistics, Department of Health, Box 3000, Charlottetown, Prince Edward Island C1A 7P1. The office also has custody of some baptismal records taken from most of the Island churches and dating from 1800 to 1886. Most of these records have the name of the parents and the date of birth. They are not open to a public search but a member of the staff will undertake this for a fee for each search. A complete list of these records is given at the end of this section.

PROVINCIAL ARCHIVES
These are located at Box 1000, Charlottetown. They have a few church registers on microfilm and these are listed later in this section. (Their holdings are very small because the Division of Vital Statistics holds the bulk of the early church records.) The Archives also have marriage licences from 1831 to 1907 and marriage bonds dating from 1849 to 1902. These are in chronological order but are not indexed. There are also a number of family genealogies and histories in MS form.

LIBRARIES
The Confederation Centre Library in Charlottetown has probate records (wills) from 1800 to 1900. These are on microfilm and may possibly be borrowed through your local library. The originals are in the Probate Office in Charlottetown.

The Provincial Library, University Avenue, Charlottetown, states they can be of little assistance to the ancestor-hunter as all their genealogical material has been given to the Provincial Archives.

GENEALOGICAL SOCIETY
The address is Box 922, Charlottetown, P.E.I. C1A 7L9. The following also have genealogical records:

The Heritage Foundation, 2 Kent Street, Charlottetown:
This organization has the Foundation Index. This includes alphabetical indexes to the censuses of 1798, 1841, and 1861; all Island newspapers to 1825; inquests to 1850; and land petitions to 1836. It also has a collection of Island genealogies.
The Abegweit Research Group, P.O. Box 20, Winsloe.
The United Empire Loyalists (Mr. L. Linkletter, Archivist, Malpeque Road, P.E.I.)

LAND TITLES
All land grants, including Crown grants, are held in the Office of the Registrar of Deeds, Charlottetown, from 1900 onwards. No fees are charged for searching. Records prior to 1900 are in the Provincial Archives.

CENSUSES: Please see Note 2 on p. 46.
So far as Prince Edward Island is concerned, the Public Archives have custody of the census returns for 1798, 1841, and 1861. (Prince Edward Island did not enter Confederation until 1873.) Unfortunately, these censuses only listed the name

of the head of the family and so are not of too much help so far as the Island is concerned. The 1798 census is not on microfilm.

CHURCH RECORDS

As mentioned above, the Department of Vital Statistics has baptismal records from most of the churches from 1800 to 1886. These are listed below exactly as supplied by the Department. They are not in alphabetical order since in many cases they cover a number of districts, nor are they separated by denomination as, in some cases, this does not appear. The dates shown are starting dates of the registers:

St. Johns Anglican Church 1837 – includes Milton, Rustico, North and South Winsloe, Brookfield, Cherry Valley, Wheatley River, Riverside, North Wiltshire, and North River.

United Church Winsloe Pastoral Charge 1800 – includes Winsloe, Highfield, Glasgow Road, Prince Town Road.

United Church York 1806 – includes West Covehead and York, Brackley, Harrington, Pleasant Grove, Grand Tradie, East Royalty, Marshfield, Dunstaffnage, Bedford, Suffolk, North Rustico, French Fort, Ten Mile House, Black River, Union Road, and St. Peters Road.

St. John United Church, Mount Stewart 1871 – includes East St. Peters, Mt. Stewart, and West St. Peters.

United Church, Cornwall 1857 – includes Kingston, Meadowbank, Clyde River, New Dominion, Nine Mile Creek, Rocky Point, Wiltshire, West River, Little York, Union Road, Brackley Pt. Rd., Tracadie Rd., Winsloe Rd., New Dominion.

Breadalbane United 1845 – includes Rose Valley, Hartsville, Pleasant Valley, North Granville, Breadalbane, Hunter River, and Stanley Bridge.

Kirk of St. James, Charlottetown 1849 –

St. Peters Cathedral, Charlottetown 1869 – includes Charlottetown, Georgetown, Winsloe Road, Southport, Little Sands, New Glasgow, Cherry Valley, North River, Morell, Keppoch, and Little York.

Trinity United Church, Charlottetown 1836 – includes Grace Church Records and First Methodist, Charlottetown.

Georgetown Anglican Church 1842 – includes Cardigan,
Georgetown, Montague, Souris, Harmony, Morell, Malpeque,
Murray Harbor, New Perth, Peakes Station, Sturgeon, St. Peters
Road, and Darnley.

Free Church of Scotland 1868 – includes Birch Hill, Mount
Albion, Pownal, Mount Mellick, Kinross, Murray River,
Freetown, Searletown, Wilmot Creek, Summerside, Carleton
Point, Tryon, Central Bedeque, Seal River, Albany, Vernon River,
Pleasant Valley, Brooklyn, Murray Harbor, and Wood Island.

St. Paul's Anglican Church 1777 – includes Southport, Morell,
Souris, N. Wiltshire, Mt. Edward Rd., Vernon River, New
Glasgow, Marshfield, Milton, Keppoch, and Saint John, N.B.

Zion Presbyterian Church 1868 –

Pownal United Church 1856 – includes Pownal, Bunbury-Clifton,
Village Green, Albany Plains, Squaw Bay, Mt. Albion, Lots 48, 49,
50, Baltic Road, Southport, Cherry Valley, Hillsborough River,
Millview, Orwell, Roseneath, Vernon River, Birch Hill, Alexandra,
Mt. Herbert.

Marshfield Presbyterian 1862 –

United Church, Montague 1828 – includes Montague, Valleyfield,
Georgetown, Methodist Church, Montague.

St. Davids United Church, Georgetown 1854 – includes
Georgetown, Alliston, Cambridge, Sturgeon, Milltown Cross, and
Albany.

Presbyterian Church, Belfast 1823 – includes Flat River, Pinette,
Mt. Buchanan, Point Prim, Eldon, Garfield, Rosebury, Ocean
View, Souris, Newtown Cross, and Orwell Cove.

Wood Islands Presbyterian 1851 –

United Church, Hampton and Crapaud 1831 – includes Bonshaw,
Appin Road, Tryon, Victoria, DeSable, and Bedeque.

St. Johns Anglican Church, Crapaud 1843 – includes Crapaud,
Springfield, Westmoreland, Hampton, Victoria, Albany, Borden,
Long Creek, Breadalbane, Emerald, and Granville.

United Church, Bedeque 1843 – includes Borden, Bedeque,
Central and Lower Bedeque, Fernwood, Searletown, Albany,

Chilton, Tryon, Cape Traverse, Augustin Cove, Carleton, and
South Shore.

United Church, North Bedeque 1826 – includes Travellers Rest,
North Bedeque, Freetown, Wilmot Valley, and Lower Bedeque.

St. Marys Anglican Church, Summerside 1865 – St. Eleanors,
Miscouche, Travellers Rest, Sherbrooke, and Summerside.

St. Marks Anglican Church, Kensington 1821 – includes New
London and St. Eleanors.

Kensington Presbyterian Church 1855 – includes New London,
Granville, Summerfield, Grahams Road, Springfield, Breadalbane,
Long River, Park Corner, Sea View, French River, Kensington,
Indian River, Spring Valley, and Norboro.

United Church of Margate 1860 – includes Clinton, New London,
Long River, French River, Stanley Bridge, Granville, Margate,
Pleasant Valley, Searletown, Malpeque, Norborough, Burlington,
Baltic, South Freetown, Darnley, Cavendish, and Sea View.

St. Augustine's R.C. Church, South Rustico 1817 –

St. Anns, Hope River 1881 –

Bideford United Church 1875 – includes Conway, Bideford, Tyne
Valley, Lot 14, Egmont Circuit, Sheep River, Lot 16, Union Corner,
Enmore River, and territory from Miscouche to Mt. Pleasant.

St. Dunstans Basilica, Charlottetown 1830 –
St. Patricks Church, Fort Augustus 1854 –
St. Joachims, Vernon River 1837 –
St. Michaels, Iona 1868 –
St. Georges, St. Georges 1836 –
St. Marys Church, Souris 1864 –
St. Alexis, Rollo Bay 1847 –
St. Columba, St. Columba 1836 –
St. James, Georgetown 1855 –
St. Pauls Church, Sturgeon 1867 –
St. Anns R.C., Lot 65 (no starting date given)
St. Josephs Parish, Kelly Cross (no starting date given)
St. Peters R.C. Church, Seven Mile Bay 1846
St. Malachys R.C. Church, Kinkora (S.W. Bedeque) 1860 –
St. Pauls R.C. Church, Summerside 1854 –
Trinity United Church, Summerside 1866 –
Anglican Church, Port Hill 1842 –

St. Bonaventure R.C. Church, Tracadie 1845 –
St. Andrews R.C. Church, St. Andrews 1856 –
St. Lawrence R.C. Church, Morell 1881 –
St. Teresas R.C. Church, St. Teresas (Cardigan Parish) 1868 –
Presbyterian Church, Murray Harbour North 1876 –
St. John the Baptist, Miscouche 1817 –
St. Marys R.C. Church, Indian River 1838 –
St. Patricks R.C. Church, Grand River 1878
St. Anns R.C. Church, Lennox Island 1842 –
Notre Dame du Mont Carmel 1820 –
St. Peters Bay R.C. Church 1850 –
St. Francis de Sales, Little Pond Parish 1865-85
St. Margarets R.C. Church, St. Margarets 1881-5
St. Jacques R.C. Church, Egmont Bay 1821 –
St. Marys Parish, Brae, Lot 9 1833 –
St. Brigids Parish 1876 –
Immaculate Conception, Wellington Parish 1884-5
St. Anthony Church, Bloomfield Parish 1839-86
West Cape United Church Records, at O'Leary 1847 –
Sacred Heart Church, Alberton 1879 –
St. Peters Anglican Church, Alberton 1859 –
United Church, Alberton 1895 –
Saints Simon and Jude R.C. Church, Tignish 1831 –
Immaculate Conception Church, Palmer Road 1882 –
St. Marks R.C. Church, Lot 7, Burton 1871 –
St. Michaels Parish (Launching) 1840 –

CHURCH REGISTERS

In addition to the above, the following registers or microfilm copies are held in various archives. Please reread Note 1 on pp. 45-6.

AAM   Archives Acadiennes, Université de Moncton, N.-Brunswick.
MBA   Maritime Baptist Archives, Acadia University, Wolfville, N.S.
PAC   Public Archives of Canada, 395 Wellington Street, Ottawa.
PEIA   Provincial Archives of P.E.I., Box 100, Charlottetown, P.E.I.
ANS   Provincial Archives of Nova Scotia, Coburg Rd., Halifax, N.S.

Church	Denomination	Dates	Archives
Alberton	A	BMD 1859-	PEIA
Alexandra	B	BMD 1843-73	MBA

Church	Denomi- nation	Dates	Archives
Belfast	B	BMD 1822-	MBA
Belfast (St. Johns)	P	B 1823-49	PEIA
Breadalbane	UC	BMD 1845-	PEIA
Cascumpeque	RC	BMD 1839-68	PEIA
Charlottetown (St. James)	P	BMD 1849-	PEIA
Charlottetown (Cathedral)	A	BMD 1869-	PEIA
Charlottetown (Trinity)	UC	BMD 1836-	PEIA
Cornwall	UC	B 1857-74, 1880, 1886 M 1857-76 D 1867-70	PEIA
Georgetown	A	BMD 1842-	PEIA
Malpeque	RC	BMD 1817-35	PEIA
Mont Carmel	RC	BMD 1844-	AAM
North River	B	BMD 1865-	MBA
Palmer Road	RC	BMD 1878-90	AAM
Port Hill	A	BMD 1842-	PEIA
Port Lajoie	RC	See St-Pierre-du-Nord	PEIA
Rustico	RC	BMD 1812-24	PEIA
St-Pierre-du-Nord (Notre Dame)	RC	BMD 1724-58 (inc. Port Lajoie)	PEIA
St-Pierre-du-Nord (St. Pierre)	RC	BMD 1721-24, 1749-58	PEIA
Tignish	RC	BMD 1844-69	PEIA
Lot 10	B	BMD 1885-	MBA
Belfast (inc. records of baptism for parts of Pictou County)	—	B 1823-49	ANS

THE ACADIANS

The Acadians are people of French descent living in the Atlantic Provinces, Quebec, Louisiana, and New England. Their ancestors were the victims of one of the most brutal expulsions in history. Their original home was what is now known as Nova Scotia.

Emery LeBlanc, in his book *Les Acadiens* (Montreal, 1963), estimated there were then 350,000 people of Acadian descent in the Atlantic Provinces, 300,000 in Quebec, 600,000 in Louisiana (where they are known as Cajuns – a corruption of Acadians), and 75,000 in New England.

The first settlement in what the French called Acadie, and what is now known as Nova Scotia, was begun by the Sieur de Monts and Samuel de Champlain in 1604. It was on an island in Passamaquoddy Bay, but was moved a year later to the mainland and was named Port Royal. English and Scottish settlers arrived in other parts of the peninsula a few years later.

From this time on the Acadians were the victims of power politics and of the wars and rivalry between France and England. Neither country showed the slightest regard for the welfare of the inhabitants of Acadia, and ownership of the peninsula went from one country to the other between the early seventeenth century and the final Peace Treaty in 1763. It was only then, with the end of French rule in North America, that the Acadians, while still a neglected minority, were left in comparative peace.

The original two hundred settlers from France, plus another fifty who arrived soon after, are the ancestors of the present-day Acadians. It has been said that every Acadian today could trace his ancestry back to the original two hundred and fifty. It is believed that at least half of the settlers came from the area of Aulnay, in the Department of Vienne, in France.

By 1750 the Acadians numbered 12,000 and, as the result of the Treaty of Utrecht, they were under the rule of England. Charles Lawrence, the lieutenant-governor, was unhappy about the presence of this large body of French-speaking settlers in what was now known as Nova Scotia. He made numerous representations to London and was finally instructed to obtain from each Acadian an Oath of Allegiance to the Crown. The Acadian leaders agreed to this, provided they would be excused military service against their fellow French in Quebec. The lieutenant-governor refused to accept this and demanded the full oath. The Acadians, who had already proved their loyalty by refusing to join a French attack on Nova Scotia, remained firm. Lawrence then decided on the mass expulsion of all the Acadians and the seizure of their lands and houses.

The expulsion started in 1755 and continued until 1763, when the Peace Treaty ended French rule in Canada. Six thousand Acadians were rounded up, placed on ships, and taken to various English settlements along the coast from Massachusetts to Georgia. Families were separated, houses and settlements were burned, and the survivors were set ashore in settlements where their language was not spoken and their religion was not tolerated.

Others fled into the forests and later made their way to Quebec, Louisiana, and the Ohio Valley. Many returned to France. Although the English government did not specifically authorize the expulsion, it certainly approved the end result. Lawrence was congratulated on his actions and promoted to Governor.

After the Peace Treaty in 1763 the Acadians started trickling back home – even though their houses and lands had been given to English settlers. Many, of course, stayed in Louisiana and Quebec. Some enlisted in the American army at the time of the Revolutionary War and were later granted land in Clinton County, New York State. Others, believing there was no future as a landless settler in Nova Scotia, also went to France to join those who had fled there during the expulsion.

In France they lived near French ports and on a large tract of land twenty miles northwest of Poitiers – in the parishes of

Archigny, Cenan, La Puye, and St-Pierre-de-Maillé. From time to time some of them returned to Canada, and others went to the Caribbean and the islands of St. Pierre and Miquelon. In 1785, the King of Spain financed the transportation of a hundred or so Acadians to Louisiana – then Spanish territory.

The Archives of France (Archives Nationales, 60 rue des Francs-Bourgeois, Paris) contain a great deal of Acadian information in a section called Archives des Colonies. These include:

CENSUSES
Besides the usual information these, in many cases, listed the parish of origin in Acadia. The censuses were held in the period from 1762 to 1773, and in 1783 and 1784.

FINANCIAL LISTS
These give details of government assistance to Acadians arriving in France. The period covered is from 1773 to 1797.

PASSENGER LISTS
These cover the period from 1775 to 1776 and are basically a census of four convoys from Acadia, giving names, ages, relationship, and occupations.

SETTLEMENT
This covers the period from 1764 to 1769 and lists the arrival and settlement in Louisiana of many families from Halifax, New York, and Santo Domingo. It gives details of their place of origin and final destination.

COURT RECORDS
These date from 1711 to 1758 and give details of court actions in that period in Acadia.

NOTARIAL RECORDS
These include wills, marriage contracts, land grants, sales, legacies, contracts, and leases for the period from 1687 to 1728.

All the above records are in the Archives Nationales. Other sources of information in France are:

CHURCH REGISTERS
These date from 1758 to about 1800 and cover the areas in

France where the displaced Acadians settled. They are to be found in departmental archives or in the local Mairie (Town Hall). (For fuller details of local archives in France please refer to Chapter Thirteen.) The main districts of settlement were Le Havre, Nantes, Boulogne, Cherbourg, St. Malo, St. Servan, Paramé, Pleudihan, Plouer, Pleslin, Morlaix, Lorient, Sauzon, Port Louis, Ile de Belle-Ile, and Chatellerault, Archigny, Bonneuil-Matours, Cenan, Chauvigny, Leigné-les-Bois, La Puye, St-Pierre-de-Maillé.

CENSUSES OF ACADIANS IN FRANCE
These cover the period from 1763 to 1789 and are in the Archives Départementales, Caen, France.

The main source of information about Acadian records in Canada is Les Archives Acadiennes, Université de Moncton, Nouveau-Brunswick (Ronald LeBlanc, Librarian). The abbreviation for these Archives is AAM.

These archives contain microfilms of nearly all the Acadian parish registers. You will find these registers listed in the Roman Catholic registers under New Brunswick, Nova Scotia, and Prince Edward Island. They have also published *Inventaire général des sources documentaires sur les Acadiens*. This costs $15 and can be bought from the publishers, Les Éditions d'Acadie, rue Victoria 120, Moncton.

The Public Archives of Canada in Ottawa have on microfilm "Gaudet's Notes". These were compiled by Placide Gaudet from various sources and list births, marriages, and deaths from the various parishes. There are some errors in them and they should not be accepted as official records.

The Public Archives also have on microfilm the registers of various parishes in Louisiana:

Atakapas (Martinville) (including Pointe-Coupée)	BMD 1756-94
Fort du Biloxi	D 1720-3
Fort Condé	*See* Mobile
Iberville (St. Gabriel)	B 1773-4 M 1773-1859
Mobile (Notre Dame)	BM 1704, 1707, 1717, 1726-8, 1732-9, 1741-8, 1750-1, 1754, 1762, 1764
Natchitoches	BMD 1729, 1734-92
Nouvelle-Orléans	B 1724, 1728-30 D 1725-30, 1734
Opelousas (St. Landry)	B 1776-85 M 1784-95 D 1779-1806
Pointe-Coupée	*See* Atakapas

The public Archives also have copies of other records in the United States. Although these are not strictly Acadian registers, there is always the possibility of a connection, and so they also are listed:

Arkansas (St. Philippe)	BMD 1744, 1761-5
Crown Point, New York	*See* Fort St. Frédéric
Détroit, Michigan	
Fort Pontchartrain	BMD 1704-1800
L'Assomption de Détroit	BMD 1781-99
L'Assomption de la	
Pointe-de-Montréal	BMD 1761-83
Fort Beauharnois, N.Y.	*See* Fort St. Frédéric
Fort de Chartres, Illinois	BMD 1721-65
Fort Duquesne, Ohio	BD 1753-6
Fort Pontchartrain	*See* Détroit
Fort St. Frédéric, N.Y.	BMD 1732-60
Kaskaskias, Illinois	BMD 1695-1834
Michilimackinac, Michigan	BMD 1695-1799
Ouabache, Indiana	BMD 1749-86
Petersham, Mass.	M 1767-73 (civil registers)
Prairie-du-Rocher, Illinois	BMD 1761-99

The Provincial Archives of Nova Scotia also have the following Acadian records in addition to the registers listed under Nova Scotia in this section:

Argyle: Register in French of families of Ste. Anne and St. Pierre Parish, Argyle, N.S., from 1816 to 1819.

St. Mary's Bay: Two registers in French containing lists of families from St. Mary's Bay, N.S., from 1818 to 1844.

Bona Arsenault, *Histoire et Généalogie des Acadiens* (Quebec, 1965).

Placide Gaudet, *Acadian Genealogy and Notes* (Ottawa, 1906).

GENEALOGICAL SOCIETY

A newly formed subsidiary of the American-Canadian Genealogical Society is the Acadian Genealogical and Historical Association of New England (P.O. Box 668, Manchester, New Hampshire 03105).

6. QUEBEC

CIVIL REGISTRATION

Registration of baptisms, marriages, and deaths has been compulsory in the province since 1621. The local priests of the Catholic Church were responsible for this, and in the more remote districts the records are neither complete nor accurate. In 1760 the same system was introduced for Protestants in the province.

A duplicate entry of each registration was made and sent to the office of the prothonotary of the superior court in each judicial district of the province. These districts are listed below.

Since 1926 civil registration in Quebec has been in line with that of the other provinces. The records are in the custody of the Registrar General, Population Register, Department of Social Affairs, Quebec City.

In 1851 the responsibility for registering the above events was extended to other Protestant denominations – including the Baptists. Until a few years ago it was necessary to register all births in Quebec at a church, but now it can be done at a City Hall or a Municipal Office if the parents of the child prefer this.

In order to get a copy of a birth certificate in Quebec it is almost essential to know in which parish the ancestor was born and baptized. If you know the exact district you should write to the correct office of those listed below. If you do not know the district, but you do know the name of the town or village, then you should write to the Registrar General mentioned above and ask him to tell you which judicial district covers the area in which you are interested.

If you do not know the name of the town or village, you will have problems, but if you read on you will get some help about overcoming or avoiding these problems. En avant, mon ami!

District Judiciaire (Judicial District)	Chef-lieu (Town)
Abitibi	Amos
Arthabaska	Arthabaska
Beauce	Saint-Joseph
Beauharnois	Valleyfield
Bedford	Cowansville

District Judiciaire (Judicial District)	Chef-lieu (Town)
Bonaventure	New Carlisle
Chicoutimi	Chicoutimi
Drummond	Drummondville
Gaspé	Percé
Hauterive	Baie Comeau
Hull	Hull
Iberville	Saint-Jean
Joliette	Joliette
Kamouraska	Rivière-du-Loup
Labelle	Mont-Laurier
Mégantic	Thetford Mines
Montmagny	Montmagny
Montréal	Montréal
Nicolet	Nicolet
Pontiac	Campbell's Bay
Québec	Québec
Richelieu	Sorel
Rimouski	Rimouski
Roberval	Roberval
Rouyn-Noranda	Rouyn
Saguenay	La Malbaie
Saint-François	Sherbrooke
Saint-Hyacinthe	Saint-Hyacinthe
Saint-Maurice	Shawinigan
Témiscamingue	Ville-Marie
Terrebonne	Saint-Jérôme
Trois-Rivières	Trois-Rivières

Letters should be addressed to The Prothonotary, The Superior Court, at the city or town above.

Although the records of the Prothonotaries go back in many cases to 1621, you must bear in mind there will be gaps in the early years. It was not until about 1870 that the records really became dependable. Also remember that the Registrar General in Quebec City does not have records before 1926.

PROVINCIAL ARCHIVES
The holdings of the Archives in Quebec and Montreal are so vast that only a very brief description can be given. Several books have been written on this one aspect of ancestor-hunting in the Province of Quebec. Two of the best to consult are published by the Archives Nationales du Québec:

État Général des Archives Publiques et Privées, 1968.
État Sommaire des Archives Nationales du Québec à Montréal, 1973.

A more comprehensive list of books to consult will be found in the bibliography at the end of this book.

The Provincial Archives are in two separate locations:

Archives Nationales (Montréal), 1 Notre Dame Est, Montréal.
Archives Nationales (Québec), La Section de Généalogie, 1180 rue Berthelot, Québec.

Some of the main records in the custody of these two Archives are listed below (holdings of church registers in their files are listed later in this chapter):

1. *Marriage contracts (Contrats de mariage)*: These date from 1636 and the Archives have lists of over thirty thousand marriage contracts for the Judicial Districts of Montreal, Trois-Rivières, and Montmagny. These are indexed. In addition, lists of such contracts for Quebec City and Charlevoix have been published and are obtainable through the regional library system:

   P. G. Roy, *Inventaire des contrats de mariage du régime français, conservé aux Archives Judiciaires de Québec.*
   Éloi-Gérard, *Inventaire des contrats de mariage au greffe de Charlevoix.*

2. *Inheritance records (Partages de biens)*: These date from 1634 and give details of names and residences of deceased persons and their heirs – with dates and relationship.

3. *Orphan records (Tutelles et curatelles)*: These start in 1637 and record the names and ages of orphans; names of parents and other relatives; dates and places of their residence.

4. *Inventories (Inventaires après décès)*: These date from 1637 to the mid nineteenth century and contain details of inventories of estates of deceased persons, with details of their families.

5. *Donations (Donations entre vifs)*: These records are unique to Quebec and date from about 1650. It was the custom for elderly people – approaching a time when they might expect to die – to divide the property which they had inherited from their parents among their own children.

6. *Fealty and homage records (Foi et homage)*: This was a relic of the seigneurial system set up in Quebec by the early settlers. It covered the period from the earliest settlement in the mid seventeenth century up to the middle of the nineteenth century. The records give details of the seigneurs and their tenants and often include family details, occupations, and places of residence.

7. *Avowals and enumerations (Aveux et dénombrements)*: This is a similar record to the previous one and gives the names of the seigneurs and of the heads of the families living on their land. It covers the districts of Montréal,

Portneuf, Sillery, Ile d'Orléans, St. Sulpice, Varennes, Tremblay, and Cap St. Ignace.

8. *Cemetery records (Registres des cimetières)*: These lists date from about 1740 and give names, dates, and places of burial.

9. *Poll books (Listes électorales)*: These contain the names, occupations, and residences of voters from 1815 onwards.

10. *Court records:* These date from 1651 and give the names and addresses of persons who engaged in litigation in the Bailiff's Court (Registres du baillage); in the Courts of Common Pleas (Plaidoyers communs); and in the Superior Court (Conseil Supérieur). These records often include wills (if in dispute), marriage contracts, etc.

11. *Indenture records (Engagements)*: These date from the days of the original settlement and give many details about the early arrivals — who often came as an indentured servant or apprentice to a settler already in Quebec. They give details of names, dates of arrival, and quite often place of origin.

12. *Lists of early colonists:* These have been gathered together from various sources and cover the period from 1608 to 1700. They give names, year and place of marriage, date of arrival, and place of origin in France.

13. *Genealogical collections (Titres de familles, et manuscrits généalogiques)*: Printed and MS genealogies covering hundreds of Quebec families over the past three centuries.

OTHER SOURCES
Each judicial district listed above also has its own archives and these can be a useful source of information for the ancestor-hunter. Of course, they include the registers of births, marriages, and deaths. In addition, most dioceses of the Catholic Church preserve a number of miscellaneous church records — such as confirmation records, dispensations (permission for a Catholic to marry a non-Catholic), and marriage banns.

The Genealogical Society of the Church of Jesus Christ of Latter-Day Saints (Mormons) also has on microfilm in Salt Lake City a card index to most marriages in Quebec between 1640 and the present day. The information includes the date and place, the names of the bride and groom and of their parents, and often the place of origin of the families.

The Public Archives of Canada in Ottawa have records of marriage bonds for Quebec for the period from 1818 to 1867 (with a few for 1779), and these are indexed. Do not expect too much of these — bonds were only used when the marriage took place by special licence, instead of the normal proclamation of the banns, and so not too many of these are likely to appear in your ancestry.

LIBRARIES

The Public Library of Montreal, 1210 Sherbrooke Street East, has a very large collection of books of value to the ancestor-hunter, plus many miscellaneous records. The books are among those listed in the bibliography at the end of this book. The other records include marriage records – mostly by county (comté) and in alphabetical or chronological order. There are also a considerable number of MS genealogies and family histories.

GENEALOGICAL SOCIETIES

There are least four genealogical societies in the province:

    Société Généalogique Canadienne-Française, Case Postale 335, Place d'Armes, Montréal, Québec H2Y 3H1.

    Société Canadienne de Généalogie (Québec), Case Postale 2234, Québec, Québec.

    Société Généalogique des Cantons de l'Est, Case Postale 635, Sherbrooke, Québec.

    Québec Family History Society, P.O. Box 1026, Pointe Claire, Québec H9S 4H9. (This is the only English-language genealogical society in the province.)

HISTORICAL SOCIETIES

There are a number of historical societies in various parts of the province. I am not listing all the addresses because usually these lists give the address of the secretary for the current year and, therefore, change very frequently. I have listed the places where I know societies exist. If one of them is in an area in which you are interested I suggest you write to the Provincial Archives for the current address:

    Québec, Sherbrooke, Chicoutimi, Baie Comeau, La Pocatière, Matane, Gaspé, Montréal, Longueuil, Boucherville, Châteauguay, Hull, Rimouski, Saint-Boniface.

Most of the genealogical historical societies have their own archives and libraries, and once you have found the area from which your ancestors came, you should consider membership in the local society.

DIRECTORIES AND NEWSPAPERS

Do not neglect these as a source of information. The Bibliothèque St. Sulpice, 1700 rue St. Denis, Montréal, has directories of Montreal from 1842 and of Quebec City from 1848. They can also be found in local libraries. You will find details of heads of households, occupations, and addresses. With this information it is possible to trace the movements of a family over many years. The main libraries also have many early newspapers dating back to 1750. These include notices of births, marriages, and deaths, and obituaries of people who have been at all prominent in the district. The Public Archives of Canada have a name and subject index of the *Gazette du Québec* from 1764 to 1823.

There is also a directory of available newspapers and their locations in various archives and libraries: *Les Journaux du Québec de 1764 à 1964* by André Beaulieu and Jean Hamelin. It was published in 1967 by Les Presses de l'Université Laval.

TELEPHONE DIRECTORIES
Bell Canada has donated to the National Archives of Quebec microfilm copies of every telephone directory published in Quebec. The earliest directory appeared in 1879, for the city of Montreal. Copies of these reels have also been given to the Public Archives of Canada in Ottawa and to the Metropolitan Toronto Library.

WILLS
These are located in the various Registrar's offices covering the district in which the testator lived. They can be referred to for a small fee, and copies can be supplied. Further information can be obtained from Service des Testaments, 630 Dorchester Ouest, Suite 1700, Montréal.

LAND TITLES
These records are located in the same Registrar's offices mentioned above, and the charges are similar.

The names of the various districts are listed below, with the name of the chief town and the address.

Abitibi	101–3e Avenue est, Amos
Arthabaska	800 boul. Bois Franc sud, Arthabaska
Beauce	297 avenue du Palais, St. Joseph
Beauharnois	80 rue Salaberry, Valleyfield
Bedford	Palais de Justice, Cowansville
Bonaventure	Palais de Justice, New Carlisle
Chicoutimi	202 Jacques Cartier est, Chicoutimi
Drummond	1680 boul. St. Joseph, Drummondville
Gaspé	Palais de Justice, rue Principale, Percé
Hauterive	71 avenue Mance, Baie Comeau
Hull	103 rue Montcalm, Hull
Iberville	Palais de Justice, St. Jean
Kamouraska	33 de la Cour, Rivière-du-Loup
Labelle	645 de la Madone, Mont Laurier
Mégantic	693 St. Alphonse ouest, Thetford Mines
Mingan	425 rue Laure, Sept-Iles
Montmagny	25 rue du Palais de Justice, Montmagny
Montréal	1 Notre Dame est, Montréal

Pontiac	Palais de Justice, John's Street, Campbell's Bay
Québec	12 rue St. Louis, Québec
Richelieu	46 rue Charlotte, Sorel
Rimouski	183 de la Cathédrale, Rimouski
Roberval	850 boul. St. Joseph, Roberval
Rouyn-Noranda	4 avenue du Palais, Rouyn
Saguenay	30 Chemin de la Vallée, La Malbaie
St. François	191 avenue du Palais, Sherbrooke
St. Hyacinthe	1550 rue Dessaules, St. Hyacinthe
St. Maurice	795–5e rue, Shawinigan
Témiscamingue	51 rue St. Gabriel, Ville Marie
Terrebonne	400 rue Laviolette, St. Jérôme
Trois-Rivières	250 rue Laviolette, Trois-Rivières

CENSUSES: Please see Note 2 on p. 46.
In Quebec there were some early censuses dating back to the seventeenth century but only covering a small part of the province as it is nowadays. In 1666 there was a census of Quebec City and this is on microfilm in the Public Archives and in print in the Provincial Archives. The same applies to the censuses of 1681 and 1716. The first census of Montreal was in 1731, and it lists the heads of families and gives details of their land. In 1744 there was another census in Quebec City and this listed all family members. This census is in print and is in the Provincial Archives.

In 1762 and 1765 the governments of Quebec, Trois-Rivières, and Montreal joined together in their censuses, and thus covered almost the whole of the settled areas. These censuses gave the name of the head of the family and the number of family members in the house. Further censuses were made by the Catholic Church in 1792, 1795, 1798, and 1805, and these are in the Provincial Archives and in print. From 1795 onwards, these Church censuses also recorded Protestants.

The Canadian censuses started in 1851 and the information given includes the names and ages of all family members, occupation, country of birth, and the age and cause of death of all family members who died during the previous year.

CHURCH REGISTERS
Before referring to any of the church registers listed below please reread Note 1 on pp. 45-6.

Anglican

ANG(O) Anglican Diocese of Ontario, 90 Johnson Street, Kingston, Ont.
ANG(M) Anglican Diocese of Montreal, 1444 Union Avenue, Montreal.

ANG(Q) Anglican Diocese of Quebec, 36 Garden Street, Quebec.

AQM Quebec Provincial Archives (Montreal), 1 Notre Dame E., Montreal.

PAC Public Archives of Canada, 395 Wellington Street, Ottawa.

CBA Cape Bretonia Archives, St. Francis Xavier University, Sydney, N.S.

Church	Dates	Archives
Arichat (Ile Madame)	M 1828-	CBA
Bristol	BMD 1668-1849	AQM
Bedford	BMD 1862-81	ANG(M)
Berthier	BMD 1823-	ANG(M)
Beauharnois	BMD 1842-6	ANG(Q)
Beauce	See St. Sylvestre	ANG(Q)
Cookshire	BMD 1815-66	ANG(Q)
Cape Cove	BMD 1864-89	ANG(Q)
Campbell's Bay	BMD 1857-	PAC
Chambly	BMD 1819-	AQM
Charteris	See Clarendon	PAC
Clarenceville (Noyan)	BMD 1805-74	ANG(M)
Clarendon (Bristol and Litchfield)	BMD 1823-98	PAC
Coteau-du-Lac	BMD 1829-89	ANG(M)
Edwardstown	BMD 1848 only	ANG(M)
Franklin and Havelock	BMD 1861-93	ANG(M)
Frampton	BMD 1889-	ANG(Q)
Glen Sutton	BMD 1876-	ANG(M)
Grenville	BMD 1831-	ANG(M)
Grosse Ile	BMD 1853- (1861 missing)	ANG(Q)
Hatley and District	BMD 1817-36	ANG(Q)
Hemison	BMD 1876-	ANG(Q)
Havelock and Franklin	BMD 1861-93	ANG(M)
Hemmingford	BMD 1845-	ANG(M)
Hull	BMD 1831-53	PAC
Inverness	BMD 1854-85	ANG(Q)
Lachine	BMD 1835-	AQM
Laprairie	BMD 1830-	AQM
Lake Beauport	See Stoneham	ANG(Q)
Leeds Rear	B 1853- M 1851- D 1852-	ANG(O)
Leeds (St. James)	BMD 1831-92	ANG(Q)
Lévis (Holy Trinity)	BMD 1873-88	ANG(Q)
Mascoule-Terrebonne	BMD 1896-	ANG(M)
Montebello	BMD 1875-	ANG(M)
Montmorency (St. Mary)	BMD 1861-	ANG(Q)
Malbay Mission	BMD 1823-62	ANG(Q)
Montreal (Christ Church)	BMD 1766-	AQM
Montreal (Garrison)	BMD 1760-4	AQM
Montreal (St. George)	BMD 1843-	AQM
Montreal (St. Stephen)	BMD 1844-	AQM
New Liverpool	BMD 1820-	ANG(Q)
Nicolet	BMD 1823 only	ANG(Q)
New Glasgow	BMD 1847-	ANG(M)
Philipsburg	BMD 1802-	ANG(M)
Percé	BMD 1823-48, 1862-6	ANG(Q)

Church	Dates	Archives
Portneuf	BMD 1840-68	ANG(Q)
Quebec (St. Peter)	BMD 1834-	ANG(Q)
Quebec (St. Paul)	BMD 1833-	ANG(Q)
Quebec (Holy Trinity)	BMD 1768-1800	PAC
Quyon	DMD 1857-	PAC
Redemption	BMD 1883-	ANG(M)
Rivière-du-Loup (Brandon)	BMD 1821-63	ANG(M)
Richmond (Grand Trunk R.R.)	BMD 1853-4	ANG(Q)
Rectory Hill	BMD 1860-71	ANG(Q)
St. Andrews East	BMD 1812-49	PAC
St. Andrews (Ahuntsic)	BMD 1896-	ANG(M)
St. Bartholomew	BMD 1877-	ANG(M)
St. Giles	BMD 1841-3, 1846-9	ANG(M)
St. Jude	BMD 1872-	ANG(M)
St. Martin	BMD 1840-	ANG(M)
St. Mary	BMD 1864-	ANG(M)
St. Simon	BMD 1892-	ANG(M)
St. Sylvestre	BMD 1850-93	ANG(Q)
St-Vincent-de-Paul	BMD 1863-	ANG(M)
Sorel	BMD 1784-1862	ANG(M)
Stoneham	BMD 1860-77	ANG(Q)
Thorne	See Clarendon	PAC
Trinity	BMD 1840-	PAC
Vaudreuil	BMD 1841-50	AQM
Waterloo (St Luke)	BMD 1821 only	ANG(M)
Mariners' Hospital (Quebec)	D 1856-89	ANG(Q)
Travelling Missionary	BMD 1808-26, 1838-40, 1853-76	ANG(Q)

Note: There are also Anglicans included in the Protestant registers of the Quebec and Trois-Rivières garrison churches:

Quebec	BMD 1797-1800, 1817-26	PAC
Trois-Rivières	BMD 1768-92	PAC

Baptist

AQM   Quebec Provincial Archives (Montreal), 1 Notre
      Dame E., Montreal.

BAP   Baptist Archives, McMaster Divinity College,
      Hamilton, Ontario.

PAC   Public Archives of Canada, 395 Wellington
      Street, Ottawa.

Church	Dates	Archives
Barnston	BM 1838-	BAP
Barnston (Township)	BMD 1843-	BAP
Clarendon	See Shawville (United Church)	PAC
Hatley	BMD 1844-	BAP
Montreal	BMD 1833-50	AQM
Sutton	BMD 1865-	BAP

Roman Catholic

AAM   Archives Acadiennes, Université de Moncton, N.-Brunswick.

AQM   Quebec Provincial Archives (Montreal), 1 Notre Dame E., Montreal.

ADQ   Archives de l'Archdiocese de Québec, Québec.

CBA   Cape Bretonia Archives, St. Francis Xavier University, Sydney, N.S.

PAC   Public Archives of Canada, 395 Wellington Street, Ottawa.

UM   Université de Montréal (Département de Démographie), Montréal

Church	Dates	Archives
Allumette Island	*See* Aylmer et Gatineau	PAC
Arichat, Ile Madame	BMD 1811-	CBA
Aylmer et Gatineau	BMD 1841-8	PAC
Aylmer (St. Paul)	BMD 1841-52	PAC
Baie St. Paul	BMD 1681-	UM
Batiscan	BMD 1756-	AAM
Beauharnois	BMD 1819-50	PAC
Beaumont	BMD 1692-1790	UM
Beauport	BMD 1673-1790	UM
Bécancour	BMD 1757-1800	AAM
Belledune	BMD 1836-	AAM
Beloeil	BMD 1772-1847	AQM
Berthierville	BMD 1760-80	AAM
Boucherville	BMD 1668-1849	AQM
Buckingham	*See* Petite-Nation (Notre Dame)	PAC
Cap-de-la-Madeleine	BMD 1673-1790	UM
Cap-St-Ignace	BMD 1679-1790	UM
Cap-Santé	BMD 1679-1790	UM
Caughnawaga	BMD 1716-	AQM
Chambly	BMD 1706-	AQM
Champlain	BMD 1679-	UM
Charlesbourg	BMD 1679-	UM
Châteauguay	BMD 1727-1849	PAC
Château-Richer	BMD 1661-1702	PAC
Chelsea	*See* Aylmer et Gatineau	PAC
Coteau-du-Lac	BMD 1833-45	AQM
Deschambault	BMD 1760-80	AAM
Fort St. Jean	BMD 1757-60	PAC
Gaspésie	BMD 1751-7	UM
Grenville	*See* Petite-Nation (Notre Dame)	PAC
Grondines	BMD 1680-	AAM
Havre-Aubert	BMD 1793-	AAM
Ile-Jésus	BMD 1702-	AQM
Ile-Perrot	BMD 1786-	AQM
Iles-de-la-Madeleine	BMD 1793-	AAM
Lac-des-Deux-Montagnes	BMD 1727-87	PAC
Lachine (St. Michel)	BMD 1832-	AQM

Church	Dates	Archives
Lachine (St. Agnes)	BMD 1676-	AQM
L'Ange-Gardien	BMD 1670-7	UM
Laprairie (La Nativité)	BMD 1729-	AQM
Laprairie (Notre Dame)	BMD 1670-	UM
L'Assomption	BMD 1760-	AAM
Lauzon	BMD 1679-	UM
Laval	BMD 1796-	PAC
Lavaltrie	BMD 1760-	AAM
Les Cèdres	BMD 1760-	AAM
Les Écureuils	BMD 1755-	AAM
L'Étang-du-Nord	BMD 1845-	AAM
Lévis	BMD 1763-	AAM
L'Islet	BMD 1679-	UM
Longue-Pointe	BMD 1724-	AQM
Longueuil	BMD 1669-	AQM
Louiseville	BMD 1778-	AAM
Maskinonge	BMD 1774-85	AAM
Montmagny	BMD 1679-	UM
Montréal (Notre Dame)	BMD 1642-1728	PAC
Neuville	BMD 1679-	UM
Oka	BMD 1721-1850	PAC
Petite-Nation	BMD 1836-	UM
Petite-Nation (Notre Dame)	BMD 1830-51	PAC
Pointe-aux-Trembles (L'Enfant Jésus)	BMD 1674-	UM
Pointe-aux-Trembles (St. François)	BMD 1755-	AAM
Pointe-Claire	BMD 1713-	AQM
Pointe-du-Lac (La Visitation)	BMD 1787-	AAM
Pointe-du-Lac	BMD 1748-	UM
Québec (Notre Dame)	BMD 1621-1737	PAC
Québec (Notre Dames des Anges)	BMD 1728-83	PAC
Repentigny	BMD 1679-	UM
Rigaud	BMD 1802-50	PAC
Rivière-des-Prairies	BMD 1687-	AQM
Ristigouche	BMD 1759-95	PAC
Rivière-Ouelle	BMD 1685-	UM
Saguenay	BMD 1686-1848	UM
St-Alexis-de-Matapédia	BMD 1871-92	AAM
St-André-d'Argenteuil	BMD 1833-50	PAC
St-Antoine-de-Tilly	BMD 1755-80	AAM
St-Augustin-de-Desmaures	BMD 1693-	UM
St-Augustin-de-Portneuf	BMD 1755-	AAM
St-Benoît	BMD 1799-1850	PAC
St-Bruno-de-Montarville	BMD 1843-	AQM
St-Constant	BMD 1752-	AQM
St-Dunstan-du-Lac Beauport	BMD 1834-	UM
Ste-Anne-au-Petit-Cap	BMD 1682-	UM
Ste-Anne-de-Beaupré	BMD 1657-1719	PAC
Ste-Anne-de-Bellevue	BMD 1760-	AAM
Ste-Anne-de-la-Pérade	BMD 1693-	UM
Ste-Anne-des-Plaines	BMD 1788-1850	PAC
Ste-Anne-du-Bout-de-l'Ile	BMD 1703-	AQM
Ste-Croix-de-Lotbinière	BMD 1755-	AAM
Ste-Famille-de-l'Ile-d'Orléans	BMD 1766-	UM

Church	Dates	Archives
Ste-Foy	BMD 1699-1790	UM
Ste-Geneviève	BMD 1741-	AQM
Ste-Geneviève-de-Batiscan	BMD 1760-	AAM
Ste-Marthe	BMD 1844-	AQM
Ste-Rose-de-Laval	BMD 1796-1850	PAC
Ste-Rose-de-Lima	BMD 1745-	AQM
Ste-Scholastique	BMD 1825-50	PAC
St-Eustache-de-la-Rivière-du-Chêne	BMD 1769-1850	PAC
St-François-de-l'Ile-d'Orléans	BMD 1679-1790	UM
St-François-de-Sales	BMD 1760-	AAM
St-François-du-Lac	BMD 1687-1836	UM
St-Hermas	BMD 1837-50	PAC
St-Isidore	BMD 1833-	AQM
St-Jacques-de-l'Achigan	BMD 1777-	AAM
St-Jacques-le-Mineur	BMD 1840-	AQM
St-Jean-de-l'Ile-d'Orléans	BMD 1679-1790	UM
St-Jean-Deschaillons	BMD 1755-	AAM
St-Joachim	BMD 1755-	AAM
St-Joachim-de-Montmorency	BMD 1687-	UM
St-Joseph-de-Chambly	BMD 1760-	AAM
St-Laurent	BMD 1720-	AQM
St-Laurent-de-l'Ile-d'Orléans	BMD 1679-	UM
St-Louis-de-Lotbinière	BMD 1755-	AAM
St-Marc-de-Cournoyer	BMD 1794-	AQM
St-Martin	BMD 1774-	AQM
St-Michel-de-la-Durantaye	BMD 1693-	UM
St-Michel-de-Vaudreuil	BMD 1773-	AQM
St-Nicolas-de-Lévis	BMD 1694-	UM
St-Ours	BMD 1750-	UM
St-Philippe-de-Laprairie	BMD 1752-	AQM
St-Pierre-de-l'Ile-d'Orléans	BMD 1679-	UM
St-Pierre-les-Becquets	BMD 1760-	AAM
St-Polycarpe	BMD 1819-	AQM
St-Raphael-de-l'Ile-Bizard	BMD 1844-	AQM
St-Régis (Mission Iroquoise)	BMD 1764-1830	PAC
St-Roch-de-l'Achigan	BMD 1787-	AAM
St-Roch-des-Aulnaies	BMD 1734-81	PAC
St-Sulpice	BMD 1760-	AAM
St-Thomas	BMD 1842-	AQM
St-Vincent-de-Paul-de-l'Ile-Jésus	BMD 1743-	AQM
Sault-au-Recollet	BMD 1736-1850	PAC
Sillery	BMD 1638-	ADQ
Sorel	BMD 1675-	UM
Soulanges	BMD 1752-	AQM
Templeton	*See* Aylmer et Gatineau	PAC
Terrebonne	BMD 1725-32	PAC
Trois-Rivières	BMD 1634-1763	PAC
Varennes	BMD 1693-	AQM
Vaudreuil	BMD 1783-1835	PAC
Verchères (St-Antoine)	BMD 1750-	AQM
Verchères (St-François-Xavier)	BMD 1723-	AQM
Wakefield	*See* Aylmer et Gatineau	PAC
Yamachiche	BMD 1760-	AAM
Richelieu (Parish Archives of the County)		

Church	Dates	Archives
St-Robert	BMD 1855-	PAC
St-Roch-sur-Richelieu	BMD 1859-	PAC
Ste-Victoire	BMD 1843-	PAC
St-Joseph-de-Sorel	BMD 1881-	PAC
Ste-Anne-de-Sorel	BMD 1879-	PAC

CIVIL REGISTERS

Church	Dates	Archives
Châteauguay	BMD 1751-62	PAC
Potton	BMD 1837-48	PAC
Ste-Famille-de-Pabos	BMD 1751-7	PAC

United Church and Allied Religions

AQM   Quebec Provincial Archives (Montreal), 1 Notre Dame E., Montreal.

KKC   Knox Crescent and Kensington Presbyterian Church, N.D.G., Montreal.

PAC   Public Archives of Canada, 395 Wellington Street, Ottawa.

PCM   Presbyterian College, Montreal.

PTE   Mrs. A. W. Mackay, St. Urbain, Quebec.

UCM   United Church Centre, 3480 Decarie Boulevard, Montreal.

Church	Denomi-nation	Dates	Archives
Allumette Island	WM	BMD 1858-	PAC
Beauharnois	P	BMD 1834-	PCM
Beechridge	P	BMD 1837-43, 1855-71	PTE
Belle Rivière	C	BMD 1842-60	UCM
Côte St. George	P	BMD 1843-74	PAC
Dalhousie Station	P	BMD 1843-74, 1883	PAC
Dundee (Zion)	C	BMD 1833-66	UCM
Harrington	C	BMD 1857-70	UCM
Laprairie	P	BMD 1828-	AQM
Litchfield	CS	*See* Shawville (UC)	PAC
Montreal (American)	P	BMD 1832-	AQM
Montreal (Côte St.)	P	BMD 1845-62	KKC
Montreal (Crescent)	P	BMD 1845-	AQM
Montreal (Garrison)	CS	BMD 1862-9	PAC
Montreal (Garrison)	C	BMD 1845-50	AQM
Montreal (Erskine)	P	BMD 1833-50	AQM
Montreal (Erskine)	P	BMD 1766-87	PAC
Montreal (Erskine)	UN	BMD 1845-50	AQM
Montreal (Erskine)	M	BMD 1846-50	AQM
Montreal (Mountain)	M	BMD 1843-81	AQM
Montreal (Mountain)	MNC	BMD 1839-45	AQM
Montreal (Mountain)	WMNC	BMD 1855-71	UCM
Montreal (St. Andrew)	P	BMD 1815-	AQM
Montreal (St. Gabriel)	P	BMD 1779 only	AQM
Montreal (St. James)	M	BMD 1818-	AQM
Montreal (St. Jean)	P	BMD 1841-	AQM

Church	Denomi- nation	Dates	Archives
Montreal (St. Joseph)	P	**BMD** 1863-8	UCM
Montreal (St. Paul)	P	**BMD** 1830-	AQM
Montreal (Second)	C	**BMD** 1843-57	UCM
Montreal (United Free)	C	**BMD** 1836-	AQM
Montreal (Zion)	C	**BMD** 1834-71	UCM
New Glasgow	P	**BMD** 1842-	UCM
Ormstown	P	**BMD** 1832-70	UCM
Ormstown	M	**BMD** 1856-	UCM
Pointe-Fortune	M	**BMD** 1848-49	AQM
Portage-du-Fort	M	*See* Clarendon (Shawville)	PAC
Quebec (Garrison)	PR	**BMD** 1797-1800, 1817-26	PAC
Quebec (Garrison)	P	**BMD** 1770-1829	PAC
Quyon	WM	**BMD** 1859-	PAC
St. Andrews East	P	**BMD** 1818-50, 1846-77 (UCM)	PAC
St. Eustache (and Grand Frenière)	P	**BMD** 1853-7, 1863-8	UCM
Ste-Thérèse-de- Blainville	P	**BMD** 1837-90	UCM
Shawville (Clarendon)	UC	**BMD** 1851-	PAC
Soulanges	P	**BMD** 1847-	AQM
Soulanges (Comté)	P	**BMD** 1862-	PAC
Trois-Rivières (Garrison)	PR	**BMD** 1768-92	PAC
Ulverton	C	**BMD** 1837-64	UCM

Abbreviations:

- C Congregational
- UC United Church
- CS Church of Scotland
- MNC Methodist New Connection
- M Methodist
- P Presbyterian
- PR Protestant (interdenominational)
- UN Unitarian
- WM Wesleyan Methodist
- WMNC Wesleyan Methodist New Connection

7. ONTARIO

When searching various archives for Ontario records do not forget the province has also been known in the past as Upper Canada and Canada West – these names are often abbreviated as UC and CW.

CIVIL REGISTRATION
This started in 1869 and the records are in the custody of the Registrar General, Macdonald Block, Parliament Buildings, Toronto. The office does not undertake genealogical research, and records are not filed by families. Provided the applicant can supply enough information, the Registrar General will supply extracts. All records are indexed alphabetically for the whole province by year This means if your ancestor was William Pearson and he was born in 1874 in Ontario you might find several people with the same name, and no means of knowing which one was yours! Of course, if you have a place, or an exact date, or a middle name, or the first name of a parent, then the odds against you are considerably reduced!

The Registrar General emphasizes that when an extract is issued he does not guarantee it is the right one. If you have not given him full information he will issue the extract and leave it to you to decide if it is the right one. (Bear in mind that in the early years the law was not always observed, and not all vital events were registered.)

PROVINCIAL ARCHIVES
These are at 77 Grenville Street, Toronto, Ontario M7A 1C7. The holdings include not only the usual government documents, but also some early marriage registers from the early 1800s to 1869, early newspapers, and maps. There are most of the standard histories and biographies relating to the province, and magazines and publications of local genealogical and historical societies. There are also microfilm copies of material from the Public Archives in Ottawa.

Finally – and probably most valuable of all – there are microfilm copies of Ontario wills (1785-1912) which were given by the Genealogical Society of the Church of Jesus Christ of Latter-Day Saints (The Mormons).

LIBRARIES

The following information about their holdings was supplied by the public libraries in the main cities in Ontario. (There are also genealogical collections in major universities, for example Queen's, Toronto, Trent, and Western.)

Hamilton

55 Main Street West, Hamilton. Their collection includes a comprehensive selection of local histories and a partial collection of township records from the various municipalities which merged to form the new Regional Municipality of Hamilton-Wentworth. However, not all the townships have donated their records so far.

Kingston

240 Bagot Street, Kingston K7L 3G2. The library holds numerous books on genealogy that refer to this part of Ontario. There is also under way a most valuable project of indexing names mentioned in Kingston newspapers from 1810 onwards.

London

305 Queens Avenue, London N6B 1X2. The library contains all the records of the Ontario Historical Society from 1899 to the present day. Indexed cemetery records of Middlesex County are being collected by the London branch of the Ontario Genealogical Society and then deposited in the library.

There are also some church records in MS form, including:
1. Register of St. Paul's Church, London (Anglican). Baptisms from 1829 to 1846.
2. Baptisms and marriages for the Mission of London, 1831.
3. Marriage register of St. Paul's for 1829 to 1834.
4. The Rev. Proudfoot's marriage records (Presbyterian) from 1848 to 1880.
5. "History of the County of Middlesex (1889-1974)" containing marriage records for various denominations (pages 52-65).

Toronto

789 Yonge St., Toronto M4W 2G8. The library has manuscripts and documents of use to genealogists but is not prepared to list them. They have an MS record of Anglican baptisms in the York area for the period from 1830 to 1834.

Windsor

850 Ouellette Avenue, Windsor N9A 4M9. The library has some locally produced family genealogies (the Wigles, McCormicks, Babys, Ilers, etc.) There are also microfilms of early Essex County newspapers.

An example of what you may find in a small local library is that of Meaford, which has almost complete details of the families of the early settlers. This was the life-work of a local resident who donated it to the library.

GENEALOGICAL SOCIETY
The Ontario Genealogical Society is a large and very active organization with its headquarters in Toronto (P.O. Box 66, Station Q, Toronto M4T 2L7) and local branches in a number of centres. These are listed below. Please check with the OGS for the current address of the branch you want:

Brant	Leeds and Gren-	Simcoe County
Bruce and Grey	ville	(Barrie)
Essex	London	Sudbury
Halton-Peel	Niagara	Thunder Bay
Hamilton	Nipissing	Toronto
Huron	Ottawa	Waterloo-Welling-
Kawartha	Oxford	ton
Kent	Quinte	Whitby-Oshawa
Kingston		

The OGS also has a large and invaluable library in the Canadiana Section of the North York Public Library, Willowdale, Ontario M2J 4S4. In addition, it publishes many booklets of vital interest to the ancestor-hunter. If your ancestral interest is in Ontario you should most certainly become a member. All branches hold regular meetings.

TELEPHONE DIRECTORIES
Bell Canada has donated microfilm copies of every telephone directory published in Ontario since 1878 to the Provincial Archives of Ontario and the Metropolitan Toronto Library. The 317 reels represent about 600,000 pages of directories. More than 1900 directories have been published in Ontario since the first one appeared in Hamilton in 1878.

Similar reels have also been given to the Public Archives of Canada in Ottawa.

ATLASES AND MAPS
Many of the Ontario county atlases have been reprinted, by various publishers; most of them by Mika Publishing Company, 200 Stanley Street, Belleville, Ontario, L8N 5B2. A few of them have been indexed by Ron Hazelgrove, and these are available from Mika Publishing or from Hazelgrove Indexes, Douglas Library, Queen's University, Kingston, Ontario K7L 5C4.

UNITED EMPIRE LOYALISTS
These early settlers were colonists in what is now the United States. They came to Canada during and after the American

Revolution and settled in Ontario, Nova Scotia, and New Brunswick.

There are various lists of these people, but the Executive Council List in the Public Archives is regarded by most people as the "official" list. If you are descended from one of these settlers you will find information about him or her in this list, and probably also in "The Old United Empire Loyalists List". There is also a United Empire Loyalist Association with a number of branches across Canada. The address is 23 Prince Arthur Avenue, Toronto, Ontario M5R 1B2. You will find a great deal of information there about the UEL and in a number of books written about them.

CEMETERIES

There are four thousand old burial-grounds in Ontario. Some of these are quite large, but many consist of half a dozen graves in one of the homestead or settlement cemeteries – usually where the boundaries of several farms met. A list of the old cemeteries was compiled many years ago by the Cemeteries Branch of the provincial government. It was later given to the Ottawa branch of the Ontario Genealogical Society on the understanding it would be made available to anyone requiring access to it. (See above for the address of this branch of the society.) The major project of the Ontario Society at the moment is the listing of the old burial-grounds.

WILLS

The probate of wills comes under the jurisdiction of the Surrogate Court – to be found in the Court House of each county capital. Some of these are now on microfilm in the Provincial Archives.

LAND TITLES

Copies of the Letters Patent for the original land grants are in the custody of the Provincial Secretary. References to land grants are to be found in the Office Documents Section, Ministry of Government Services, Hearst Block, Queen's Park, Toronto, Ontario M7A 1N3. All correspondence relating to land grants before 1857 is in the custody of the Provincial Archives. All later transactions are recorded in the various land registry offices throughout the province. As there are sixty-seven of these, I suggest you write to the Provincial Secretary's Office for the address of the Office for the area in which you are interested.

LAND PETITIONS

Early settlers, in order to obtain Crown Land, were required to submit petitions to the Governor stating their claims to free grants. These petitions are often a useful source of information because the petitioner would state where he was born (often just the country), his marital status, etc. The land petitions for Ontario for the period from 1791 to 1867 are in the custody of the Public Archives of Canada in Ottawa. They are indexed and available on microfilm through inter-library loan. If you know the township in which your ancestor first settled, you should check the township papers in the Provincial Archives in Toronto. These are filed by lot and concession number, and contain many letters from early settlers to the government of the day.

CENSUSES: See Note 2 on p. 46.
So far as early Ontario is concerned, if your ancestor came from Augusta Township you are very lucky because this area started its own census in 1796 and held further ones in 1806, 1813, 1823, 1824, 1842, 1848, and 1850. These records are held by the Public Archives of Canada in Ottawa, and are on microfilm. However, they only show the name of the head of the family.

HUGUENOT SOCIETY OF CANADA

Descendants of the Huguenot refugees from France should contact this society (Miss R. Loft, 136 Tollgate Road, Brantford, Ontario N3R 4Z7).

CHURCH REGISTERS

Before referring to any of the church registers listed below please reread Note 1 on pp. 45-6.

Anglican

ANG(K) The Anglican Diocese of Keewatin, Box 118, Kenora, Ontario.

ANG(M) The Anglican Diocese of Montreal, 1444 Union Avenue, Montreal, Quebec.

ANG(N) The Anglican Diocese of Niagara, 67 Victoria Ave. S., Hamilton.

ANG(O) The Anglican Diocese of Ontario, 90 Johnson Street, Kingston.

ANG(Ot) The Anglican Diocese of Ottawa, 71 Bronson Avenue, Ottawa.

ANG(T) The Anglican Diocese of Toronto, 135 Adelaide St. E., Toronto.

AO Provincial Archives of Ontario, 77 Grenville Street, Toronto.

HWM Hiram Walker Museum, 254 Pitt Street West, Windsor.

100

ONTARIO

Church	Dates	Archives
Adelaide	*See* Strathroy	PAC
Adolphustown	B 1823- M 1873- D 1847-	ANG(O)
Almonte and Clayton	BMD 1863-	ANG(Ot)
Ameliasburg	BM 1833- D 1835-	ANG(O)
Amherst Island	BMD 1841-	ANG(O)
Amherstburg	BMD 1829-	HWM
Arnprior	B 1863- M 1870- D 1868-	ANG(Ot)
Ashton	BMD 1856-	ANG(Ot)
Augusta	B 1801- MD 1821-	ANG(O)
Barriefield	BM 1844- D 1853-	ANG(O)
Barton and Glanford	B 1849- MD 1850 only	ANG(N)

(A separate Marriage Register for 1858-72 includes Barton, Glanford (St. Paul), Hannon (St. George), Tapleyton (St. George), and Woodburn (Christ Church).)

Church	Dates	Archives
Bath and Ernestown	BD 1788- M 1787-	ANG(O)
Bearbrook	BMD 1863-	ANG(Ot)
Belleville (Christ Church)	BMD 1865-	ANG(O)
Belleville (St. Thomas)	B 1819- D 1821-	ANG(O)
Bradford	*See* West Gwillimbury	AO
Brockville	B 1820- M 1811- D 1826-	ANG(O)
Brooklin	*See* Port Perry	ANG(T)
Burritt's Rapids	*See* Merrickville	ANG(O)
Caledon East (St. James)	M 1843-57	ANG(T)
Camden East	B 1842- M 1843- D 1841-	ANG(O)
Campbellford (Christ Church)	B 1849- MD 1858-	ANG(T)
Carleton Place	BM 1834- D 1858-	ANG(Ot)
Cavan	BMD 1819-	ANG(T)
Chatham	BMD 1829-41	HWM
Chippawa (Trinity)	B 1820-37 M 1820-35 D 1862-	ANG(N)
Churchill	BMD 1860-	ANG(K)
Cobden	BM 1868- D 1867-	ANG(Ot)
Cobourg (St. Peter)	BMD 1851-	ANG(T)
Cornwall	BM 1803-46 D 1813-46	PAC
Coulson	*See* West Gwillimbury	AO
Craighurst (St. John)	B 1851- M 1854- D 1850-	ANG(T)
Crysler and Finch	BMD 1864-	ANG(Ot)
Delaware	BM 1834-47	AO
Edwardsburg	*See* Williamsburg	PAC
Elizabethtown	BM 1868- D 1869-	ANG(O)
Elora (St. John)	M 1858-72	ANG(N)
Etobicoke	B 1831-51 M 1832-52 D 1833-51	ANG(T)
Exeter	BMD 1860-	UWO
Farnham (Puslinch Plains)	B 1861- M 1863- D 1862 only	ANG(N)
Fitzroy Harbour	BMD 1854-	ANG(Ot)
Fort Albany	BMD 1859-	AO
Fort Alexander	BMD 1864-	ANG(K)

Church	Dates	Archives
Fort Severn	BMD 1865-	ANG(K)
Franktown	B 1835- MD 1841-	ANG(Ot)
Fredericksburg	B 1787- M 1788- D 1797-	ANG(O)
Gananoque	BM 1855- D 1854-	ANG(O)
Granton	*See* Kirkton	PAC
Hamilton (St. Thomas)	BMD 1857-	ANG(N)
Hannon (St. George)	*See* Barton and Glanford	ANG(N)
Hawkesbury	BM 1846- D 1873-	ANG(Ot)
Holland Landing	BD 1866- M 1867-	ANG(T)
Huntley	BMD 1852-	ANG(Ot)
Kemptville	BMD 1829-	ANG(O)
Kingston (All Saints)	BD 1868- M 1869-	ANG(O)
Kingston (St. George)	B 1788- M 1789- D 1791-	ANG(O)
Kingston (St. James)	B 1844- M 1845- D 1846-	ANG(O)
Kingston (St. John)	BMD 1852-	ANG(O)
Kingston (St. Paul)	BM 1848- D 1857-	ANG(O)
Kirkton	BMD 1862-	PAC
Lamb's Pond	BM 1830- D 1831-	ANG(O)
Lansdowne Rear	BD 1862- M 1882-	ANG(O)
Lindsay (St. Paul)	BMD 1856-	ANG(T)
Loughborough	BMD 1848-	ANG(O)
Madoc	BM 1865- D 1863-	ANG(O)
Manvers (St. Mary)	BD 1857- M 1863-	ANG(T)
March	BM 1824- D 1833-	ANG(Ot)
Matilda	*See* Williamsburg	PAC
Matilda and Edwardsburg	BMD 1859-	ANG(Ot)
Merrickville	BM 1849- D 1856-	ANG(O)
Middleton	*See* West Gwillimbury	AO
Moose Factory	BMD 1780-	AO
Moulinette and Osnabruck	BMD 1852-	ANG(Ot)
Mountain, Matilda, and Edwardsburg	B 1848- M 1853- D 1847 only	ANG(Ot)
Mulmur	B 1861- MD 1862-	ANG(T)
Napanee	BMD 1837-	ANG(O)
Newborough	B 1839- M 1856- D 1843-	ANG(O)
Newboyne and Lombardy	BM 1851- D 1860-	ANG(O)
North Augusta	BD 1853- M 1851-	ANG(O)
North Essa	B 1852- M 1858-	ANG(T)
North Gower and Kars	BMD 1860-	ANG(Ot)
Osgoode and Metcalfe	BMD 1856-	ANG(Ot)
Osnabruck	BMD 1801-	ANG(Ot)
Ottawa	BMD 1832-	ANG(Ot)
Ottawa (Christ Church)	B 1852- M 1858-	PAC
Packenham	BMD 1829-	ANG(Ot)
Pembroke	BMD 1854-	ANG(Ot)
Penetanguishene	B 1835- M 1836- D 1837-	AO
Perth	BMD 1819-	ANG(Ot)
Philipsburg	BMD 1802-	ANG(M)
Pickering (St. George)	B 1867- M 1858- D 1868-	ANG(T)
Picton	B 1827- M 1825- D 1828-	ANG(O)
Port Perry and Brooklin	B 1865-	ANG(T)
Prescott	BMD 1821-	ANG(O)
Prospect Hill	*See* Kirkton	PAC
Renfrew	BMD 1868-	ANG(Ot)
Richmond	BM 1825- D 1836-	ANG(Ot)
Roslin	B 1860- M 1859- D 1874-	ANG(O)

Church	Dates	Archives
Saintsbury	*See* Kirkton	PAC
Saltfleet	*See* Barton, Glanford, Stoney Creek	ANG(N)
Sandwich	BMD 1802-27, 1842-60	HWM
Scarborough	B 1841- M 1844- D 1846-	ANG(T)
Shannonville	BM 1864-	ANG(O)
Smith's Falls	BMD 1849-	ANG(Ot)
South Mountain	BMD 1865-	ANG(Ot)
Stoney Creek	B 1869- MD 1868-	ANG(N)
Strathroy	BMD 1833-	PAC
Streetsville (Trinity)	BMD 1846-	ANG(T)
Tamworth	BM 1863- D 1860-	ANG(O)
Tapleytown (St. George)	*See* Stoney Creek	ANG(M)
Tecumseh	BMD 1850-	ANG(T)
Toronto (St. George)	B 1847- M 1848-	ANG(T)
Toronto (St. John)	M 1858-	ANG(T)
Toronto (Trinity)	B 1844- M 1847-	ANG(T)
Toronto (Misc.) There are some Toronto entries in the Glanford baptismal register for 1850 to 1881.		ANG(N)
Trenton	BMD 1848-	ANG(O)
Tyendinaga	BMD 1831-	ANG(O)
Uxbridge (St. Paul)	BMD 1850-	ANG(T)
Unionville (St. Philip)	BD 1819-49 M 1821-49	ANG(T)
Wellington and Hillier	B 1847- M 1851- D 1854-	ANG(O)
Wellington and Hillier	*See* North Gower and Kars	ANG(Ot)
West Gwillimbury	BD 1849-	AO
Whitby (All Saints)	BD 1863- M 1864-	ANG(T)
Whitby (St. John)	BD 1842- M 1849-	ANG(T)
Williamsburg and Osnabruck	BM 1790- D 1797-	ANG(Ot)
Williamsburg and Matilda	BM 1790- D 1797-	PAC
Wolfe Island	BD 1851- M 1852-	ANG(O)
Woodbridge and Vaughan	B 1850- M 1851-	ANG(T)
Woodburn	*See* Stoney Creek	ANG(N)
Woodstock	*See* Barton and Glanford	ANG(N)
York Factory	BMD 1864-	ANG(K)

Baptists

AO   Provincial Archives of Ontario, 77 Grenville St., Toronto M7A 1C7.

BAP   Canadian Baptist Archives, McMaster Divinity College, Hamilton L8S 4K1.

PAC   Public Archives of Canada, 395 Wellington Street, Ottawa.

Church	Dates	Archives
Binbrook	M 1859-	BAP
Breadalbane	M 1858-	BAP
Drumbo	M 1857-	BAP
Hartford	BMD 1783-	PAC
Kingston	M 1858-	BAP
Picton	BM 1817, 1826, 1832	AO
St. Thomas	M 1858 only	BAP
Waterford	M 1858-	BAP
York Mills	MD 1832-	BAP

Lutheran

AO   Provincial Archives of Ontario, 77 Grenville St., M7A 1C7.

PAC   Public Archives of Canada, 395 Wellington Street, Ottawa.

Church	Dates	Archives
Cambridge (St. Peter)	BMD 1834-	PAC
Fredericksburg*	BMD 1826-31	AO
Morrisburg (St. Lawrence)	BMD 1826-	PAC
Morrisburg (St. John)	BMD 1840-	PAC
Morrisburg (St. Paul)	BMD 1840-	PAC
Morrisburg (St. Peter)	BMD 1858-	PAC
Osnabruck (St. John)	BD 1837-53	PAC
Preston (St. Peter)	See Cambridge	PAC
Williamsburg (St. John)	BMD 1843-	PAC

*Evangelical Lutheran

Roman Catholic

AO   Provincial Archives of Ontario, 77 Grenville Street, Toronto M7A 1C7.

HWM   Hiram Walker Museum, Windsor, Ontario.

PAC   Public Archives of Canada, 395 Wellington Street, Ottawa.

Church	Dates	Archives
Centreville (St. Anthony)	BMD 1846-	PAC
Dwyer Hill (St. Clare)	See Richmond	PAC
Embrun (St. James)	BMD 1841-	PAC
Glengarry (St. Raphael)	BMD 1805-37	AO
Goulbourn (St. Clare)	See Richmond	PAC
Kemptville (Ste. Croix)	BMD 1844-68	PAC
Kent County (St. Peter)	B 1802- M 1806- D 1803-	HWM
Ottawa (St. Joseph)	BMD 1858-	PAC
Perth (St. John the Baptist)	BMD 1823-	PAC
Richmond (St. Philip)	BMD 1836-	PAC
St. Andrews West	BMD 1837-61	AO

Society of Friends (Quakers)

AO   Provincial Archives of Ontario, 77 Grenville St., Toronto M7A 1C7.

UWO   University of Western Ontario, London, Ontario.

Church		Dates	Archives
Newmarket		BD 1803-66 M 1804-40,	
(Yonge Street)	H	1859	UWO
Pelham	H	M 1845-	UWO
Pickering	O	M 1844-	UWO

Church		Dates	Archives
Pickering	H	BM 1829- D 1829-66	UWO
West Lake	H	M 1855-	UWO
West Lake	O	M 1859-	UWO
Yarmouth	O	BD 1803-	UWO
York County	H	BD 1803-	AO

O Orthodox Quakers H Hicks-ite Quakers

United Church and Associated Denominations

Please note that the various denominations listed below in this section are not necessarily "associated" theologically and I do not intend to suggest they are. It is simply that they have more in common than not — and since a change of religion was quite common you may well need to check the registers and records of several of these denominations. Changes were usually made between the various Nonconformist religions — Methodist to Wesleyan, Methodist to United Church, for example, rather than Methodist to Anglican or Roman Catholic.

The various denominations and the abbreviations used are as follows:

UC	United Church
CS	Church of Scotland
C	Congregational
M	Methodist
ME	Methodist Episcopalian
MN	Mennonite
MNC	Methodist New Connection
MO	Moravian
PM	Primitive Methodist
WM	Wesleyan Methodist
BWM	British Wesleyan Methodist
P	Presbyterian
FP	Free Presbyterian
UP	United Presbyterian
EUB	Evangelical United Brethren

The following abbreviations are used for the various Archives listed:

PAC	Public Archives of Canada, 395 Wellington Street, Ottawa.
AO	Provincial Archives of Ontario, 77 Grenville Street, Toronto.
UCA	United Church Archives, Victoria University, Toronto.
MA	Mennonite Archives, Conrad Grebel College, Waterloo, Ontario.

PAK   Presbyterian Archives, Knox College, St. George
         Street, Toronto.
QU   Queen's University, Kingston, Ontario.
UWO   University of Western Ontario, London, Ontario.
UCM   United Church Centre, 3480 Decarie Blvd.,
         Montreal, Quebec.
HWM   Hiram Walker Museum, 254 Pitt Street West,
         Windsor, Ontario.

Church	Denomi-nation	Dates	Archives
Aberfoyle		*See* Morriston	UCA
Agincourt	UC	**BD** 1830-57 **M** 1848-	UCA
Allan Park	P	**B** 1862-3	UCA
Almonte	UC	**BMD** 1833-	PAC
Amherstburg (St. Andrew)	P	**M** 1837 (one only)	HWM
Ancaster	P	*See* Dundas	PAC
Annan	M	**B** 1864-9	UCA
Appleton	M & P	*See* Carleton Place (UC)	AO
Ashton	P	*See* Almonte (UC)	PAC
Beamsville	C	**B** 1824-35	UCA
Beckwith	P	**B** 1822- **MD** 1834	UCA
Beckwith	M & P	*See* Carleton Place (UC)	AO
Bell's Corners	WM	*See* Carp (UC)	PAC
Bell's Corners	M	**M** 1858-	UCA
Bobcaygeon	M	**M** 1858-	UCA
Bolton	ME	**M** 1860-3	UCA
Bond Head	P	**B** 1822-	AO
Bothwell	M	**B** 1861-	UCA
Bowmanville	P	**BD** 1853-5 **M** 1853-	UCA
Brampton	P	**M** 1858-	UCA
Brant	PM	**M** 1858-	UCA
Brinston	ME	**B** 1844-54	UCA
Brockville	P	**BM** 1812-	QU
Buxton	UC	**B** 1859- **M** 1857-	UCA
Caledon	C	**B** 1866-	UCA
Caledon	P	**B** 1866 only	UCA
Caledonia	P	**M** 1853-	UCA
Canboro	ME	**M** 1858-	UCA
Cannington	WM	**B** 1832-41	UCA
Carleton Place	UC	**M** 1834-55	AO
Carleton Place	WM	*See* Almonte (UC)	PAC
Carleton Place	M	**B** 1829-43	UCA
Carp	UC	**BMD** 1858-	PAC
Castleford	P	*See* Lochwinnoch (P)	PAC
Chatham	M	**M** 1858-	UCA
Claremont	M	**B** 1868-	UCA
Cobourg	M	**M** 1867-	UCA
Collingwood	P	**B** 1856-61	UCA
Cornwall	P	**BMD** 1833-	AP
Dewar's Settlement	P	*See* Lochwinnoch (P)	PAC

Church	Denomination	Dates	Archives
Don Mills	M	M 1868-	UCA
Dorchester	P	M 1858-	UCA
Drummondville West	P	B 1822-44	AO
Dundas	P	M 1848-52	PAC
Eastern District	CS	M 1858-69	PAC
Ernestown	P	B 1800-40 M 1800-36	QU
Ernestown	M	BMD 1855-9	PAC
Fort Frances	WM	B 1840-	UCA
Franktown	P	B 1823- M 1834-55 D 1863-	UCA
Gainsborough	ME	See Niagara Circuit	UCA
Georgetown	C	M 1858-	UCA
Glencoe	P	B 1842-53	UCA
Gorrie	M	B 1862-	UCA
Guelph	P	B 1868-	UCA
Guelph	PM	M 1858-	UCA
Gwillimbury West	P	M 1857-	PAK
Hallowell Circuit	M	B 1836-8	UCA
Hamilton (Barton Stone)	P	B 1842-50 D 1841-3	UCA
Hamilton (St. Andrew's)	P	B 1833-68 M 1834-60 D 1841-67	PAK
Hamilton (St. Andrew's)	WM	B 1840-57 M 1842-8	UCA
Hamilton (Knox)	P	BMD 1834-68	PAK
Hamilton (Knox)	C	B 1848-	UCA
Harrington	P	M 1859-	PAK
Inglewood	P	M 1857-	UCA
Innisfil and Essa	P	B 1856-	PAK
Kemble	P	B 1868-	UCA
King Township	P	M 1859-	AO
Kingston	P	M 1858-	UCA
Kingston	C	B 1849- M 1858-	UCA
Kingston	M	M 1831-50	UCA
Kirkhill	CS	See Lochiel	PAC
Laurel	PM	B 1852-	UCA
Lochiel	CS	BMD 1820-	PAC
Lochwinnoch	P	M 1833-	PAC
London	MNC	M 1865-	UCA
London	C	M 1862-	UCA
London	P	M 1835-50	AO
London Circuit	PM	B 1861- M 1858-	UWO
L'Orignal	P	See Dundas and Lochiel	PAC
Lowry	P	See Carp (UC)	PAC
Lucan	P	B 1869-	UCA
Lunenburg	P	See Osnabruck and Lunenburg	PAC
Malahide	ME & WM	B 1822- M 1833- D 1829-	UCA

Church	Denomination	Dates	Archives
Malcolm	P	B 1854-67	UCA
Mallorytown	ME	B 1859-68 D 1866-	UCA
Malton	P	M 1858-69	UCA
Markham	P	B 1806- M 1840- D 1854-6	UCA
Markham	PM	B 1868- M 1857-	UCA
Mayfield	UC	B 1832-	UCA
Meaford	C	M 1862-	UCA
Middleville	P	B 1858-65	UCA
Milton	WM	M 1858-	UCA
Milverton	M	M 1860-	UCA
Mississauga	M	M 1857-	UCA
Moraviantown	MO	B 1800-	AO
Morriston	EUB	M 1862-	UCA
Napanee	M	B 1854 only	UCA
Napanee	P	M 1853-	UCA
Nelson Circuit	ME & WM	B 1832-43	UCA
New Hamburg	MN	BMD 1863	MA
Niagara Circuit	ME	B 1795-1855 M 1835-55	UCA
Niagara Falls	P	M 1857-	UCA
Orangeville	P	M 1859-	UCA
Osnabruck and Lunenburg	FP	BD 1849- M 1860	PAC
Osnabruck and Lunenburg	P	B 1852-	PAC
Ottawa	P	B 1829- M 1830- D 1836-	PAC
Owen Sound	P	B 1856- M 1856-7	UCA
Pembroke	M	B 1841-	PAC
Perth	WM	M 1858-	PAC
Perth	P	BM 1817- D 1848-	PAC
Perth	FP	BMD 1858-	PAC
Peterborough	P	BM 1817- D 1848-	PAC
Playfair	M	M 1859-	UCA
Port Dalhousie	UC	B 1855-63 D 1853-5	UCA
Port Dover	P	M 1858-	PAK
Port Elgin	UC	M 1868-	UWO
Prescott	P	B 1825- M 1834-68 D 1852-7	PAK
Ramsay	P	B 1795-1835	PAK
Riceville	ME	B 1864- M 1858-	UCA
Riceville	UC	BMD 1840-	UCM
Rideau Circuit	ME	B 1824-43	UCA
Rockwood Circuit	WM	BMD 1861-	UCA
Romney-Glenwood	P	M 1859-	UCA
Seaforth	P	B 1865-	UCA
Shannonville	P	M 1858-	UCA
Shelburne	ME	B 1864- M 1858-	UCA
Simcoe	P	See Port Dover	PAK
Smith's Falls	M	See Rideau Circuit (ME)	UCA
Springville	P	B 1854-	UCA
Stewartville	P	See Lochwinnoch	PAC
Sydenham	ME	B 1839-49	UCA

Church	Denomi-nation	Dates	Archives
Toronto (Alice St.)	PM	B 1869- M 1858-	UCA
Toronto (Bay St.)	PM	B 1832-	UCA
Toronto (Bond)	UC	B 1863- M 1858-	UCA
Toronto (Carlton)	PM	B 1869-	UCA
Toronto (Cooke's)	P	M 1858-	PAK
Toronto (Elm)	M	M 1865-	UCA
Toronto (George)	BWM	B 1842-51 M 1833-51	UCA
Toronto (Gould)	P	MD 1865-	UCA
Toronto (Knox)	P	B 1823-38 M 1826-31	UCA
Toronto (Zion)	C	BMD 1834-	UCA
Trafalgar	C	B 1840-54	UCA
Vankleek Hill	CS	*See* Lochiel	PAC
Vaughan	P	B 1845-	PAK
Vaughan	UP	B 1847-	PAK
Warkworth	M	BM 1856-67	UCA
Waterdown	MNC	M 1858-	UCA
Wellandport	P	B 1860-	PAK
West Flamboro	P	*See* Dundas	PAC
Whitby	M	B 1848-57 M 1864-	UCA
Williamsburg	P	BM 1779-1810 D 1811-17	PAC
Williamstown	P	BMD 1779-	PAC
Wilton	M	M 1858-	AO
Wolfe Island	P	M 1862- D 1856-	UCA
Wolfe Island	M	B 1855-	UCA
Woodhouse	P	*See* Port Dover	PAK
Eastern District	all*	M 1831-65	UCA
Marriage Certificates	ME	M 1849-80	UCA

*This includes Baptist, Church of Scotland, Congregational, Independent, Lutheran, Mennonite, Methodist, Moravian, Presbyterian, and Tunker.

The United Church Archives also contain the following:
1. Baptismal records of the Wesleyan Methodist Church 1834-74, by Township (until 1854 only for Ontario and Pontiac County in Quebec).
2. Methodist circuit registers from 1792.

Cemetery Lists and Civil Registers

AO	Provincial Archives of Ontario, 77 Grenville Street, Toronto M7A 1C7.
PAC	Public Archives of Canada, 395 Wellington Street, Ottawa.
UWO	University of Western Ontario, London, Ontario.

Church	Dates	Archives
Alnwick	M 1858-82	PAC
Avondale	D 1871-	AO

Church	Dates	Archives
Eastern District	M 1831-65	PAC
Goderich	D 1866-	UWO
Grenville	D 1769-	PAC
Johnstown	M 1801-51	PAC
London (Woodland)	D 1879	UWO
London (District)	M 1784-1833	PAC
Peterborough County	M 1859-73	PAC
Norfolk County	M 1810-13, 1826, 1832-50	PAC
Roxborough, Kenyon, Maxwell	D 1813-	PAC

8. THE WESTERN PROVINCES

ALBERTA

CIVIL REGISTRATION
Originally part of the North-West Territories, Alberta became a province in 1905. Civil registration of births, marriages, and deaths in what is now Alberta started in 1897, but these records are not complete before 1905. There are some birth records as far back as 1853 and deaths from 1893. The custodian is the Director of Vital Statistics, Department of Social Services and Community Health, Hillhurst Building, 301–14th Street N.W., Calgary, Alberta.

For genealogical purposes, birth records are available to the immediate members of the subject's family; marriage records are available to the persons mentioned in the registration, and there is no restriction on the issue of death certificates.

PROVINCIAL ARCHIVES
These are located at 12845–102 Avenue, Edmonton, Alberta T5N 0M6. They have a large collection of records and documents of great help to the ancestor-hunter. There are a number of church registers which include those of the Anglican Church dioceses of Athabasca and Edmonton, and of the Oblate Fathers of Mary Immaculate (where these pre-date civil registration they are listed below).

The Archives were established in 1963 and the building, now known as the Provincial Museum and Archives of Alberta, was opened in 1967. Before this the only collection of historical and genealogical records was that of a semi-private organization – the Glenbow-Alberta Institute, Glenbow Centre, Ninth Avenue and First Street S.E., Calgary, Alberta T2G 0P3. Details of the holdings of this body are listed later.

The Provincial Archives now contain a mass of material – not all of it useful to the genealogist, but some parts are well worth checking. The various municipal records include information about land ownership, school records, and early maps showing location of farms. The provincial government records include homestead files dating back to the early settlement of the province. These contain applications for grants of land, and show the age, place of birth, residence, occupation, and family of the applicant.

Another very useful collection in the Archives is that of official documents presented as proof of age by applicants for pensions. There are five thousand of these, dating back to the early 1860s and containing birth and baptismal certificates, and immigration records arranged alphabetically. There is also a "Change of Name" index for the period from 1916 to 1950. Although this does not go back very far it may be useful, since some immigrants with names very difficult to pronounce often changed them to a more simplified form. There are also tape recordings of reminiscences by "old timers" and pioneers, and there is an index of people mentioned in these recordings.

GLENBOW-ALBERTA INSTITUTE
This extremely efficient and well-organized place includes a museum, an art gallery, and an historical library and archives (Twelfth Avenue and Second Street S.W., Calgary). The Archivist is Shelagh S. Jameson. The Institute's genealogical collections include the following:

Original MS histories and family papers of several families

Three or four hundred local histories covering Alberta, Saskatchewan, interior British Columbia, and – to a small extent – Manitoba

Some biographical dictionaries

City and county directories

A few wills of Hudson's Bay Company staff (nineteenth century)

Very detailed land records from the Canadian Pacific Railway– land grants and sales, homesteads and ranches, and general settlement records

Church registers (listed later in this section)

Records of fraternal groups and clubs; school registers and records; municipal records, etc.

LIBRARIES
The Calgary Public Library has some basic books of information that are of help to the ancestor-hunter. The Edmonton Public Library has produced a small leaflet listing various books of interest. A copy can be obtained by writing to the information desk of the Library. The Cameron and Rutherford libraries at the University of Alberta, Edmonton, also have many old books of interest to the ancestor-hunter.

OTHER SOURCES
The Church of Jesus Christ of Latter-Day Saints (the Mormons) had a branch genealogical society at 9010–85 Street,

Edmonton, and another one at 348–3rd Street W., Cardston, Alberta T0K 0K0. Nearly all the massive records of the Society can be inspected at these addresses by previous arrangement. Whatever your religious views may be, don't ignore the Mormons as an invaluable source of information. Towards the end of this book you will find full details of the church's genealogical holdings, and a thorough check of their records is vital to you before writing or going overseas.

There are City Archives in Edmonton (10165–112 Avenue); the Cemetery Office there (12420–104 Street) has burial records for the three Edmonton cemeteries, and there are other cemetery offices in Edmonton, including:

Catholic Cemetery, 11237 Jasper Avenue

Jewish Cemetery, 7622–101 Avenue

Ukrainian Cemetery, 137 Avenue and 82 Street

plus several more recent memorial gardens. In Calgary the main cemetery office is at 3425–4th Street N.W.

Nearly all the towns and villages in the province have municipal cemeteries in addition to church burial-grounds. There are a number of small, disused graveyards throughout the province. These are the so-called homestead or settlement cemeteries and were usually located where the boundaries of several farms met. Many have disappeared or been ploughed under, but the Alberta Genealogical Society is trying to list and preserve the remaining ones before they, too, disappear.

GENEALOGICAL SOCIETIES
The Alberta Genealogical Society, Box 3151, Station A, Edmonton T5J 2G7; and the Alberta Family History Society, Box 302070, Station B, Calgary, Alberta T2M 4P1.

WILLS
All wills probated in Alberta are retained in the Court House in the judicial district in which probate is granted. There is a small charge made by the Probate Clerk for every search made in the office of the Surrogate Court. Starting at the northern end of the province, the judicial districts and their court houses are as follows:

Judicial District	Address
Peace River	Court House, Peace River
Grande Prairie	Court House, Grande Prairie
Edmonton	Law Courts Building, Sir Winston Churchill Square, Edmonton
Vegreville	Court House, Vegreville
Wetaskiwin	Court House, Wetaskiwin
Red Deer	Court House, Red Deer

Calgary	Court House, 611–4th Street S.W., Calgary
Drumheller	Court House, Drumheller
Hanna	Court House, Hanna
Lethbridge	Court House, Lethbridge
Medicine Hat	Court House, Medicine Hat
Fort Macleod	Court House, Fort Macleod

LAND TITLES

These can be searched at the Land Titles Office in Edmonton for the Northern Alberta Land Registration District. Write to The Registrar, Land Titles Office, P.O. Box 2380, Edmonton, Alberta T5J 2T3. For the Southern Alberta Land Registration District, the address is: The Registrar, Land Titles Office, P.O. Box 7575, Calgary, Alberta T2P 0Y8.

The province is divided into two parts, and that portion north of the ninth correction line is in the Northern District, and the portion south of Innisfail is in the Southern District. There is a small charge for search of any documents in the Land Titles offices.

CENSUSES: Please see Note 2 on p. 46.

Censuses, as we know them today, started in 1851, and those for that year and for 1861, 1871, and 1881 are in the custody of the Public Archives of Canada, Ottawa. Because Alberta was sparsely settled in those years it is unlikely the returns will be of much use, but it is certainly worth writing to the Public Archives.

CHURCH REGISTERS: Before referring to any of the church registers listed below please reread Note 1 on pp. 45-6.

The following abbreviations given refer to the various archives:

AA   Alberta Provincial Archives, 12845–102 Avenue, Edmonton.

ACO   Archives des Châtelets, Ottawa.

ANG(C) Anglican Diocese of Calgary, 218–7th Avenue S.E., Calgary.

GA   Glenbow-Alberta Institute, 9th Avenue and 1st St. S.E., Calgary.

UC   United Church Archives, Victoria University, Toronto.

UCE   United Church Archives, University of Alberta, Edmonton.

(*Note:* All the early registers of the Anglican dioceses of Athabasca, Edmonton, and Mackenzie River – later the Arctic – are in the Provincial Archives.)

Church	Denomination	Dates	Archives
Athabasca (All Saints)	A	B 1893- M 1895- D 1894-	AA
Athabasca (St. Matthew)	A	BMD 1893-	AA
Banff (St. George)	A	BMD 1897-	ANG(C)
Calgary (Cathedral)	A	B 1884- M 1883- D 1885-	GA
Calgary (St. Dunstan)	A	B 1897- M 1901-	ANG(C)
Calgary (Knox)	P	B 1884- MD 1885-	GA
Camrose	M	BMD 1904-	GA
Canmore (St. Michael)	A	B 1892- M 1895- D 1893-	ANG(C)
Cochrane (All Saints)	A	B 1892- M 1893- D 1894-	ANG(C)
De Winton (Saints Philip and James)	A	B 1897-	GA
Edmonton (Knox)	UC	BMD 1890-	UC
Edmonton (McDougall)	M	BMD 1879-	UCE
Edmonton (Oblates)	RC	B 1842-	ACO
Edmonton (All Saints)	A	BMD 1893-	AA
Edmonton (Strathcona)	A	BMD 1895-	AA
Fort Chipeywan (St. Paul)	A	BMD 1871-	AA
Fort Norman (Holy Trinity)	A	B 1859- M 1882- D 1887-	AA
Fort Vermilion (St. Luke)	A	BM 1876- D 1871-	AA
Fort Wrigley (St. Philip)	A	B 1881- M 1893- D 1900-	AA
Gleichen (St. Andrew)	A	BD 1887- M 1886-	ANG(C)
Hay River (St. Peter)	A	B 1893- M 1898- D 1894-	AA
Lacombe (St. Cyprian)	A	BM 1901-	ANG(C)
Lesser Slave Lake (St. Peter)	A	B 1887- M 1892- D 1894-	AA
Livingstone (St. Martin)	A	B 1903- M 1899-	ANG(C)
Midnapore (St. Paul)	A	BM 1884- D 1886-	GA
Millarville (Christ Church)	A	B 1895- M 1896-	GA
Peace River (St. James)	A	B 1881- M 1890- D 1888-	AA
Pincher Creek	P	B 1889- MD 1905-	UCE
Priddis	P	BMD 1895-	UCE
Wetaskiwin	A	BMD 1894-	AA

Abbreviations:
   A Anglican
   M Methodist
   P Presbyterian
   RC Roman Catholic
   UC United Church (may include M, P, and Congregational)

BRITISH COLUMBIA

CIVIL REGISTRATION
This province was also settled comparatively recently and entered Confederation in 1871. The civil registration of births, marriages, and deaths started in 1872, but the early records are incomplete. The custodian is the Director of Vital Statistics, Parliament Buildings, Victoria. He has a few baptismal records dating back to 1849. His office will not make extended searches over many years but will cover a three-year period. The cost includes a Certificate of Birth, Marriage, or Death. There is an additional charge for each three-year period.

PROVINCIAL ARCHIVES
These are also located in the Parliament Buildings, Victoria. They have a large holding of various documents and records of great help to the genealogist. There are a number of church registers (those pre-dating civil registration are listed below); early marriage licences (also listed); some wills; early newspapers; ship's passenger lists; and some genealogies in MS form.

LIBRARIES AND MUSEUMS
The public libraries in Victoria and Vancouver tell me they have no material of interest to the ancestor-hunter. If this is so, it must be some kind of record – since I know of no libraries in other provinces which have made the same claim. I suggest you ignore these statements and make your own approach to the libraries – they may well have some early directories and newspapers, and probably a number of local histories.

If your ancestor is likely to have taken part in the 1858 Gold Rush you should contact the Barkerville Museum, Barkerville. There is also an old Anglican church and burial-ground nearby.

GENEALOGICAL SOCIETY
The address is Box 94371, Richmond, British Columbia V6Y 2A8.

WILLS
When searching for a will there are three places to contact:
Supreme Court Registry, Law Courts, Victoria.
Division of Vital Statistics, Victoria.
Succession Duty Department, Parliament Buildings, Victoria.

The majority of them are in the Supreme Court Registry, which contains all the wills from probated estates in British Columbia. The Registry requires to know the full name and year of death of the person in question. The search fee is small and a photocopy can be supplied at a cost of 20¢ per page. The wills held date back to 1867.

LAND TITLES

Full information can be obtained from the Land Registry Office, The Law Courts, Victoria. Original Crown Grants are retained by the Lands Branch, Department of Lands, Forests, and Water Resources, Victoria. Records of subsequent transactions are kept in the various Land Registry offices in Prince Rupert, Prince George, Kamloops, Nelson, New Westminster, Vancouver, and Victoria. The tax assessment rolls in the custody of the Surveyor of Taxes, Department of Finance, Victoria, are also a useful source of information about land in unincorporated areas.

CENSUSES: Please see Note 2 on p. 42.

CHURCH RECORDS (ANGLICAN)

There are five Anglican dioceses in the province but there is no common policy among them about the custody of early registers of baptism, marriage, and death. Details are:

Diocese of British Columbia

Registers up to 1915 are in the Synod Office, 912 Vancouver Street, Victoria. No list of these registers is made available, but if application is made to the Synod Office they will inform you if they have a particular register. A search of it will cost $2, including a certificate.

Diocese of Caledonia

A number of early registers are in the Synod Office, 208 Fourth Avenue West, Prince Rupert. Some of these are listed below, but a complete list is not available, and no searches will be undertaken due to lack of staff.

Diocese of Cariboo

There are no registers which pre-date civil registration.

Diocese of Kootenay

There are no registers in the Synod Office.

Diocese of New Westminster

There are no registers in the Synod Office.

There is also an Anglican Provincial Synod Office, with an Archivist (Rev. C. E. H. Williams, 6050 Chancellor Boulevard, Vancouver V6T 1L4), but he tells me that he has no early registers in his custody.

CHURCH REGISTERS

Before referring to any of the church registers listed below please reread Note 1 on pp. 45-6.

The following abbreviations given refer to the various archives:

ABC	Provincial Archives, Parliament Buildings, Victoria V8V 1X4.
ANG(Cal)	Anglican Diocese of Caledonia, 208–4th Avenue W., Prince Rupert.
UCA	United Church Archives, Victoria University, Queen's Park, Toronto.

Church	Denomination	Dates	Archives
Barkerville (St. Savior)	A	BMD 1869 only	ABC
Bella Coola	UC	B 1880- M 1881-	UCA
Cowichan District	A	BMD 1866-	ABC
Kincolith (Christ Church)	A	B 1864- M 1867- D 1869-	ANG(Cal)
Kuper Island	A	BMD 1831-	ABC
Lillooet (St. Mary)	A	BMD 1861-	ABC
Metlakatla (St. Paul)	A	BD 1861- M 1864-	ANG(Cal)
New Westminster	WM	M 1859-	ABC
Quamichan (St. Peter)	A	BMD 1866-	ABC
Saanich (St. Stephen)	A	M 1863-	ABC
Victoria (Christ Church)	A	B 1836- MD 1837-	ABC
Victoria (Church of Our Lord)	RE	M 1847- D 1876-	ABC
Victoria (Church of Our Lord)	P	BD 1870- M 1865-	ABC
Yale (St. John the Divine)	A	B 1869- MD 1859-	ABC

Abbreviations:
- A Anglican
- P Presbyterian
- RE Reformed Episcopalian
- UC United Church (inc. Congregational, Methodist, and Presbyterian)
- WM Wesleyan Methodist

MANITOBA

CIVIL REGISTRATION

The province joined Confederation in 1870 and at that time the name Manitoba was first used – before that it was known as the Red River Settlement. The area was bought by the Canadian government in 1870. Civil registration of births, marriages, and deaths became law in 1882. The custodian is The Recorder, Office of Vital Statistics, Department of Health and Social Development, 104 Norquay Building, Winnipeg, Manitoba R3C 0P8. The office is not prepared to make extended searches. The Recorder states that for birth records he needs to know date and place of birth, and names of parents; for marriages, names of both parties and date and place of marriage; for deaths, name, date, and place of death.

With these very tight restrictions – which seem to be unique in Canada – it seems doubtful whether the Office of Vital Statistics is likely to be of much help to the ancestor-hunter. It will probably be best to try church records first. The Recorder does have some incomplete church records, but for the latter the actual denomination must be known.

PROVINCIAL ARCHIVES
These are located at 200 Vaughan Street, Winnipeg, Manitoba R3C 0P8. They hold no original church registers. However, they do have microfilm copies of some Anglican registers dating from 1820, some Roman Catholic registers from 1834, and some Presbyterian registers from 1852. Details of these are given later in this section.

LIBRARIES
The Winnipeg Public Library, 380 William Avenue, Winnipeg, Manitoba R3A 0J1, has a clipping and pamphlet file referring to early pioneer families, and also *Henderson's Directory of Manitoba, the City of Winnipeg, and the Towns of Manitoba,* dating back to 1880.

GENEALOGICAL SOCIETY
The address is Box 2066, Winnipeg, Manitoba R3C 3R4.

WILLS
These date back to 1879 and are deposited in the Surrogate Courts of the judicial districts; the Central at Portage la Prairie; the Western at Brandon; the Northern at The Pas; the Eastern at Winnipeg; and the Dauphin at Dauphin.

LAND TITLES
Land grants, land sales, and transfers are all filed within the Land Titles offices of the area in which the land is located. These documents date back to the 1800s and indicate original grants from the Crown. A fee is payable for every search. The mailing addresses for the various offices are as follows:

Land Titles Office, Winnipeg, Manitoba R3C 0V8.
Land Titles Office, Boissevain R0K 0E0.
Land Titles Office, Brandon R7A 0P4.
Land Titles Office, Dauphin R7N 1K7.
Land Titles Office, Morden R0G 1J8.

Land Titles Office, Neepawa R0J 1H0.
Land Titles Office, Portage la Prairie R1N 1N8.

CENSUSES: Please see Note 2 on p. 46.
The area now known as Manitoba had censuses starting in
1832, and these are in the custody of the public Archives of
Canada. Details are as follows:

HF   lists heads of families only
N   lists all members of the household
Assiniboia and Red River: 1832 HF
                           1834 HF
                           1835 HF
                           1840 HF
                           1843 HF
                           1846 HF
                           1849 HF
                           1856 incomplete
                           1870 N
All of these, except 1856, are available on microfilm.

CHURCH REGISTERS
Before referring to any of the church registers listed below
please reread Note 1 on pp. 45-6.
The following abbreviations given refer to the various
archives:

AM   Provincial Archives of Manitoba, 200 Vaughan
       Street, Winnipeg, Manitoba R3C 0P8.
ASR Provincial Archives of Saskatchewan, University
       of Regina, Regina, Saskatchewan S4S 0A2.
PAC Public Archives of Canada, 395 Wellington Street,
       Ottawa.

Church	Denomination	Dates	Archives
Baie St. Paul	RC	BMD 1874-	AM
Dynevor (St. Peter)	A	BD 1839- M 1851-	AM
Kildonan	P	BM 1851- D 1852-	AM
Little Britain	P	BMD 1884-	AM
Marquette (West Circuit)	P	BMD 1876-	PAC
Middlechurch (St. Paul)	A	BD 1850- M 1853-	AM
Portage la Prairie	M	B 1890- M 1884-	AM
Portage la Prairie (St. Mary)	A	BMD 1855-	AM
Portage la Prairie (Knox)	P	BMD 1884-	AM
St. Boniface	RC	BMD 1825-34, 1860-	AM
St. Eustache	RC	BMD 1874-	AM

Church	Denomination	Dates	Archives
St. François Xavier	RC	BMD 1834-	AM
Winnipeg (St. Andrew)	A	B 1845- MD 1835-	AM
Winnipeg (St. Clement)	A	BD 1839- M 1851-	AM
Winnipeg (St. John)	A	B 1813- M 1820 D 1821-	AM
Winnipeg (St. Paul)	A	B 1850- M 1853-	AS
Winnipeg (St. Peter)	A	B 1839- M 1850	AS

SASKATCHEWAN

CIVIL REGISTRATION

Saskatchewan became a province in 1905 and civil registration of births, marriages, and deaths became law in that year. It can be seen how young a province it is when we realize there was no settlement at all in the Regina area before 1882 and the only major settlements at that time were in the vicinity of Prince Albert and North Battleford. There are some civil registration records dating back to 1878, and some of the records between 1889 and 1920 are incomplete. If you cannot trace your ancestor because of these incomplete entries you will have to depend on other sources such as church registers, censuses, wills, and land titles.

The custodian of the registers of birth, marriage, and death is The Director, Office of Vital Statistics, Department of Public Health, 3475 Albert Street, Regina, Saskatchewan S4S 6X6. The department is not organized to make protracted searches but will cover a period of three years for a fee. After that, an additional fee is charged for each further three-year period.

The information contained in the various registrations varies over the years. For example, the following table shows the basic information required in 1889, plus later changes:

Births	1889	Name, date, place, sex, name of father, maiden name of mother
	1898	Birthplace of parents (usually just the province or the country)
	1916	Age of parents, number of children born to mother
Marriages	1899	Name, age, residence, religion, birthplace of bride and groom, place and date of marriage, names of witnesses and clergyman, name of parents of bride and groom
	1900	Religion of clergyman
	1916	Maiden names of mothers

	1920	Birthplace of both fathers
Deaths	1947	Birthplace of both mothers
	1889	Names, date, place, sex, birthplace, age, occupation
	1898	Marital status
	1916	Residence, name and birthplace of father, maiden name and birthplace of mother
	1920	Date of birth
	1947	Name of husband or maiden name of wife

PROVINCIAL ARCHIVES

Saskatchewan and Quebec are the only provinces which split their archives between the two major cities. The Saskatchewan Archives are located in the University of Regina, Regina S4S 0A2, and in the University of Saskatchewan, Saskatoon S7N 0W0. The basic reason for the divided archives is to provide access in the two main centres and at the two universities. As early as 1937 the University of Saskatchewan had set up an Historic Public Records Office in Saskatoon. In 1945 the Archives Act established an office in Regina. To some extent the Regina office acquires material in the southern half of the province, and Saskatoon acquires that in the north. However, just to confuse matters, although Regina is the capital of the province, governmental records are lodged in the archives in Saskatoon. Documents for genealogical research can be sent, upon advance request, from one office to the other – unless the donor of the material refuses permission.

The early registers of the Anglican Diocese of Saskatoon are in the Saskatoon office, and the miscellaneous records of the Anglican Diocese of Qu'Appelle are in the Regina office (but the registers of births, marriages, and deaths are still in the Synod Office of the diocese). The early registers (in cases where they pre-date civil registration) are listed later in this section.

A little-known source of information in the Provincial Archives is the homestead files. These are in the Saskatoon office, and cover the period from 1871 up to the present day. The files for the period from 1871 to 1930 were created by the Dominion government (as it was then called) and were transferred to the province in 1956. Since 1930, when natural resources were transferred to the province, the files have been maintained by the provincial government.

Each file contains three basic documents, showing how the settlers complied with regulations of the various land acts. These documents are: an application for entry on the land; an application for letters patent; and a notification that the patent has been granted. The documents contain information about the place and date of birth of the applicant and some information about his family. There is a name index for the files prior to 1930.

LIBRARIES

The Regina Public Library has no genealogical records. However, the Saskatoon Public Library, 311–23rd Street East, Saskatoon, Saskatchewan S7K 0J6, has several books of interest on Saskatchewan families including the Carrs, the Fowlers, and the Masseys. It also has a copy of D. D. Rempel's *Family Chronicle*, a two-volume account of Mennonite migration to Canada, with detailed coverage of a number of families.

GENEALOGICAL SOCIETY

There is a Saskatchewan Genealogical Society (Secretary: Mrs. L. S. Meeres, P.O. Box 1894, Regina, Saskatchewan S4P 3E1). The main project of the Society at the present time is locating all the old burial-grounds in the province. The members are also collecting cemetery inscriptions and publishing them in their regular bulletin. The Society also maintains a library in the Canadian Plains Research Centre at the University of Regina. Membership will be worth your while if you are ancestor-hunting in Saskatchewan.

WILLS

Wills which have been probated are kept on file at the Court House in the centre where the probate was issued. The public may inspect the complete file relating to probate, including the will itself, for a search fee depending on the date of death of the person in question. It is not necessary for a will to go to probate if all the property was held jointly. A will probated before 1958 will be found at the judicial centre nearest the place of residence of the deceased.

After 1958 the rules were changed so that any judicial centre could issue probate regardless of the place of residence of the deceased. The Surrogate Court at the Court House in Regina has a central index covering all wills probated in the province at each judicial centre. The Registrar will conduct a search for a fee depending on the date of death of the person in question, if you can provide information about the residence and date of death of the ancestor which will pinpoint the judicial centre at which the will is on file. In addition, the Surrogate Court Registrar at Regina has copies of wills which direct that a right or interest in land be utilized for religious, educational, charitable, or public purposes.

The judicial centres in the province at which wills may be found are listed below.

Correspondence should be sent to The Sheriff-Local Registrar, the Court House:

Arcola S0C 0G0
Assiniboia S0H 0B0
Battleford* S0M 0E0
Estevan S4A 0W5
Gravelbourg S0H 1X0
Humboldt* S0K 2A0
Kerrobert S0L 1R0
Melfort S0E 1A0
Melville S0A 2P0
Moose Jaw* S6H 4P1

Moosomin S0G 3N0
Prince Albert* S6V 4W7
Regina* S4P 3E4
Saskatoon* S7K 3G7
Shaunavon S0N 2M0
Swift Current* S9H 0J4
Weyburn S4H 0L4
Wynyard S0A 4T0
Yorkton* S3N 0C2

LAND TITLES

There are eight Land Registration Districts which have records of the transactions in land since the province was formed in 1905. Records before that date are in the Land Titles Office in Regina. The records are open for public inspection at a cost of 50¢ per document. The offices of the eight districts mentioned are in the locations marked with an asterisk(*) in the list above under Wills.

If you have only a vague idea of the district in which your ancestor held land you should get in touch with the Provincial Archives at Saskatoon. They have alphabetical indexes available.

CENSUSES: Please see Note 2 on p. 46.

CHURCH REGISTERS

Only a very small number of registers of births, marriages, and deaths have been lodged with various archives, or have been microfilmed. In cases where they pre-date civil registration they are listed below. Before you refer to any of the church registers mentioned please reread Note 1 on pp. 45-6.

The letters AS under Archives refer to the Provincial Archives of Saskatchewan – the only archives holding early church registers in the province. AS(R) means the Regina office.

Church	Denomi-nation	Dates	Archives
Asissippe (St. Mark)	A	BMD 1876-94	AS(R)
Duck Lake (St. Laurent)	RC	BMD 1871-96	AS(R)
Duck Lake (St. Michael)	RC	BMD 1894-	AS(R)
Duck Lake (St. Sacrement)	RC	BMD 1870-93	AS(R)
English River		*See under* Stanley	
Nepowewin-Prince Albert	A	B 1853-91 D 1854-91	AS(R)

Church	Denomi-nation	Dates	Archives
Nepowewin-Prince Albert	A	D 1879-87	AS(R)
Nepowewin-Prince Albert (Saints James and Mary)	A	M 1854-83	AS(R)
Prince Albert (St. Mary)	A	B 1875-91	AS(R)
Qu'Appelle (Imm. Conception)	RC	BMD 1888-	AS(R)
Rupert's Land (Diocese)	A	BM 1813-90	AS(R)
St. Catherine's	A	D 1884-7	AS(R)
Stanley (District)	A	M 1850-	AS(R)
Stanley (English River)	A	M 1857-71 D 1850-89	AS(R)
Stanley (Trinity Church)	A	B 1847-78	AS(R)
Wolseley (St. Anne)	RC	BMD 1883-	AS(R)

A Anglican RC Roman Catholic

Remember that the early registers of the Anglican Diocese of Qu'Appelle have not been lodged with the archives but are still in the Synod Office, 1501 College Avenue, Regina. Several of them date back to 1882. You will find details of the parishes of this diocese in Chapter Four (Canadian Church Records).

INTRODUCTORY NOTE TO CHAPTERS 9 TO 17

The time will come sooner or later when you will have traced your ancestors to a country overseas. At this point, fired with enthusiasm, you will be tempted to book passage on a plane or a ship to the Old Country. *Don't*! Or at least, don't rush into it. Be absolutely sure that you have discovered enough about your emigrant ancestor to make your journey worth while, and the expense of the expedition justifiable. You must have a name and an approximate date and – when you get back into the mists before civil registration – you must have a place of origin.

Don't take off for Scotland or Italy or Sweden with no information beyond the fact that "my grandfather came from there." If you do, then the chances are you will have a frustrating and fruitless journey because you will discover nothing new. Don't go until you are good and ready and have some solid facts available.

Put all your facts in order. Write down the name of your immigrant ancestor, his place of origin, the date of his arrival in Canada, his religion, his wife's name (if he was married before he emigrated), the names of his parents (if known), his occupation, and whatever you have discovered about the relatives he left behind "over there". If all you know is that his name was Carlo Fabiano and he came from Italy, or that he was Alexander McDonald and he came from Scotland, then *don't go*. Stay home and find out more about him.

Reread the chapter about the country from which he came and check that you have tried all possible sources. Look through the bibliography at the end of the book. Recheck with your relatives. Search the family papers once more. Talk again to that very old aunt or uncle. If this produces nothing new, then try two more things:

1. Find out the name of the newspaper in the capital of the country in which you are interested. You can get this from the nearest Embassy or Consulate. Then write to the editor along the following lines:

Dear Sir,

I am trying to trace my Norwegian ancestors. My grandfather, Lars Nielsen, emigrated from Norway to Canada in 1895. He was a farmer. I believe he left behind a brother, Nils, in Norway. If any of your readers are related, or know anything about him, I would be very happy to hear from them.

Yours sincerely,

Of course, there is a chance the newspaper will not print your letter, and since you will get no acknowledgement, you will not know for sure about this. However, in my experience, most Old Country newspapers will print your letter, providing it is short and to the point and does contain a couple of facts.

You should get a number of replies and you may hit pay-dirt – at least you will make contact with people over there and this may be useful to you when you do cross the ocean.

2. Write to the state library, or genealogical society, or whatever source is suggested in the section of this book for your country, and try and find out if anyone has already done any ancestor-hunting in your family. I was lucky once – I was tracing my wife's ancestors in Scotland and had got back to 1710. At this point I ran into major problems, but by a series of lucky breaks I was able to find a complete family tree which took the family back to 1476. With this as a base I was able to go even further back – to 1296 – and getting back that far is quite an achievement. You will find more details about this in the final chapter, entitled "Personal Experiences".

When you do have all your basic facts, and you do go overseas, you may well discover a great deal about your ancestors. You may discover long-lost relatives, and even find the house or farm (or castle!) where your ancestors lived for many generations. It is a wonderful and eerie experience to stand, as I once did, in the living room of a farmhouse built in 1450 by one of my ancestors and inhabited by his Baxter descendants for the next three hundred and fifty years.

The following chapters will give you the main sources of information in the countries from which we all came.

Important Note about Genealogical Records in Great Britain and Ireland

REGNAL YEARS

Dates in older records are often given in what is called the *regnal year*. For example, you may find a reference in a will to an ancestor having died "on the 15th day of July in the 10th year of the reign of our Gracious Queen, Anne". This does not tell you very much, unless you know the exact date of the commencement of each reign, and so here they are, set out below (for example, the reign of Queen Anne began on 8 March 1702. So, from 8 March 1702 to 7 March 1703 was the regnal year 1 Anne):

William I	25 Dec. 1066	Mary	6 July 1553
William II	26 Sept. 1087	Philip and Mary	25 July 1554
Henry I	5 Aug. 1100	Elizabeth I	17 Nov. 1558
Stephen	26 Dec. 1135	James I†	24 Mar. 1603
Henry II	19 Dec. 1154	Charles I	27 Mar. 1625
Richard I	3 Sept. 1189	Commonwealth‡	
John*	27 May 1199	Charles II	30 Jan. 1649
Henry III	28 Oct. 1216	James II	6 Feb. 1685
Edward I	20 Nov. 1272	(Interregnum	12 Dec. 1688
Edward II	8 July 1307		to 12 Feb. 1689)
Edward III	25 Jan. 1327	William III and	
Richard II	22 June 1377	Mary	13 Feb. 1689
Henry IV	30 Sept. 1399	William III	28 Dec. 1694
Henry V	21 Mar. 1413	Anne	8 Mar. 1702
Henry VI	1 Sept. 1422	George I	1 Aug. 1714
Edward IV	4 Mar. 1461	George II	11 June 1727
Edward V	9 Apr. 1483	George III	25 Oct. 1760
Richard III	26 June 1483	George IV	29 Jan. 1820
Henry VII	22 Aug. 1485	William IV	26 June 1830
Henry VIII	22 Apr. 1509	Victoria	20 June 1837
Edward VI	28 Jan. 1547	(The regnal year discontinued)	

*In the case of John, regnal years are calculated from Ascension Day each year.

†Also known as James VI of Scotland.

‡No regnal year was used during the Commonwealth, 30 Jan. 1649 to 29 May 1660. At the Restoration on that date, the years of the reign of Charles II were back-dated to the death of Charles I, on the principle he had been king *de jure* since then.

THE CALENDAR

In trying to pinpoint an exact date of birth, marriage, or death, in searching British records, there are two traps for the unwary:

1. There was a major change in the calendar in 1752.
2. In addition, in that year, the New Year was changed from March 25 to January 1.

How all this came about is a little complicated, but, unless you understand what happened, you will make some mistakes in the dates you attribute to your ancestors. (This also applies in the British colonies of that period – including those in North America.)

Before 1582 the Julian Calendar was used throughout the Christian world. It had been set up by Julius Caesar – hence the name. This calendar divided the year into three hundred and sixty-five days, plus an extra day every fourth year. This system was in operation until 1582, but astronomers discovered that it exceeded the solar year by eleven minutes, or three days every four hundred years. Between the date when the Julian Calendar was instituted in 325 and the year 1582, the difference amounted to ten days. Since this affected the calculations for Easter, Pope Gregory XIII decreed that ten days be dropped from the calendar in order to bring Easter to the correct date. To prevent a recurrence of the variation he also ordered that in every four hundred years Leap Year's extra day be omitted in a centennial year when the first two digits could not be divided by four without a remainder.

Are you still with me? Well, it means that it was omitted in 1700, 1800, and 1900, but will not be omitted in 2000. The Pope also changed the beginning of the New Year from March 25 to January 1, and this new system became known as the Gregorian Calendar. All Roman Catholic countries adopted the new system, effective from 1582. Protestant ones did so later.

However, England (a) was having a fight with the Pope at that time, and (b) was suspicious of new ideas, anyway, and so she ignored the whole idea. She continued to ignore it for another hundred and seventy years – never let it be said the English rush into new-fangled systems! So, up until 1752 in Britain and her colonies the New Year still started on March 25, while the rest of the Christian world started it on January 1. To further complicate matters, many educated people thought the change should have been made, and so you will occasionally find entries in church registers and other records dated, for example, 8 January 1686/7, thus showing that although it was 1686, they thought it really should be 1687.

Finally, in 1752, the English government changed from the Julian Calendar to the Gregorian Calendar and ordered that eleven days be dropped between September 2 and 14 in that year. This prompted riots in various parts of the country, with mobs of people waving banners and crying "Give us back our eleven days." Yes, that really did happen!

As a result, you will find entries like 11 June O.S. (Old Style), 22 June N.S. (New Style). In addition, the change of the New Year to January 1 meant that people born on 27 March 1692 (O.S.) had to change their date of birth to 7 April 1691 (N.S.).

Once all this is clear to you you will not be confused to find that an ancestress of yours had one child born in one year and a second born a few months later. It was the calendar which changed and not the nine-month gestation period, so all is well!

9. ENGLAND AND WALES

The problem with records in the United Kingdom is not scarcity but plenty! Nothing has been thrown out and records go back in many cases for a thousand years. The real problem is to discover where they are located.

You may have heard of "Somerset House" in London. It used to be the location of the General Register Office, but the new address is St. Catherine's House, 10 Kingsway, London WC2B 6JP. This is the office which has on file the certificates of birth, marriage, and death since 1 July 1837, the date when registration of these events became compulsory in England and Wales (see Chapter Ten for Scotland and Chapter Eleven for Ireland).

The details of registers and records in the General Register Office are as follows:

1. RECORDS OF BIRTHS, MARRIAGES, AND DEATHS

This is the main series of national records. Indexes completed to within about the last twelve months are available. The indexes cover the whole of England and Wales in one alphabetical order for each quarterly volume. To cover one year you must, of course, search all four volumes. They each measure 2 feet by 18 inches and weigh about 10 lbs. (the earlier parchment ones weigh twice this amount), so start getting into good physical shape. If you are searching a five-year period you will have to haul twenty volumes off the shelves and then lift them onto the reading racks provided.

If the surname for which you are searching is a common one, and the first name is also, you will be astonished to discover a number of people with those same names being born in the same year in different parts of the country. Of course, if you have the exact address this will not make too much difference, but if you do find it impossible to distinguish between two or more individuals, then you will have to note them all and go to other sources (such as wills) to identify the one in which you are interested.

Of course, you do not need to search the indexes yourself. You can apply by mail. The fee for a certificate of birth, marriage, or death, when applied for by mail (search in the indexes will be restricted to cover a period not exceeding five years), is at least £10. If you make the search yourself it will cost less. (The search rooms are open between 08 30 hours and 16 30 hours from Monday to Friday.) Your fee includes a certificate of the event.

Remember that the fee applies to each separate event; i.e., births, marriages, and deaths are quite separate from each other and separate applications are needed for each one.

The birth certificate gives the place and date of birth; sex and names of the child; name and occupation of father; name and maiden name of the mother; and the name, description, and address of the informant.

The marriage certificate gives the place and date of the marriage; the names, ages, occupations, addresses, and marital status of the bride and bridegroom; the names and occupations of the fathers of the bride and groom; and the names of the witnesses. (The latter names are often very useful, as they are usually relatives of either the bride or the groom.)

The death certificate gives the name, sex, age, and occupation of the deceased; the place, date, and cause of death; and the name and address of the informant.

The great advantage of a personal search, apart from the saving in cost, is that you can follow up clues on the spot. For example, in searching for one relative you may find references to others, and you can search for them.

You can call for your certificate the next day, or arrange for it to be mailed to you.

It should be noted that, in addition to the registers mentioned above, which are kept at the General Register Office, there are also district registers kept in the District Registry of births, marriages, and deaths in each locality. If you are quite certain that your ancestors came from a particular district, you can always search the local registers instead of those in London. They are, of course, much smaller, and one index can cover five or more years. They are also cheaper to consult.

2. RECORDS OF STILL-BIRTHS SINCE 1 JULY 1927

Certified copies of these records can only be obtained with the special permission of the Registrar General.

3. RECORDS OF BIRTHS AND DEATHS AT SEA SINCE 1 JULY 1837 (MARINE REGISTER BOOK)

These returns relate chiefly to persons of British nationality belonging to England and Wales.

4. RECORDS OF BIRTHS AND DEATHS IN AIRCRAFT (AIR REGISTER BOOK)

These returns commence in 1949 and relate to births and deaths occurring in any part of the world in any aircraft registered in Great Britain and Northern Ireland.

5. SERVICE RECORDS

Births, marriages, and deaths occurring out of the United Kingdom among members of the armed forces and certain other persons, or occurring aboard certain ships and aircraft. The entries in the army registers date mainly from 1881, but some entries go back to 1796. The Royal Air Force Returns commenced in 1920.

6. CONSULAR RETURNS

Births, marriages, and deaths of British subjects in foreign countries, recorded by Consular Officers since July 1849.

7. MISCELLANEOUS

Births, baptisms, marriages, deaths, and burials, in a large series of miscellaneous records (army, colonial, and foreign), some dating back to 1627, including births and deaths registered by, and marriage certificates forwarded by, the British High Commissioners for India and Pakistan from 1950, and by High Commissioners in other Commonwealth countries at a later date.

8. RECORDS OF ADOPTION SINCE 1 JANUARY 1927

These records consist of entries of adoption made in the Adopted Children Register in accordance with the Adoption Acts. The fees for certificates are the same as those for births, marriages, and deaths. When applying for a search to be made, the applicant should give as much of the following information as possible:

a) Date of the adoption order and name of the court making the order;
b) Name of the child;
c) Full name and surname of the adoptive parents.

Applications by mail for these certificates should be sent to the General Register Office, Registration Division, Titchfield, Fareham, Hampshire.

Note: All fees sent to the General Register Office for any kind of search or certificate should be paid by international money order, cheque, or draft, payable to the Registrar General in sterling funds.

Before we go further into the location of records in England and Wales, it should be mentioned that in 1975 there were considerable changes in the structure of local government. As a result of this, several counties disappeared and others were divided or renamed. The new county of Cumbria, for example, includes the old counties of Cumberland and Westmorland, parts of Lancashire, parts of the old West Riding of Yorkshire, and the County Borough Councils of Carlisle and Barrow-in-Furness. This can be confusing when you are searching for a particular county and find it no longer exists. Details of the changes for England and Wales are given below:

ENGLAND: M after the county name indicates a Metropolitan County, CBC means County Borough Council, C stands for City. The name of the county town and seat of government is shown in brackets:

AVON: Bath and Bristol CBCs, parts of Gloucestershire and Somerset (Bristol)

BEDFORDSHIRE: Luton CBC and Bedfordshire (Bedford)

BERKSHIRE: Reading CBC, most of Berkshire, parts of Buckinghamshire (Reading)

BUCKINGHAMSHIRE: Most of Buckinghamshire (Aylesbury)

CAMBRIDGESHIRE: Cambridgeshire, Isle of Ely, Huntingdon, and Peterborough (Cambridge)

CHESHIRE: Chester and Warrington CBCs, most of Cheshire, parts of Lancashire (Chester)

CLEVELAND: Hartlepool and Teesside CBCs, parts of Durham, parts of North Riding of Yorkshire (Middlesbrough)

CORNWALL: Cornwall (Truro)

CUMBRIA: Barrow-in-Furness and Carlisle CBCs, Cumberland, Westmorland, parts of Lancashire, parts of West Riding of Yorkshire (Carlisle)

DERBYSHIRE: Derby CBC, Derbyshire, parts of Cheshire (Matlock)

DEVON: Exeter, Plymouth, and Torbay CBCs, Devon (Exeter)

DORSET: Bournemouth CBC, Dorset, parts of Hampshire (Dorchester)

DURHAM: Darlington CBC, most of Durham, parts of North Riding of Yorkshire (Durham)

EAST SUSSEX: Brighton, Eastbourne, and Hastings CBCs, most of East Sussex (Lewes)

ESSEX: Southend-on-Sea CBC, Essex (Chelmsford)

GLOUCESTERSHIRE: Gloucester CBC, most of Gloucestershire (Gloucester)

GREATER MANCHESTER M: Wigan, Bolton, Bury, Rochdale, Salford, Manchester, Oldham, and Stockport CBCs, parts of Lancashire, parts of Cheshire (Manchester)

HAMPSHIRE: Portsmouth and Southampton CBCs, most of Hampshire (Winchester)

HEREFORD and **WORCESTER:** Worcester CBC, Herefordshire, most of Worcestershire (Worcester)

HERTFORDSHIRE: Hertfordshire (Hertford)

HUMBERSIDE: Grimsby and Kingston-upon-Hull CBCs, most of the East Riding of Yorkshire, parts of Lindsey (Lincolnshire), and parts of the West Riding of Yorkshire (Kingston-upon-Hull)

ISLE OF WIGHT: Isle of Wight (Newport)

KENT: Canterbury CBC, Kent (Maidstone)

LANCASHIRE: Blackburn, Blackpool, Burnley, and Preston CBCs, most of Lancashire, parts of the West Riding of Yorkshire (Preston)

LEICESTERSHIRE: Leicester CBC, Leicestershire, Rutland (Leicester)

LINCOLNSHIRE: Lincoln CBC, Holland, Kesteven, some of Lindsey (Lincoln)

MERSEYSIDE M: Bootle, Southport, Liverpool, and St. Helens CBCs, parts of Lancashire, parts of Cheshire (Liverpool)

NORFOLK: Great Yarmouth and Norwich CBCs, Norfolk, parts of East Suffolk (Norwich)

NORTHAMPTONSHIRE: Northamptonshire and Northampton CBC (Northampton)

NORTHUMBERLAND: Most of Northumberland (Newcastle)

NORTH YORKSHIRE: York CBC, most of the North Riding of Yorkshire, part of the East Riding of Yorkshire (Northallerton)

NOTTINGHAMSHIRE: Nottingham CBC, most of Nottinghamshire (Nottingham)

OXFORDSHIRE: Oxford CBC, Oxfordshire, part of Berkshire (Oxford)

SALOP: Salop (Shrewsbury)

SOMERSET: Most of Somerset (Taunton)

SOUTH YORKSHIRE M: Barnsley, Doncaster, Rotherham, Sheffield CBCs, part of the West Riding of Yorkshire (Barnsley)

STAFFORDSHIRE: Burton-upon-Trent and Stoke-on-Trent CBCs, most of Staffordshire (Stafford)

SUFFOLK: Ipswich CBC, West Suffolk, most of East Suffolk (Ipswich)

SURREY: Most of Surrey (Kingston-upon-Thames)

TYNE AND WEAR M: Gateshead, Newcastle-upon-Tyne, South Shields, Sunderland, Tynemouth CBCs, parts of Northumberland, parts of Durham (Newcastle-upon-Tyne)

WARWICKSHIRE: Most of Warwickshire (Warwick)

WEST MIDLANDS M: Birmingham, Coventry, Dudley, Solihull, Walsall, Warley, West Bromwich, Wolverhampton CBCs, parts of Staffordshire, parts of Warwickshire, parts of Worcestershire (Birmingham)

WEST SUSSEX: West Sussex, parts of East Sussex (Chichester)

WEST YORKSHIRE M: Bradford, Dewsbury, Halifax, Huddersfield, Leeds, Wakefield CBCs, parts of the West Riding of Yorkshire (Wakefield)

WILTSHIRE: Wiltshire (Trowbridge)

It will be seen from the above that the two smallest counties in England (Rutland and Isle of Ely) have disappeared, as have Huntingdon and Westmorland, Cumberland and Middlesex. Only Bedfordshire, Cornwall, Essex, Hertfordshire, Isle of Wight, Kent, Northamptonshire, Salop, and Wiltshire have no boundary changes.

WALES

CLWYD: Flintshire, most of Denbighshire, part of Merioneth (Mold)

DYFED: Cardiganshire, Carmarthenshire, Pembrokeshire (Carmarthen)

GWENT: Newport CBC, most of Monmouthshire, part of Breconshire (Newport)

GWYNEDD: Anglesey, Caernarvonshire, most of Merioneth, part of Denbighshire (Caernarvon)

MID GLAMORGAN: Merthyr Tydfil CBC, parts of Breconshire, parts of Glamorgan, parts of Monmouthshire (Cardiff)

POWYS: Montgomeryshire, Radnorshire, most of Breconshire (Llandrindod Wells)

SOUTH GLAMORGAN: Cardiff CBC, parts of Glamorgan, parts of Monmouthshire (Cardiff)

WEST GLAMORGAN: Swansea CBC, parts of Glamorgan (Swansea)

To contact the CRO for each county, you should write to the County Archivist, County Record Office, in the county town, i.e., the place which appears in brackets after the county description above.

Before we leave the General Register Office and pass on to other sources of information, it is worth while to emphasize that the Office does not possess family trees. No one is going to provide you with a complete, ready-made family tree, unless (a) you are descended from a Peer, in which case you will find it in several books of reference, such as Debrett or Burke (more about these later); or (b) your family has played a prominent part in the public life of the district, and its family tree is included in a local history book; or (c) someone else has already researched your family.

Once you have obtained all possible information from the General Register Office (St. Catherine's House) you must decide whether to search parish registers, census returns, or wills. Personally, I would go for the census returns first. This means you now go round the corner to another great source of information – the Public Record Office. This is located in Chancery Lane, London, a short distance away from the General Register Office. Actually, the PRO now has two locations. At Chancery Lane you will find censuses, probate records, and non-parochial registers. At the new headquarters in

Kew (Ruskin Avenue, Kew, Richmond) the records of government departments are kept. These include many military and naval records of vital interest to the ancestor-hunter.

The Public Record Office contains many millions of documents relating to the actions of the government and the Courts of Law in England and Wales from the eleventh century, of Great Britain from 1707, and of the United Kingdom from 1801 to the present day.

The Office is open from 09 30 hours to 17 00 hours from Monday to Friday. All Search Rooms are closed during the last week in September and the first week of October for stock-taking.

People are expected to carry out their own searches, although the search-room officers will give advice. If you are unable to make a personal visit to the Public Record Office, they can supply information about professional record agents who will undertake research for a fee. In a limited number of cases, the Office will undertake searches, i.e. census returns and non-parochial parish registers, naval and military service records, and probate records.

A person wishing to inspect the records must fill in an application form for a reader's ticket (valid for five years, if you plan to stay that long!). This requires a recommendation from "someone of recognized position" to whom the applicant is known personally, or, more simply, a signature from someone in the High Commissioner's office at Canada House.

A majority of the records are of no interest to the ancestor-hunter and so I will only list those that are:

NON-PAROCHIAL REGISTERS

The parish registers often contain entries relating not only to members of the Church of England, but also to Dissenters, since the Registration Act of 1695 required notice of all births to be given to the parish clergyman. The later Marriage Act of 1753 restricted marriages to parish churches, even if those being married did not belong to the Church of England. This did not apply to Quakers and Jews, and was usually ignored by Roman Catholics. Many dissenting churches retained their own registers of births, marriages, and burials. As the result of several acts of Parliament, all these dissenting, or non-parochial, registers and records have been lodged with the Public Record Office. There are seven thousand volumes and files and no index, so if you are searching for an ancestor who was not a member of the Church of England you must at least know the approximate locality from whence he came. These registers are confined to England and Wales. The great majority are from Protestant Nonconformist churches; they include several registers of Huguenot and other foreign Protestant churches in England, and registers of the Society of Friends (Quakers). An index to the latter is in the library of the Society of Friends, Friends' House, Euston Road, London. The few Roman Catholic registers are mostly from the north of England. There are no Jewish registers. Most of the registers are within the period 1775-1837, although a few continue up until 1857, and several go back as far as the middle of the seventeenth century or even, in the case of foreign Protestant churches, to the sixteenth century.

Many of the non-parochial registers are now on microfilm in the County Record Offices of England and Wales.

CENSUS RETURNS

The first census of England and Wales took place in 1801. There had been several attempts before that to establish a regular census of the population, but the opposition to the idea was based on the belief it would give valuable information to England's enemies, and the various proposals were always defeated.

Since 1801 the censuses have been held every ten years (except in 1941, during the Second World War). The early censuses are of no interest to the ancestor-hunter because they gave only the numbers in each household, and not the names.

The 1841 census is the first of interest. It gave the name of all persons in the household, with their approximate age (to the nearest five years below), their sex, their occupation, and whether they were born in the same county or not. Unfortunately it did not give the relationship of each person listed to the head of the household.

The 1851 census is far more valuable. It gave the exact address or location of the house; the names of all the people in the house; their condition (single, married, widowed, etc.); their exact age; their occupation; and (praise be!) their exact place of birth. It also showed the head of the household (this was in the days before Women's Lib.) and the relationship of each person to him (i.e., wife, son, daughter, mother, visitor, servant). The same information is given in the census returns of 1861 and 1871, which are also available for inspection in the Public Record Office. Census returns are produced free of charge to the holders of readers' tickets. Searches will be undertaken for a small fee for persons not able to visit the office in person.

The census returns for 1881 and subsequent years are in the custody of the Registrar General, St. Catherine's House, 10 Kingsway, London, and are not available to the public until a hundred years after the date of the census (the 1881 census became available in 1982).

The main problems in using the census returns is in finding

the exact address of the person you are looking for. In a village this does not matter because the entire return for that area will not be more than a few pages. The cities will present the main problem. If you know that your ancestor, William Adams, came from Bristol, for example, but you have no address, then you can probably find this in a local directory. Most major cities published directories as far back as the late eighteenth or early nineteenth centuries, and they are to be found in local libraries, in the Guildhall Library in London, and in the British Museum.

You may find several William Adamses listed in the directory and you will have to note them all and check each one out in the census returns. (Presumably you know the name of William's wife or son, and this will show up in the census and enable you to forget about the others.)

The census returns can sometimes be the key to taking your family a long way back. For example, you may find William Adams in the 1851 census living at 403 Gloucester Road, Bristol, with his wife and children. His place of birth is shown as Bristol, *but* you also find he had an aunt, Mary Adams, spinster, living with him. She was eighty years old and was born in the village of Alveston, Gloucestershire. Do you realize the value of this one entry? It means that if Mary Adams was born in Alveston, then it is ninety-nine per cent certain that her brother (the father of William) was born there too. Without this census return you might never have made the link between Bristol and Alveston.

So, the censuses lead you to the parish registers, and we will talk about them after we have finished with the information you can find at the Public Record Office.

Before we finish with census returns it should be mentioned that no returns for British colonies have been preserved, except for the 1828 census of New South Wales, Australia. This gives the name, age, information as to whether the person is free or in bondage, ship and year of arrival, length of sentence (for criminals), religion, employment, residence, and details of land and stock. The return is in alphabetical order.

BRITISH MILITARY RECORDS

Before the Civil War (1642-9) there was no regular standing army in England. Regiments were raised to meet special occasions and were usually known by the names of the colonels who raised them. There are no records of such regiments, although occasional reference to individual officers and soldiers is found in state papers and Privy Council registers. It would be very exceptional to find in these records any reference to any individual's birthplace or family.

For the period of the Civil War and of the Commonwealth

which followed it, the officers of both sides are listed in *The Army List of Roundheads and Cavaliers* by Edward Peacock (1865), and for Parliamentary troops much detailed information can be found in *The Regimental History of Cromwell's Army* by Firth and Davies (1940).

After the restoration of the monarchy in 1660, records are far more plentiful. The main War Office Records contain a great deal of information about military operations and administration, finance, supplies, courts martial, etc.

The service records of commissioned officers of the British Army are almost complete from 1660. Family details and places of birth were recorded from the end of the eighteenth century. The date of an officer's death can be found in the Paymaster General's records of full and half pay.

The records of other ranks are arranged by regiments, so it is essential to know the name of the regiment in which the soldier served in order to trace his record. When his regiment is known, the best records for information about a soldier are regular soldiers' documents. These date back to 1756 and include the discharge certificates. These record his place of birth and his age at date of enlistment. After 1883, details of the next-of-kin, wife and children, are sometimes given.

Other good sources of information are the pay lists and muster rolls. These date from 1760 and are useful for finding out the date of the soldier's enlistment, his movements throughout the world while in the army, and the date of his discharge or death. There are also the description books. These contain the soldier's date of birth and his physical description. They were used by the authorities to trace and identify deserters.

NAVAL RECORDS

The Admiralty Records are also to be found in the Public Record Office. Information about officers is easier to find than that about naval ratings. From 1789 all candidates for officer rank had to file copies of their baptismal certificates. These are attached to copies of the lieutenants' passing certificates, and are indexed for the period 1777 to 1832.

The bounty papers (1675 to 1822) give the name and address of the next-of-kin to whom the bounty is to be paid if the officer or rating was killed in action or died. The baptismal certificate of the next-of-kin is also included.

The register of lieutenants soliciting employment, which was kept from 1799 on, is another source of information because it lists the address of the lieutenant.

There are also such sources of information as the ships' muster rolls; passing certificates for officers; and the returns of midshipmen's services.

In addition to these records at the Public Record Office,

there are several published books which give detailed information, and these are listed in the bibliography at the end of this book.

ROYAL MARINES

The records of the Royal Marines are also at the Public Record Office. Many of the early documents have been lost, including most of the description books. The attestation forms (1790-1883) give the age, place of birth, and physical appearance of each recruit. These are arranged alphabetically. The description books that remain cover the period 1750 to 1888 and, here again, they are in alphabetical order. The registers of service (1842-1905) give similar information.

The Public Record Office also has in its custody a number of wills, but since the whole complicated question of wills and where to find them is dealt with later in this chapter, I will not attempt to talk about the PRO holdings at this stage.

PARISH REGISTERS

Now we are ready to go into the whole story of parish registers – the single most important item for the ancestor-hunter, because without the parish registers no completely accurate and verifiable family tree is possible.

In mediaeval times there were no official parish registers, although some monasteries and parish priests did keep some sort of record of births, marriages, and deaths of leading local families. Records which have been preserved were kept in a small village in Derbyshire (Crich) as far back as 1344. However, this is exceptional, and for the average ancestor-hunter the starting date for parish registers is 5 September 1538. All parsons, vicars, and curates were ordered to enter in a book every wedding, christening, and burial in the parish, with the names of the people concerned. They were further ordered to provide a "sure coffer" with two locks. The parson kept the key to one, and the churchwardens the key to the other.

These entries were made on paper, and often just on loose sheets. In 1598 all the entries were supposed to be copied into parchment books. When this was done the paper books and sheets could be destroyed. Unfortunately the wording of the Act said the entries should be copied from the beginning, "but especially since the first year of Her Majesty's reign". In most cases this loose phrase was taken to mean that entries *before* the first year of Queen Elizabeth's reign need not be copied, and so few records exist before that year (1558).

The Act of 1598 also specified that once a year a copy of all the entries for that year should be sent to the diocesan registry – these are now known as the *bishop's transcripts*. In many cases, where parish registers have been lost or destroyed, the bishop's transcripts have been preserved.

The bishop's transcripts are now nearly all deposited in the County Record Offices most nearly concerned with the areas of jurisdiction of the bishops. A notable exception is Kent, where those of the Diocese of Canterbury remain at Canterbury Cathedral. Those for the Diocese of Lichfield, which covered several counties, are all at the County Record Office for Lincoln. In the Diocese of London none were kept before 1800, and in that of Winchester none were kept before 1770. (This latter diocese also covered the Channel Islands, so searchers in that area should remember this.)

The Civil War and the subsequent Commonwealth disrupted life in England and Wales from 1642 to 1660, and very many registers have gaps in their entries for this period.

From 1660 the parish registers are, generally speaking, complete. The only exceptions are caused by local disasters such as fire or flood. Here again, the bishop's transcripts are very useful – depending on the date of the disaster and the date on which the transcripts were sent to the bishop (they were supposed to be sent after Easter in each year). In 1753 the Marriage Act tightened the regulations for a church marriage. Among other provisions, it set out that one of the parties must reside in the parish, and that the marriage was not valid unless the banns had been read or a special licence issued. This assured more dependable marriage records.

In 1812 Rose's Act, as it is known, set out stringent rules for the preservation and safe custody of the parish registers. It also legislated the end of the parchment registers and had them replaced with the typeset form of book in use today.

If your ancestors belonged to the Church of England the parish registers will, if you are lucky, provide you with much information about them. By and large, there was not a great deal of movement of the population before the latter half of the eighteenth century – then the start of the Industrial Revolution meant a general drift from the countryside into the towns. This static population over many centuries meant that men and women were most likely to marry someone from their own village, or at least from the neighbouring one.

Let me quote from my own family, as an example. The first Baxter appeared in the valley of Swindale, Westmorland, in 1195, when John Bacastre was mentioned in a tax roll. The family was mentioned again in 1362 when John Baxter and his wife, Beatrice, were left forty sheep in the will of Sir Thomas Legleys. From then on descent was proved right down to the present day, and from 1195 to 1795 – six hundred years – the Baxters lived in that remote little valley.

The parish registers, until recently, were always in the original church. However, in 1978, a new act directed that all registers more than one hundred years old were to be deposited in the County Record Offices, or such other archives as were designated for the purpose. As a result, very few now remain in the churches. Although, as I mentioned earlier in this chapter, there were changes in county boundaries in 1975, the location of the various county record offices has not been changed. For example, the record office of Westmorland is still in Kendal, although Westmorland is merged with Cumberland to form Cumbria, with headquarters at Carlisle.

When starting your search of parish registers there are a number of things you must bear in mind:

If you are unable to visit England or Wales, but have discovered the place where your family originated, you can apply by mail to the CRO for a search of the parish registers. If they have been published or indexed, the CRO will know about this. If all you want is a single entry, probably no charge will be made. If you need a long search, you will be referred to a local researcher, who will do this for a fee and negotiate the price with you directly. When writing to the CRO, be sure you enclose a self-addressed airmail envelope and two International Reply Coupons (obtainable from your post office); otherwise, you are unlikely to get a reply.

An alternative source of printed or microfilmed copies of parish registers and bishop's transcripts is the Genealogical Library of the Church of Jesus Christ of Latter-Day Saints (Mormons) in Salt Lake City, Utah. Part of the religious observances of this church is the baptism of previous generations so that, by proxy, they become church members. As a result, the Church has embarked on a massive campaign of copying all church records in all European countries and now possesses the largest genealogical collection in the world.

Some of the statistics are staggering — 200,000 books on the open shelves, 1,100,000 rolls of microfilm. For information about parish registers write to the Genealogical Society of the Church of Jesus Christ of Latter-Day Saints, 50 East North Temple, Salt Lake City, Utah 84111.

However, there are ten thousand parish registers in England and Wales, and the odds are that your particular register has not yet been printed or microfilmed. In any case, a visit to the parish is essential for filling in the gaps by looking at the tombstones in the graveyard. In many cases they have been transferred to the wall of the church or the interior; in some cases they have been piled one on top of the other in a corner; in more cases the weathering of centuries has made them unreadable; and yet, in many other cases, they are a vast fund of information. Here again, check with the parson or the local library because quite often local historians have copied and listed and indexed all the readable inscriptions. Frequently, this was done when the graveyard was to be disturbed by road-widening or removal of the stones.

The reaction of the church parson to your visit, or to your letter, will vary. Tread gently in your dealings with him. If you are writing, go to your local library and look up the parish in *Crockford's Clerical Directory*. This will give you the parson's name, his full address, *and* any degrees or decorations he possesses – some of them are very sensitive about the omission of these. When you write, bear in mind that he is not bound to search the registers for you and so you must ask him politely if he would be willing to do you this favour. There is also a scale of fees for such searches. The whole question of these fees is under discussion in England and Wales at the moment, and so any figure I quote would not necessarily be the right one for you. In any case, if you want a search over a period of years, rather than one particular entry, the amount is usually negotiable. So, tell him what you want done, and ask him what it will cost. Also, be sure you enclose a self-addressed airmail envelope and an international reply coupon for the correct postage. (Postage in Great Britain increases very often, so check with your post office.) I should emphasize *airmail* because the British seem to have a mental block about writing by airmail, and surface mail can take many weeks.

It is usually wise to ask him for any entries under the particular surname because this will give you brothers and sisters as well, and will not usually cost you any more.

If you are searching the registers personally you must be prepared to do it under difficult conditions and under close supervision by the parson, unless he decides that you look quite trustworthy. You may find you are searching the registers by candlelight in a damp cellar, or by oil lamp in a draughty tower, or with a Scotch in your hand by a roaring fire – all these things have happened to me!

You will meet parsons who regard you with the deepest suspicion and question you closely as to whether you are a Mormon. You will meet parsons who ask you to lunch. You will meet parsons who tell you to come back *after* lunch. You will meet parsons who – at ten in the morning – appear to have been into the sacramental wine. All these things, too, have happened to me.

When you search the registers yourself you will usually find that the parson will quote you an inclusive fee for a morning's search, or an afternoon's, or whatever.

It must also be remembered, when searching the earlier registers, that until 1 January 1752 the year began on 25

March, the Feast of the Annunciation, so that before that date any dates in January, February, and March, up to March 24, were included in the previous year. (See pp. 127-8.)

Another fact to remember is that, although you may have discovered that your ancestor lived at a farm in a certain parish, he did not necessarily attend the church in that parish – he may have found that the church of a neighbouring parish was, in fact, much nearer if he took a short-cut over the fields. So try and find a large-scale map of the district – one that shows the location of individual farms and local footpaths and churches. The ordnance survey maps with a scale of six inches to the mile are admirable for this purpose and can usually be bought at a stationer's or bookseller's in the local county town, or at HM Stationery Office in London, or other large centres.

Be prepared for difficulty in deciphering the writing in the early registers. Sometimes it is "copper-plate" and easy to read, but very often great concentration is needed and a magnifying glass is a great help. Remember, until fairly recent times a double s (ss) was written fs (β). You will also find that there may be considerable variation in the spelling of the surname of your ancestor. Very often the entry was made by a church-warden or parish clerk who could not necessarily read and write, except to a limited degree. He would ask the surname and then write it down as it sounded. My own name appears in parish registers as Baxter, Backster, Baxster – all within a single generation. First names can also be a problem because, in the early registers, the name was often written in Latin, and it is not easy to realize that James and Jacobus are the same, as are William and Guglielmo. A further complication is the fact that many first names are applicable to both male and female children. Examples are Evelyn, Leslie, and Hilary.

If you find that the parish registers in which you are interested have been lost, or contain long gaps, do not forget what I told you earlier about the bishop's transcripts.

If you are lucky, you will find the surname for each entry is shown first, on the left of the page, followed by the rest of the information. I am always delighted to be able to run straight down a page when this happens, rather than painstakingly reading across each line.

You may also run into a difficult problem if there were a number of members of your family living in the town or village at any one time. Many years ago, when tracing my own family, I found two separate couples producing children in the valley at the same time – both named William and Elizabeth Baxter. This made matters very difficult, but I was able to solve it eventually by reference to wills, plus the naming patterns of that particular time (approximately 1700-1875), i.e.:

> The first son was named after the father's father
> The second son after the mother's father
> The third son after the father
> The fourth son after the father's eldest brother
> The first daughter after the mother's mother
> The second daughter after the father's mother
> The third daughter after the mother
> The fourth daughter after the mother's eldest sister

There were exceptions to this pattern when the naming sequence produced a duplication of names. In that case, the name was taken from the next on the list; i.e., if the eldest son was named John, after the father's father, and the mother's father was also John, then the second son could not be named after him and was, therefore, named after the father.

Another break in the pattern could be caused by death. A century or so ago it was not unusual for at least half the children to die in infancy. Nowadays, parents who lose a child by death are not inclined to use his name for a subsequent child, but this is a comparatively recent development. I have known cases where five sons in succession were named John because, in turn, each one died. This is why it is important to check the deaths in the register as well as the births.

You must remember, too, that you are, in fact, searching the registers of baptisms, marriages, and burials and *not* actual births, marriages, and deaths.

You may find that one of your ancestors was illegitimate, and in this case, the entry will read something like this: "Baptized this day John, the base-born son of Mary Adams." If you do find something like this, for Heaven's sake, don't let it worry you. It happened very often in those far-off days.

TITHES
Another possible source of information about any ancestors living in about 1840 is the Tithe Records in the Public Record Office in London. Because of a change in the tithe payments, a complete survey of land took place at about that time, and every owner or occupier was listed, parish by parish. Many of the CROs also hold copies of these records.

NEWSPAPERS
Another possible source of information locally may well be the newspaper files in the nearest county town, or the copies in the nearest library. The first provincial paper in England was the *Norwich Post*, begun in 1702, and this was followed soon after by newspapers in Bristol and Worcester. A list of the

dates when newspapers began and ended publication, or were merged, can be found in the *British Union Catalogue of Periodicals* in most local libraries in England and Wales. Many local libraries have superb collections of local newspapers. The public library in Northampton, for example, has a complete set of the *Northampton Mercury* from 1720 to the present day. Births, marriages, and deaths first appeared in local newspapers in the latter half of the eighteenth century; and one very useful point about the marriage entries in local newspapers is that often details were given of a marriage of a local man which took place some considerable distance away.

NON-PAROCHIAL REGISTERS

I have already mentioned the non-parochial registers in the custody of the Public Record Office. It is time now to talk about these records at greater length. If your ancestors were not members of the Church of England, then your task of tracing them will be harder. In olden days religious tolerance was nonexistent, and dissenters were either persecuted or placed under various restrictions. Of course, before the fight between Henry VIII and the Pope, the English Church was Catholic and monolithic. If there was an opposition it was not very apparent.

With the founding of the Church of England, Catholics and their religion went underground. Services and confessions were held in secret, and as a result Catholic registers were kept hidden in various places. Consequently, a great many of the early ones have disappeared. Those that did survive have been retained by the Church and are not in the custody of the Public Record Office. The Catholic Record Society has published a number of early registers for the years prior to 1754. After that year, the Hardwicke Marriage Act ordered that all Catholics were to be married in the Church of England; otherwise the marriage would not be legal. Catholics, in general, complied, but probably had a secret marriage as well within their own Church.

In general terms, current Catholic registers (and in small parishes this may mean those dating back to the early nineteenth century) are kept in the original church, and there are no microfilm copies. However, in certain dioceses, notably Westminster, Lancaster, Birmingham, and Southwark, original registers from before 1850 have been deposited in the central Diocesan Archives, or else a microfilm has been deposited, although this latter case is rare. Each diocese acts independently, some having archivists to the bishop and archbishop and some not.

Two first steps are always useful:
1. Get hold of the current Catholic Directory which lists all

Catholic churches in the country. This may be in your local library in Canada, or in the Chancery Office of the local Catholic diocese; or it may be obtained through your regional library system. With this you can locate the church you want and write to the parish priest.

2. If this produces no result, you should then write to the archivist or the bishop of the diocese to ask if the registers of that church have been deposited.

If both these steps fail, then write to the Catholic Record Society, 114 Mount Street, London W1Y 6AH.

Many Nonconformists were also married in the Church of England because before 1806 their own ministers were not permitted to officiate at marriages, and only marriages in the recognized Church were legal.

The Congregationalists are the oldest body of Nonconformists, and came into existence immediately after the Reformation. They disagreed with the idea of the king being head of the Church and did not believe church membership should be open to everyone – only to true believers and people who made open confession of their faith. The Puritans were basically on offshoot of the Congregationalists and, of course, the Church suffered accordingly when the monarchy was restored in 1660.

The Corporation Act of 1661 prevented members from holding any kind of public office, and the Conventicle Act of 1664 declared illegal all religious meetings except those of the Church of England (also known as the Anglican Church). The Five Mile Act of 1665 forbade Nonconformist ministers from teaching in schools or living within five miles of a town. In 1673 the Test Act ordered that all people holding office under the Crown should take the sacrament according to the rites of the Church of England.

During the eighteenth century there was an increase in religious tolerance, and although the Acts remained on the statute books, very little attempt was made to enforce them. By the nineteenth century they were abolished.

Many Nonconformist records have disappeared. The National Union of Congregational Churches was established in 1832 and set up the Congregational Library where many early records are preserved. The registers which did survive are, of course, in the Public Record Office. The information in them is more detailed than in the established church registers – baptismal entries included the maiden name of the child's mother, a very valuable addition.

The Methodists are of later origin and came into being as the result of the work of the two Wesley brothers – John and Charles. They did not intend to form a new church, but simply to revitalize the Church of England. However, they were overtaken by events and, even in their own life-time, ministers among their followers were baptizing, marrying, and burying their adherents. However, many members continued to use the facilities of the parish church for these events. After the deaths of the Wesley brothers in 1788 and 1791 the Methodists began to form themselves into organized churches, rather than isolated district meetings. Almost at once, splits appeared in the Methodist ranks and a number of offshoots appeared, such as the Wesleyan Methodists, the New Connection, the Primitive Methodists, the Bible Christians, the Protestant Methodists, the Wesleyan Methodist Associates, and the Wesleyan Reformers. By the end of the century there was a gradual merger of these various sects, and now there are two only – independent Methodists and the Methodists.

In 1818 a Methodist registry was set up for the central recording of baptisms being performed in the chapels throughout the country, and its register is among the records now in the Public Record Office. There are also the records of many early Methodist burial-grounds.

The Society of Friends (Quakers) kept good records from their foundation by George Fox in the seventeenth century. These were also handed over in 1840 and are in the PRO. However, before doing so, the Quakers made digests of them, indexed them, and kept them at Friends' House. There are 85 volumes, containing 260,000 births, 40,000 marriages, and 310,000 burials.

WILLS

After parish registers and census returns, wills provide the next most important information for those tracing their ancestors. They are also the most difficult to find and whole books have been written on "Wills and where to find them", "Wills and their whereabouts", and so on. Details of these and other books on the subject will be found in the bibliography at the end of this book.

Since 1858 wills in England and Wales have presented no great difficulty, as from then on they were proved in the Principal Probate Registry at Somerset House, or in one of the district probate registries set up at that time. The Principal Probate Registry is now known as the Principal Registry of the Family Division, Somerset House, Strand, London WC2R 1LP. The wills and probate records are available for inspection from 10 00 hours to 16 30 hours Monday to Friday. Individuals may make pencil copies of wills or extracts from them. The fees payable by individuals requesting copies by mail is under review at the present time.

The index at Somerset House shows, in exact alphabetical order, all wills proved from 1858 to the present day. The index gives you the name, address, and place of death of the deceased; the date of death; the names of the executors and their addresses.

When we go back before 1858 the real problems start. However, as time goes by, the discovery of wills is being made easier. More and more are being deposited in County Record Offices, irrespective of the original area of church authority. So, if you know the *original* county in which your ancestor was living, you should write directly to the CRO first, before trying any other sources.

Before 1858 the proving of wills was in the hands of the church – just as baptisms, marriages, and burials were. In earlier times a will was regarded as a sacred document and that is why all early wills start with the words "In the name of God, Amen" and continue in quasi-religious style. In theory, if a man died, leaving land or property within the area of an archdeaconry, then his will would be proved in that Archdeacon's Court. If he had property in two archdeaconries within the same diocese, then his will would be proved in the Bishop's Court. If he had property in two dioceses, then his will would be proved in the Prerogative Court of Canterbury or the Prerogative Court of York (there are two Archbishops in England – Canterbury and York). If a man had property in both the province of York and that of Canterbury, then his will was proved at Canterbury.

This is all complicated enough but there is more to come. You will have no idea whether your ancestor had property in one or two or all of the jurisdictions mentioned above and so the above rules are not much guidance to you. However, you must start by working on the assumption that he owned property in only one location and see how you get on from there. The next complication is that, although a man owning property in one place was *supposed* to have his will proved in the Archdeacon's Court, his executors could decide to have it proved in a higher Court – that of the bishop or the archbishop. This was often done to preserve secrecy as to the disposal of a man's estate.

There is another complication. A man might die in Bristol and own no property elsewhere, and in this case you might assume the will would be proved in the Archdeacon's Court there. Wrong. If the executor lived in London he could decide to have the will proved there for his own personal convenience!

The Public Record Office holds the wills proved in the Prerogative Court of Canterbury. The following records of the Court are listed below and are available to holders of a reader's ticket (now you know why it is issued for a period of five years!):

PROB. 1: Special wills (1581-1853)
2: Inventories (1417-1660)
3: Inventories (1702, 1718-82)
4: Inventories (Parchment) (Post 1660)
5: Inventories (Paper) (Post 1660)
6: Act books: Administrations (1559-1858)
7: Act books: Limited administrations (1810-58)
8: Act books: Probates (1526-1858)
9: Act books: Limited probates (1526-1858)
10: Original wills (1484-1858)
11: Registered copy wills (1384-1858)
12: Register books (Index to Prob.11) (1385-1858)

All of the above (except Prob. 10) can be produced very quickly. Photocopying is available. Prob. 10 records are stored out of London (at Hayes in Middlesex) but can be produced for inspection at the Public Record Office with three days' notice.

The inventories mentioned above are lists of the personal and household goods left by the deceased, with their appraised value at the time of his or her death.

There are a number of words you will come across in this general area of wills, and it seems a good plan to list some of these now;

Act books: an account of the officials' grants of probate of wills, letters of administration, and other business in connection with the will

Administration, letters of: a grant to the next-of-kin when no executors were specified, or if they had predeceased the man making the will

Adminstrator: a person vested with the right of administering the estate (a woman is an **Administrix**)

Bona notabilia: a Latin term meaning considerable goods

Bond: a signed and witnessed statement

Caveat: a warning announcement that a will is in dispute

Citation: a summons to court

Curation: guardianship of orphan minors

Diocese: the area over which a bishop has authority

Executor: a man appointed by the testator to see that the provisions of a will are carried out (a woman is an **Executrix**)

Intestate: a person who died without making a will

Inventory: a list of personal and household goods left by the testator, with their appraised value at that time

Jurisdiction: the area over which a court claimed the right to grant probate or letters of administration

Manor: sometimes Manorial Courts had jurisdiction over a parish

Noncupative will: a will made orally, usually by the testator on his deathbed, written down and sworn to by witnesses, but not signed by the deceased

Peculiar: a parish or a group of parishes which were exempt from the jurisdiction of one court and came under the jurisdiction of another one — even though, geographically, they were within the normal jurisdictional boundaries of the first one

Personalty: personal property (goods, chattels, etc.) as opposed to real property (real estate)

Probate: evidence that a will has been accepted and the Executor is free to carry out its provisions

Proved: a will is proved when probate is granted

See: the same as diocese

Testator: a man who makes a will (a woman is a **Testatrix**)

One final word of warning. If the place of origin of your ancestor is in a particular county, and that county is shown as being within the jurisdiction of a particular diocese or see, you must double-check very carefully. Let me give you an example from my own experience. My ancestors came from the county of Westmorland. The whole of Westmorland was in the Diocese of Carlisle, *but* Bampton (the village of my ancestors) was in the Archdeaconry of Richmond because it was in the Deanery of Kendal. Richmond was in Yorkshire, but the Archdeaconry of Richmond was in the Diocese of Chester over one hundred and fifty miles away in Cheshire — and that was where, finally, I found the wills of my Baxter ancestors! Now, do you see what I meant when I started this section of the chapter by saying the finding of wills was "difficult"?

In this chapter, devoted to England and Wales only, we have covered the main sources of civil registration, census returns, parish registers, non-parochial registers, and wills. These records are all vital to your success in tracing your ancestors in these two countries. There are other sources which may provide some additional mention of some of your ancestors, but are not of much use in establishing relationship or descent:

Feet of fines
These cover the period from 1189 to 1834. They are records of land transfer in which the vendor joined with his wife and children to overcome entail or dower. The foot of the fine was lodged with the court, and the other two pieces were held by the two parties concerned. They are in Latin until the middle of the eighteenth century, and after that in English. Located in the Public Record Office.

Manor Court rolls
Most of these are in private hands but are registered with the

Manorial Documents Register, Royal Commission on Historical Manuscripts, Quality Court, Chancery Lane, London WC2A 1HP. These record various deeds, such as mortgages and marriage settlements of an estate.

Lay subsidy rolls and hearth tax returns

These are also with the Public Record Office and are useful in showing the status and residence of a particular individual. They cover the period from the mid sixteenth century to about 1680.

There are other minor sources which you will find mentioned in the bibliography at the end of this book. These will be of more interest when you have traced your ancestors back as far as you possibly can, and are looking for a few more miscellaneous facts to decorate the tree.

THE SOCIETY OF GENEALOGISTS

This organization was formed in 1911 and its expert staff and immense collection of genealogical material can be of very great help to anyone searching for their ancestors in the United Kingdom. It has a membership of some four thousand, and occupies three floors of a large house at 37 Harrington Gardens, London. Membership in the Society costs $10 entrance fee and an annual subscription of $25. A quarterly magazine is mailed to all members.

Members' queries in the magazine cost £1 for the first twenty words and 50p for every additional ten words. In this section of the magazine you can insert the following kind of enquiry:

> SMITH, David. Believed born in Keynsham in 1820. Wife Elizabeth. Any information to John Smith, 1105 Main Street, Toronto, Canada.

This ad would cost you £1 and there is a chance it may produce some information. A member may have already traced his Smith ancestors in that district, or someone who lives at Keynsham may write and tell you he has noticed a tombstone there which gives dates of birth and death of a David and Elizabeth Smith, or someone called Jones may write and tell you he had an ancestor named Elizabeth Jones who married a David Smith. As I say, it is a chance, but if you have tried every other way of tracing your ancestor a couple of dollars is worth spending.

The Society will also undertake research for both members and non-members. For details of fees for this you should write to the Director of Research at the address above. If you are in London, as a member you will have free use of the library.

There are also a number of publications of the Society which are very useful. For example you can buy a catalogue of parish registers, or a key to *Boyd's Marriage Index*, or a catalogue of directories and poll books.

The library is open from 10 00 hours to 18 00 hours on Tuesday and Friday, 10 00 hours to 20 00 hours on Wednesday and Thursday, and 10 00 hours to 17 00 hours on Saturday. It is closed on Monday.

All the books in the library are on open shelves and this saves a considerable amount of waiting time. It has a good collection of printed and MS family histories, and an almost complete collection of every printed parish register in the country, plus very many MS copies which have been made for the Society by members and do not exist elsewhere. Its collection of city and county directories dating back to the early years of the nineteenth century is also good.

The Society is at present publishing the *National Index of Parish Registers* and eight volumes are in print so far.

The main collections of the Society are set out below:

DOCUMENTS
The document collection, built up from the donations of members and non-members, is divided into two sections. All the documents which relate to one particular family are filed in envelopes in alphabetical order of surname in eight hundred box files. A list of names in the document collection was published ten years ago and totalled eleven thousand at that time. In the second section are those documents which relate to several persons or families in some particular place. These are filed in envelopes under the name of the place, and arranged in alphabetical order by counties. The "documents" vary from complete family trees to miscellaneous notes by genealogists. In other words, it is a mass of information and among it may be something of vital importance to you.

THE GREAT CARD INDEX
This contains some three million references and is a vast store of knowledge from the Norman conquest to the nineteenth century. The index is arranged under surnames and subdivided by Christian name.

BOYD'S MARRIAGE INDEX
This was compiled by Percival Boyd between 1925 and 1955 and is an index of marriages appearing in certain parish registers. Each county is indexed. When he died, the records were left to the Mormon Church on condition that it continue the

work. This is being done and the indexes are in the various CROs and in the library of the Society of Genealogists. It is by no means complete and probably covers less than fifty per cent of the parishes — varying from ninety-eight per cent in Suffolk to two per cent in Stafford. However, it can be very useful.

WALES
This section of the library includes the Williams Collection, which consists of 104 volumes of MS notes on Welsh pedigrees.

SCOTLAND
This collection is not a particularly good one and in the main consists of the MacLeod Papers covering the period from 1880 to 1940. The MacLeods, father and son, were professional record-searchers, but the collection is of only limited value.

A visit to the Society's offices may be a worth-while trip, but do not expect a miracle. Make sure you know exactly what you are looking for before you go — otherwise you will waste a lot of time wandering from shelf to shelf. The staff are helpful within limits, but one often has the feeling one's intrusion into their little empire is not particularly welcome. However, this sort of thing is not unique in England, so do not be put off. Oddly enough, I have always found the staff most helpful by correspondence and I cannot fault them in any way on this score.

THE BRITISH LIBRARY

Another major source of information for the ancestor-hunter of British descent is the British Library. It is located in Great Russell Street, London WC1B 3DG. One important fact to note before a visit to the library is that admission is not granted for the purpose of consulting material which is available in other libraries. Applicants are frequently referred to the Society of Genealogists or to the Guildhall Library, Aldermanbury, London (a good source of genealogical information about London).

Copies of the *British Library General Catalogue of Printed Books* are held in the Metropolitan Toronto Library, the Robarts Library of the University of Toronto, and probably in other major libraries throughout Canada.

The Bibliographical Information Service, for which there is no charge, answers enquiries by mail, but cannot undertake detailed research. It will provide names of professional researchers who will undertake work for a fee.

The Department of Manuscripts holds a considerable amount of genealogical material. Anyone wishing to use the Students' Room there must apply in writing, giving details of their proposed research. The application must be accompanied by a character reference from a person of recognized position, based on a personal knowledge of the applicant, and certifying that he or she is a fit and proper person to use the Students' Room. It is open on all weekdays throughout the year from 10 00 hours to 16 45 hours.

The Department of Printed Books contains all family histories that have been printed. There are also complete runs of many newspapers from the first issue. The Reading Room is open daily from 09 00 hours until 21 00 hours on Tuesday, Wednesday, and Thursday, and until 17 00 hours on Monday, Friday, and Saturday. Books are not on open shelves. You must order them and they will be delivered to your desk by a staff member. Delivery takes from one to two hours. Tickets of admission must be applied for in advance and the same regulations apply as for the Department of Manuscripts above.

OTHER ORGANIZATIONS IN ENGLAND

CATHOLIC RECORD SOCIETY, 114 Mount Street, London W1Y 6AH
The function of the Society is to make available in print the essential sources needed for the history of Catholicism in England and Wales since the Reformation. The Society does not undertake any research but will direct enquirers to the sources available. A catalogue of the various publications will be forwarded on request. An annual subscription is $13 and this includes the regular annual publications.

THE SURNAME ARCHIVE, 108 Sea Lane, Ferring, Sussex BN12 5HB
This professional organization undertakes genealogical research for a fixed fee, as follows:

Surname Report: This provides details of the origin of the name, details of its appearance over the centuries, and its distribution today. Fee $20.

Emigrant Report (United States and Canada only): This provides details of surnames among emigrants during the past four centuries. (Bear in mind that such lists of emigrants as exist are by no means complete.) Fee $20.

Annuity Check: This is based on the Surname Archive's unique lists of the tontine and annuity records of the seventeenth and eighteenth centuries. A tontine was a form of investment which was combined with a gamble on the survival of the investor. It was very popular with wealthier people for a while. Fee $3.

PINHORN'S, BCM Pinhorns, London WC1V 6XX
This company undertakes genealogical research and also publishes leaflets of interest to the ancestor-hunter.

ACHIEVEMENTS LTD., Northgate, Canterbury, Kent, England
The company publishes maps of the counties of England and Wales setting out the boundaries of the parishes and giving the earliest dates in each parish register.

KINTRACERS LTD., 12 Dover Street, Canterbury, Kent CT1 3HD, England
This company undertakes genealogical research on a fee basis in the U.K. and many other countries.

FAMILY HISTORY SOCIETIES
In most parts of England and Wales, and in some parts of Scotland, there are such societies devoted to the history of local families. There is a parent federation, and the General Secretary is Mrs. Ann Chiswell, 96 Beaumont Street, Milehouse, Plymouth, Devon PL2 3AQ. I suggest you write to her and ask if there is a branch in the area in which you are interested. You must send a self-addressed airmail envelope and *three* International Reply Coupons.

DR. BARNARDO'S HOMES, Tanners Lane, Barkingside, Ilford, Essex IG6 1QG, England
This organization was responsible for sending some thirty thousand orphaned or abandoned children overseas between the years 1882 and 1939 – mostly to Canada, but a number of them finally settled in the United States, Australia, and other parts of the world.

In many cases the children were photographed and their parentage was recorded (if known) before they went overseas. For more information you should write to the above address, enclosing a donation of $20, and telling all you know about the child – original name, age on arrival, date of landing, etc. Success is not guaranteed, but a thorough and very conscientious search will be made.

10. SCOTLAND

For a variety of reasons, there are major differences between ancestor-hunting in Scotland and ancestor-hunting in England and Wales. The obvious one is that Scotland is a separate country, with its own laws, its own Church, and its own social history. Another major difference is in the type of records and their location.

Civil registration in Scotland commenced in 1855 – eighteen years later than in England and Wales. Before that date, the registration of baptisms, marriages, and burials was solely the responsibility of the Church authorities, just as it was south of the border.

From the point of view of genealogy the 1855 civil registration was magnificent. Unfortunately, the wealth of information demanded and received took so much effort that in future years registrations asked fewer questions. However, let us be very grateful for 1855. In that golden year the following details appeared on the various certificates:

Birth: The name, sex, year, date of month, hour of birth, and place of birth (if in lodgings, so stated) of infant; father's name, rank, profession or occupation, age and birthplace, and date and place of marriage; other children, both living and dead; mother's name and maiden name, age, place of birth; the signature of her father, or other informant, and residence if not in the house in which the birth occurred; when and where birth registered.

Marriage: The date and place of the marriage; the present and normal residence of the bride and groom; the age, rank, profession, and occupation of both parties, and, if related, the relationship between them both; the status of each (i.e., whether widower or widow, details of the previous marriages, if any, and details of the children of such marriages); the birthplaces, and the date and place of the registrations of the births of the bride and groom; the name, rank, profession, or occupation of each of the four parents; and the date and place of registration of the marriage.

Death: The name, sex, age, place of birth, rank, profession, and occupation of the deceased, and the length of time of residence in the district where death occurred; names, rank, profession, or occupation of both parents; if deceased was married, the name of the wife, the names and ages of children in order of birth, both living and dead; the year, date, and hour of death; the place of death, the cause, and how long the final illness lasted; the name of the doctor attending and the date on which he last saw the deceased; the burial place and the name of the undertaker; the signature of the informant and his relationship, if it existed, to the deceased; and the date and place of registration.

You will see at once how much more information was given than in the English and Welsh registrations and how useful the additional facts can be. Even the later years from 1856 to 1860 omit from the birth certificate only the age and place of birth of the parents, and details of their marriage and other children. In 1861 the date and place of the parents' marriage was restored. Quite often in the death certificates some of the questions could not be answered because the informant had no detailed knowledge of the early life of the deceased.

The records of civil registration are filed and indexed and located in the New Register House, Edinburgh EH1 3YT, in the custody of the Registrar General for Scotland. So are the old parish registers and many other records and this seems to be the right moment to describe just what can be found in this one central place.

GENERAL REGISTER OFFICE
The General Register Office for Scotland, as it is called, is open from Monday to Thursday from 09 30 hours to 16 30 hours, and on Friday from 09 30 hours to 16 00 hours. The main records fall into three categories – the register of births, marriages, deaths, stillbirths, and adoptions; the old parish registers; and the records of censuses of Scotland. Full copies of the entries from any of the above records can be obtained (except for those of stillbirths which require special authorization from the Registrar General himself).

The old parish registers (1553 to 1854) from all the parishes of Scotland are lodged here. A few of them are indexed. Generally speaking they are in good condition and – except for the earliest entries – quite legible. Once you have paid for a day's search you are then free to request whatever registers you require, and these are brought to you within a few minutes. Of course, there is much variety in the quality of the registers. Some contain very bare facts and others go into greater detail. Some parish registers are missing and others contain mysterious gaps. Remember that Scotland saw two major rebellions (in 1715 and 1745) and a number of minor ones. It also had some fairly bloodthirsty religious strife with consequent burning of some churches in the name of the Lord!

There are also some registers of neglected entries (1801 to 1854). These contain records of births, marriages, and deaths proved to have occurred in Scotland at that time but not entered in the old parish registers.

As mentioned, the registers of civil registration date from 1855 and are indexed. The registers and the indexes are available within a year after the current year, as soon as copying and indexing are completed.

The records of stillbirths have been kept since 1939 and are not open to public search. Copies are usually only made available for legal purposes.

The Adopted Children Register dates from 1930 and lists persons adopted under orders made by the Scottish courts.

Other registers include:

Marine Register of Births and Deaths from 1855
Air Register of Births and Deaths from 1948
Service records from 1881
War-death registers from 1899
Consular returns of births, marriages, deaths from 1914
High Commissioners' returns from 1964
Registers of births, marriages, deaths in foreign countries
    from 1860 to 1965
Foreign marriages from 1947

The census records contain the census returns for Scotland for every tenth year since 1841 (except for 1941 when no census took place). Only the returns up until 1891 are open to public search.

Before we talk about these records in more detail, I should mention that local government in Scotland was also reorganized in 1975 and many old county boundaries have changed, or counties have disappeared. The mainland of Scotland is now divided into nine regional councils:

CENTRAL: Clackmannan, most of Stirling, parts of Perth, parts of
    West Lothian (centre of government is Stirling)
DUMFRIES AND GALLOWAY: Dumfries, Kirkcudbright, and Wig-
    town (Dumfries)
FIFE: Fife (Cupar)
GRAMPIAN: Aberdeen, Kincardine, Banff, most of Moray
    (Aberdeen)
HIGHLAND: Caithness, Nairn, Sutherland, most of Inverness, most
    of Ross and Cromarty, parts of Argyll, parts of Moray
    (Inverness)

LOTHIAN: Edinburgh, East Lothian, most of Midlothian, most of West Lothian (Edinburgh)

STRATHCLYDE: Glasgow, Bute, Dunbarton, Lanark, Renfrew, Ayr, most of Argyll, part of Stirling (Glasgow)

TAYSIDE: Dundee, Angus, Kinross, most of Perth (Dundee)

BORDERS: Berwick, Peebles, Roxburgh, Selkirk, parts of Midlothian (Newtown St. Boswells)

In addition, there are the Islands Authorities:

ORKNEY: Orkney (Kirkwall)

SHETLAND: Zetland (Lerwick)

WESTERN ISLES: The Islands formerly part of Inverness and Ross and Cromarty (Stornoway)

Before you start your Scots ancestor-hunting try and make sure no one has already done some of the work for you. There is an excellent book called *Scottish Family Histories Held in Scottish Libraries* by Joan Ferguson (Edinburgh, 1960). This was first published in 1960 and a revised and up-to-date edition is expected. Its two hundred pages list all the family histories written so far – in both book and manuscript form – in alphabetical order. There is always the possibility that a member of another branch of your family has already done work on your ancestors. It would be a tragedy to search for months and finally produce your family tree – only to find someone else had done it all for you!

There is also an organization called the Scots Ancestry Research Society located at 20 York Place, Edinburgh EH1 3EP. This is a non-profit organization set up to assist people of Scots descent to trace their ancestors. In order to obtain the help of the Society you must obtain a form and complete it, giving the information you have about the ancestor you wish to trace. There is an initial registration fee and further fees for work done.

Now let us talk about the major Scots records in some detail.

PARISH REGISTERS

There is some evidence that parish registers were first kept in the fourteenth century but none of them have survived. In 1552 the General Provincial Council of Scotland ordered that each parish should keep a register which should record baptisms and marriages, but this was observed by only a few parishes. In 1616 the newly formed Church of Scotland issued an edict that every minister should keep a record of baptisms, marriages, and deaths. Here again, only a few of the parishes took any action. In fact, only twenty-one parishes kept registers before 1600, and thirty-five did not start them until 1801. Very few of the registers in Scotland have ever been printed or published. However, a check should be made with the Scottish Central Library in Edinburgh, and with the public library in the area in which you are interested.

If by chance your ancestors came from Selkirkshire, you are lucky. All the entries of baptism in the registers of the six parishes of this county (Ettrick, Galashiels, Kirkhope, Roberton, Selkirk, and Yarrow) have been listed and indexed up to 1854.

The registers in the best state of preservation and which began in the earliest year are, generally speaking, in the large cities and towns. It is, of course, a tremendous advantage that when civil registration started in 1855 all the old registers were brought to the New Register House in Edinburgh. There are over four thousand volumes from over 900 parishes. The gaps which are to be found in many of them were caused in the main by two events, apart from rebellion and civil strife. In 1733 there was a split in the Church and many of the ministers who seceded regarded registration as part of the established Church and refused to keep them for some years; and in 1783 a tax of threepence was set for each entry. As you can imagine, expenditure of this kind did not sit well with the churches, and whole areas stopped registration for a number of years.

One fascinating aspect of the parish registers – mainly in the border counties – is the wealth of social comment by the minister or the session clerk. The sins of members of the congregation (when discovered) are set out in some detail. Those brought before the kirk session and found guilty of adultery and fornication are listed in detail. Standards of morality were so rigid that even a married couple producing a child less than nine months after the marriage were called before the session to explain the reason why. If they could not come up with an explanation thought satisfactory they, too, were listed as guilty of the sin of fornication.

There is another area in which Scots parish registers are unique. Under Scots law, hand-festing was recognized. This was the custom whereby a man and a woman could hold hands over water (usually on a bridge) and declare themselves man and wife. This was legally recognized by the state but was a source of worry to the God-fearing ministers of the kirk, who regarded the whole thing as sinful in the extreme. Great pressure was brought to bear on the hand-fested couple to get married in the church, and thus you will find entries of such marriages with mention of the fact that a clandestine, or irregular, marriage had taken place previously. If there were children of the irregular marriage they were usually baptized at the same time as their parents' church wedding!

BAPTISMS

An entry in a Scots register shows the maiden name of the

mother, and usually the names of the godparents or sponsors – generally called witnesses – are also given. The general practice was to appoint two men and one woman for a boy, and one man and two women for a girl.

MARRIAGES

In Scotland the registers record the proclamation of the banns, and in many cases that is all that is recorded. The marriage itself is not specifically mentioned, although one can assume it did take place. Often the banns were published in two places if the prospective bride and groom came from separate parishes. In that case, the register of one parish simply stated the banns had been read, whereas in the other parish it stated, in addition, that the marriage had taken place – meaning it had occurred in that parish. The marriage proclamation, or banns, gave the name of the father of the bride, but the name of the father of the groom was mentioned more rarely.

BURIALS

For some reason Scots ministers often showed no great interest in recording burials, and these records are much less complete than those of baptisms and marriages. Often, though the burial was not mentioned, it was recorded that a payment had been made for the use of the "mortcloth". This cloth belonged to the parish and was loaned for burials. It was removed at the moment of interment. Tombstones are not such a source of information as in England and Wales because two hundred years ago many people were buried without headstones. The Scottish Genealogical Society and its members have been copying inscriptions from tombstones and MS lists of these can be found in the local libraries. In many cases this copying was done just before the tombstones were removed and piled in a corner of the graveyard. A great deal of this removal is taking place in Scotland, so that graveyards can be completely sodded and the cost of cutting the grass reduced.

EPISCOPAL CHURCH IN SCOTLAND REGISTERS

These are still in the custody of the original churches. **Roman Catholic registers** are also with the original churches.

CENSUS RETURNS

As already mentioned, these are located in the New Register House. For a small fee, the staff will prepare a copy of a particular entry in which all the relevant details as to name, address, and year of census can be supplied. They will not make a general search – this you will have to do yourself, or employ someone to do it for you. The New Register House can supply you with the names of experienced people in the Edinburgh area who will undertake searches of these and other records for a fee.

TESTAMENTS (OR WILLS)

Scots testaments were originally the responsibility of the Church, as in England and Wales. After the Reformation, the Church courts were abolished and replaced by the commissary courts. These were set up to deal with wills. The *commissariots*, as they were called, were abolished in 1876 when the responsibility for proving wills was transferred to the sheriff courts. The commissariot districts usually matched the boundaries of the dioceses of the bishops. They were set up in 1563 and were thirteen in number. As time went by their number was increased to twenty-two.

None of the commissariot records are complete, but they have been indexed up to 1800 by the Scottish Record Society and copies can be found in the Central Library in Edinburgh and in district libraries. The Edinburgh Commissariot covered the whole country (rather like the Prerogative Court of Canterbury in England), whereas the other commissariots only covered their particular district.

When examining Scots testaments it is important to know that in Scotland only movable property could be left by testament. Landed property descended by certain fixed laws. This means that in cases where the testator's landed property exceeded in appraised value his movable property, he would be described as "debita excedunt bona" (debts exceed the assets).

When the testator was survived by a widow and children, the movable estate was automatically divided into three – one terce (a third) would go to the widow, one terce to the children, and one terce could be left by the testator to anyone he wished. The inventory of the movable property was attached to the testament, and this is useful in telling you something about the standard of living of your ancestor.

Because, under Scots law, only movable property could be left by testament, and the disposal of the landed property was controlled, there was not such a great need for a will as there was in England or Wales, and so wills are consequently more rare.

I am indebted to my friend, Walter Reid, W.S., for the following very clear definition of the Scots Law of Succession:

1. **Heritage and movables:** There is no such thing in Scots law as "real property". Land, things attached to land (i.e. buildings), and certain rights in land are known as heritage or heritable property as distinct from movable property, which includes cash, shares, etc.
2. **Testate and intestate succession:** As you know, if people die

without making a will, their property passes to their survivors according to the rules of intestate succession. If they make a will, it will regulate the succession to part of the estate; a surviving wife and surviving children will have indefeasible claims to the rest of it. They can only exercise these rights by giving up any legacy contained in the will, and may elect to accept a legacy rather than to exercise the rights.

3. **The law before and after the Succession (Scotland) Act 1964:**
The system of succession prior to 1964 was one of restricted primogeniture. The 1964 Act ended this system and introduced important and radical reforms in the law of succession. The simplest way of looking at the mechanics of succession is to look separately at the positions before and after the 1964 Act.

Pre-1964

INTESTATE SUCCESSION

(a) *Heritage:* Essentially males were preferred to females, the eldest to the youngest, descent to ascent, no succession through the mother, in ascending the rule of the eldest first was reversed, women in the same degree took jointly. For example, A's heirs were: his eldest son, failing whom, *his* son and so on, failing whom A's second son and descendants and so on through A's sons, failing whom A's daughters, failing whom A's younger brother, failing whom his younger brother's sons, failing whom his other younger brothers and issue, failing whom A's immediately older brother and so on upwards, failing whom A's sister, failing whom A's father, failing whom his father's younger brother and so on. After father and collaterals came the paternal grandfather and his collaterals. The mother and her relatives were completely excluded.

(b) *Movables:* All those in the same degree of proximity to the intestate succeeded and if one of that degree had predeceased the intestate, then his or her children took the parent's place providing that the grade which succeeded was not more remote than brothers and sisters of the intestate. The father, failing whom the mother, took one-half where the succession fell to collaterals. The mother's relatives were excluded. The heir to the testate estate could share in the movable succession only if he collated or threw into a common stock the heritage to which he had succeeded.

The surviving spouse had overriding rights in the deceased's estate, known as *legal rights*: the husband had a *jus relicti* of one-third of his wife's movables (half if there were no children) and a life interest in her heritage, called *courtesy*; the wife was entitled to one-third (half if there were no children) of her husband's movables as *jus relictae* and a life interest, or terce, of one-third of his heritage. The children also had legal rights, known as *legitim* (formerly known as the bairn's part). They were entitled to a third, or if neither parent survived, to a half of the movable property.

TESTATE SUCCESSION

The surviving spouse and surviving children had the same legal rights as in intestate succession. The result was that a married man with children could dispose with absolute freedom of one-third of his movable property and two-thirds of his land, unless the spouse and children elected to accept a testamentary provision in satisfaction of their legal rights. So far as the estate passed under the will, there was no distinction between heritage and movables.

Post-1964

INTESTATE SUCCESSION

There is no longer any difference in the law of succession between real estate and movable property. The order of succession is

1. children of the deceased, including adopted children
2. if they are dead, their children
3. if none, then brothers and sisters of the deceased's parents or their children
4. if none on the father's side, then the same on the mother's
5. if none, then next nearest relative on either the father's or the mother's side

The legal rights of *jus relicti, jus relictae*, and *legitim* remain, payable from the movable estate. In addition, the surviving spouse now has important overriding rights, known as *prior rights* in intestacy, to the deceased's dwelling house and contents and to a cash payment, which is made from the heritage and movable property in proportion to the respective amount of each. These rights take priority over legal rights. The result is that in very many cases of intestacy the surviving spouse takes the whole estate.

TESTATE SUCCESSION

The surviving spouse and surviving children have the same legal rights as in the case of intestacy but the surviving spouse has no prior rights. As was the case before 1964, the surviving spouse and surviving children have to choose between their legal rights and any provision under the will.

In 1823 the boundaries of the commissariot districts were changed to coincide with those of the sheriffdoms, and this arrangement continued until the abolition of the commissariot districts in 1876. The records up until 1823 are now kept in the Scottish Record Office, General Register House, Edinburgh. (Do not confuse this with the New Register House where the parish registers are to be found.) In addition, many of the records *since* 1823 are now lodged with the Record Office –

the records of the commissariot districts since 1823 that are *not* there are to be found in the local sheriff court. At the time of writing these are Berwick (in the sheriff court at Duns); Caithness and Sutherland (at Wick and Dornoch); Dumfries (at Dumfries); Inverness (at Inverness); Kirkcudbright (at Kirkcudbright); Moray and Nairn (at Elgin and Nairn); Orkney and Shetland (at Kirkwall and Lerwick); Wigtown (at Wigtown).

There are certain legal terms under Scottish law which differ from those of England and Wales, and some examples of these are given below:

Commissariot: the district within the jurisdiction of a Commissary Court

Commissary: a person holding authority under the law to exercise jurisdiction over a specific area

Commissary court: a court which took over the jurisdiction of the pre-Reformation Church courts

Confirmation: the completion of the probate of a testament by the executors

Inventory: a list of personal and household goods left by the deceased, together with their appraised value

Personalty: personal property, as opposed to real or landed property. Until 1868 only movable property could be bequeathed.

Sheriff court: the court with testamentary jurisdiction over anyone dying within its district, usually a county or part of a county. There are several such districts in each modern sheriffdom. Its chief official, the sheriff clerk, has custody of current testamentary records, and also of those since 1823 which have not been handed over to the Scottish Record Office.

Sheriffdom: an administrative area, originally coinciding with a county, but now incorporating several counties and sheriff-court districts

Warrants (of testaments): usually, the drafts from which the entries in the register were made up, but sometimes including the original wills

THE SASINES REGISTERS

Land registration in Scotland depends on the existence of the notary public – an office originating in Roman times. The most important class of notarial instruments is the *sasine*. The idea that the sasine of land should be recorded by a notary started in Scotland in the fourteenth century. The notary's record of transactions in land was preserved in a book. It therefore became the custom that sasine must be proved by writing, and the notary became the chief agent in doing this. The registers in which the notaries preserved the record of their actions became known as the protocol books, and the earliest of these still in existence dates back to the early sixteenth century. The Record Office holds over two hundred of these books. In 1599 the Register of Sasines and Reversions (redemption of mortgages on land) was established, and Scotland was divided into seventeen districts for this purpose. In seven of these, a major portion of the records survive. The register was abolished in 1609 but eight years later the General and Particular Registers of Sasines was instituted. The General Register was available for sasine of land anywhere in Scotland and the Particular Register recorded lands in a particular district. The registers were put under the control of the Lord Clerk Register and form a complete record of land transactions from then until the present day. As land usually descended from one generation to another within a family, these records are invaluable for genealogical research.

The word *sasine* comes from "seize". To be seized of land means to possess it. A similar word appears in English medieval law — The Assize of Novel Disseisin, which gave occupiers protection against attempts to eject them.

There is no such thing as "a" Sasine. "Taking sasine" was the ceremony by which a man became the legal owner of land, a ceremony which was recorded in documents known as Instruments of Sasine in the Sasine Register, which was established in 1617. Eventually the recording of these writs replaced the ceremony as a means of transferring ownership.

Nearly all the land in Scotland is held on a feudal, not a freehold, basis. That is to say, it is held either directly or indirectly from the Crown. The Sasine Register is a register of all deeds transmitting feudal interests in land. Leases historically have no place in the feudal system, and were not recorded in the register until 1857. By that time a practice of granting long leases instead of extending the feudal chain had grown up to a restricted extent in certain areas. The Registration of Leases Act of 1857 recognized this fact and allowed leases for thirty-one years or more to be recorded on the Sasine Register. Shorter leases cannot be so recorded, and the proportion of long leases to feudal property is very small.

No one can have a complete title to feudal property unless the title is recorded on the Register, and nothing is recorded on the Register which does not transmit a feudal right. I have read that the registration of non-feudal rights in Scotland is voluntary. This is incorrect and is probably caused by confusion between the Sasine Register and another register known as the Books of Council and Session. This latter register is for people who simply want, on a voluntary basis, to record deeds for preservation.

The registers which really concern the ancestor-hunter are

those dating between 1617 and about 1857. These consist of:
1. the old General Register of Sasines (1617-1868) contained in 3779 volumes;
2. the Particular Registers of Sasines for the various counties which cover the same period;
3. the New General Register which began in 1869 and continues to the present day. It is kept in county divisions. This is in over 50,000 volumes.

The Record Office is gradually indexing both the General Registers and the Particular Register. There is also an abridged version of the Sasines dating from 1780, and this has been indexed. These indexes and abridged versions, too, are in the Scottish Record Office.

From the beginning the act of taking sasine of land was accompanied by the ceremony of handing over earth and stone or other symbols on the land itself. I have in my possession the copy of a sasine of 1739 involving an ancestor of my wife's. It is too long to quote in full, but it starts as follows:

At Dumfries the twelfth day of February, 1739, between the hours of four and five afternoon. The Sasine after insert written upon parchment and duly stamped was presented by James Copland, apprentice to Joseph Corrleson, Clerk of Dumfries, to be recorded in this Register, conforming to the Act of Parliament, whereof the tenor follows in the Name of God, Amen. Be it known to all men by this present Publick Instrument that upon the Twenty Day of December, 1738, and of the Reign of our Sovereign Lord, King George the Second, the twelfth year, in presence of the Nottar Publick and witnesses subscribing, appeared personally upon the Ground of the lands of Garland, after mentioned James Laidly in Corsbank, Baillie in that part specially constituted by the precept of Sasine after insert contained in the Bond of Disposition after mentioned, and also compared William Laidly in Corsbank pro, for, and in name of Alexander Telfer, Tacksman of the Mynes at Wanlockhead and whose power of attorney was sufficiently known to us, the Nottar Publick subscribing. And there the said William Laidly, the Attorney for and in name aforesaid of the said Alexander Crighton of Gareland, grants him to have borrowed and recorded from the said Alexander Telfer at the term of Martinmas preceding the date of the said Bond, the sum of one thousand merks Scots money, etc., etc.

The sasine concludes: "To the said Alexander Telfer and that by delivering to the said William Laidly prov. for and in name foresaid of the said Alexander Telfer of earth and stone of the ground of the said lands of Gareland and a penny money for the said garent . . . (etc, etc) . . . these things were done upon the ground of the said lands of Gareland betwixt the hours of two and three in the afternoon (etc, etc)."

The interpretation of the above legalese is that the document was an instrument of sasine in favour of Alexander Telfer, proceeding on a bond of annual rent for fifty merks Scots, granted by Alexander Crighton and his wife Margaret Williamson to the said Alexander Telfer. The bond is secured over the lands of Gareland, and the lands are said to be as specified in a bond granted by Crighton to Christopher Pearson in 1700.

THE SERVICE OF HEIRS

When lands were handed over to an heir the procedure was for a brieve to be issued from chancery. This ordered the sheriff of the county to empanel a jury to discover what lands the ancestor owned at his death, and whether the person claiming them was the true heir. The verdict was sent back or "retoured" to chancery and preserved in a "respond book". These records are almost complete from 1600.

REGISTERS OF DEEDS

This is one of the most valuable records in Scotland for the genealogist. It contains all the deeds which have a clause consenting to their registration and preservation. Almost anything may be recorded in this enormous register. It is part of the Court of Session. There are three series: the first, in 621 volumes, covers the period 1554 to 1657; the second runs from 1657 to 1811 and is in 959 volumes; the third, from 1812, is indexed. The earlier series are also partly indexed, and this work is still proceeding. The sort of things covered by these registers includes an agreement between neighbours over the diversion of a burn, and records of the building of churches and schools, of apprenticeships, of trade, of marriage contracts, and even copies of correspondence.

REGISTER OF HORNINGS, INHIBITIONS, AND ADJUDICATIONS

These can often be of value. The word *horning* originated in a curious way many centuries ago. A creditor was able to obtain legal satisfaction against a debtor who had refused to obey a court order to pay his just debts. He could have him denounced as a rebel against the king by having a messenger of arms give three blasts on a horn. After this the debtor's goods were held by the Crown against the claim of the creditor. The register covers the period from 1610 to 1902 and is in 1289 volumes. There is no index. It can be searched at the Scottish Record Office.

The Letters of Inhibition prevented a debtor avoiding his

just debts by disposing of his property to others.

The other records available for search at the Scottish Record Office include the acts of the lords of council in civil cases, the exchequer rolls, the Lord High Treasurer's accounts, the registers of the Privy Council, the Register of the Great Seal, the Register of the Privy Seal; burgh records; barony records; and regality records. (A barony consisted of lands held from the Crown, and a Regality was a territorial jurisdiction granted by the Crown.)

There are also the rolls of the cess tax. This was a special tax levied in the seventeenth and eighteenth centuries to raise funds for the support of troops. Some of these rolls are in the Scottish Record Office and others are in the Town Clerk's Office in the major cities and towns.

THE CLANS AND THE CLAN SYSTEM

No genealogical guide for ancestor-hunting in Scotland would be complete without a short explanation of the clan system.

The Highland Line, which divided Scotland between the Highlands and Lowlands, ran from Dumbarton in the west in a northeasterly direction almost as far as Aberdeen. There it turned north and then west, passing south of Inverness, and then headed north to a point midway between Cape Wrath and John O'Groats. Everything north and west of the line was considered Highland. The word *clan* simply means "kin", and far back in history the Highlanders grouped themselves around the leading landowner of the district. He provided them with protection against marauding bands of robbers from other areas and they, in turn, provided him with a strong force of fighting men to enable him to expand his estates or his sphere of influence. In many cases they were related to him; in other cases they adopted his name. The chiefs of the clans were soon known by the name of their estates, so there was Cameron of Lochiel, MacNeil of Barra, Macdonald of Keppoch, and so on. A Highlander living as a tenant on the estate of the chief of Clan Cameron never adopted the servile approach of the Englishman under similar circumstances. There was no bowing and scraping, no pulling the forelock — he stood straight and addressed his clan chief as "Lochiel". All the emphasis within the clan was not on land, but on the blood connection between the chief and his clansmen.

The death of the clan system was the unsuccessful Rising of 1745 when Prince Charles (Bonnie Prince Charlie) tried to regain the throne for his father, the exiled James III. His defeat at Culloden, and the subsequent destruction of the clans and their chiefs by "Butcher" Cumberland, also destroyed the clan system itself.

In the Lowlands there was the same grouping of tenants around the local great landlords – the Scots, the Maxwells, the Douglases, the Hamiltons – but this grouping was based on land tenure and not on kinship.

The differences between Highlanders and Lowlanders went deep and were largely racial. The Highlanders were descended from the Celts and the Lowlanders were of Saxon and Teutonic origin.

The great concentration of one surname in a particular district – such as the Campbells in Argyll and the MacIntoshes south of Inverness – does not make ancestor-hunting very easy for people of Highland descent. However, if your name happens to be McKenzie or Stewart or a similar common Highland name, do not assume that your ancestors came from the part of Scotland associated with that name – your ancestor could have left there centuries ago. There are more Campbells in the Glasgow telephone directory than there are in the whole of Argyllshire!

THE SCOTTISH GENEALOGY SOCIETY (Hon. Secretary, Miss Joan Ferguson, M.A., 21 Howard Place, Edinburgh EH3 5JY)
The Society was formed in 1953. Its aims are to promote research into family history and to undertake the collection and publication of genealogical material.

The Society does not undertake research for ancestor-hunters but will supply a list of professional researchers. I should mention that Miss Ferguson is the author of *Scottish Family Histories*, which I mentioned earlier in this chapter, and is a friendly, helpful, and most knowledgeable person.

One of the current projects of the Society is the compilation of a list of pre-1855 emigrants to Canada (a similar book on emigrants to the United States has already been published). If you would like to be helpful, send details of your Scots emigrant ancestors, quoting name, date, and ship, to the Chairman of the Society – Donald Whyte, F.S.A., 4 Carmel Road, Kirkliston, West Lothian.

THE SCOTTISH HISTORY SOCIETY (c/o The National Library of Scotland, George IV Bridge, Edinburgh EH1 1EW). This organization is concerned with history in the wider sense and *not* with genealogy. However, once you have traced your Scots ancestors and wish to add to your knowledge of the times in which they lived, you will find membership well worth while.

FAMILY HISTORY SOCIETIES
Aberdeen and North East Scotland (Miss B. J. Cowper, 31

Bloomfield Place, Aberdeen AB1 5AG)
Glasgow and West of Scotland (Ms. Hazel Wright, 11 Huntly
 Gardens, Glasgow G12 9AT)
Tay Valley (J. Anderson, 5 Balmossie Place, Monifeith,
 Dundee DD5 4QP)

11. EIRE, NORTHERN IRELAND, THE CHANNEL ISLANDS, AND THE ISLE OF MAN

At the start, it must be said that it is very difficult to trace ancestors in either Eire or Northern Ireland (Ulster). This is because of a major disaster affecting most of the Irish records of interest to the genealogist. In 1922 the Public Record Office in the Four Courts Building, Dublin, was taken over by one side during the Civil War. The records of Ireland were used to barricade the windows and the building was eventually destroyed by fire.

Lost were all the wills, censuses, and registers of the Church of Ireland lodged there under the terms of the Public Records Act of 1867. Safe from destruction were the Catholic and Presbyterian registers. However, many of the registers destroyed had been copied before they were sent to the building.

Since then, the Public Record Offices of both Eire and Northern Ireland have managed to collect a great deal of what is called substitute material. For example, all lawyers in the two sections of Ireland were asked to search their files for wills which were then photocopied. In addition, some of the indexes to wills had survived elsewhere, and so, in many cases, although you can obtain no details of the provisions of a will, it is possible to discover that one existed.

An Irish surname may be borne by a large number of people – Murphy is an example – so be sure you have some details about your ancestor besides that before you start searching in Ireland. Since the establishment of Eire in 1922 the Irish records have been split between the two sections of the country. The Republic of Eire has its records in the capital, Dublin, and the Province of Ulster has its records in Belfast. There is some overlapping, and if you are ancestor-hunting in Eire you may well find you have to search some records in Belfast, and vice-versa.

Details of the records in both cities are given below:

DUBLIN

Civil registration of births, marriages, and deaths
These records started in 1864, many years after England and
Wales. They are kept at the Office of the Registrar General,
The Customs House, Dublin. Marriages of non-Catholics are
recorded since 1845. The registration is on a county basis.

Parish registers
Those of the Catholic Church are in the custody of the parish
priests throughout the country. They do not go back as far as
you would expect – about two hundred years in the cities and
towns, and only about one hundred and fifty years in the
remote rural areas.

The Church of Ireland (Anglican) registers were, as mentioned above, almost totally destroyed in the fire of 1922; but
some do exist, and either the Genealogical Office at Dublin
Castle or the National Library of Ireland have lists of these
and where they are to be found.

If your ancestors were Presbyterian you should contact the
Presbyterian Historical Society, Church House, Fisherwick
Place, Belfast. They have a number of Presbyterian registers
from all over Ireland and can also tell you where other registers are kept by local ministers.

Land records
Because of the shortage of information to be got from parish
registers, the various land records become very important.
They consist of deeds, leases, mortgage foreclosures, marriage
settlements, partition of estates, and fiats. Land records are all
located in the Registry of Deeds, Henrietta Street, Dublin
(except for the fiats which are at the Public Record Office.
These refer to grants of land from the Crown to loyal pro-
English subjects.) The various land records go back to 1708.
They are indexed in the name of grantors and grantees, alphabetically, but do not mention locations before 1833. Basically,
the Irish land records are very similar to the sasines of Scotland.

Surname index
The Public Record Office in Dublin holds an Index to the
Tithe Applotment Books (1823-37) and the Primary Valuation (1848-65). These list for each parish the surnames which
appear in the Tithe Applotment Books and the Primary Valu-
ations. There is a volume for each county: one section lists
surnames for the county, and the second section lists surnames
by parish.

Census records

These are available for 1901 and 1911 in the Record Office, Four Courts Building, Dublin. The previous ones were lost in the fire, or were destroyed in error. A few survive for 1821, 1831, 1841, and 1851 for Cavan, Cork, Galway, Kings, Meath, and Waterford counties. There was a Religious Census in 1766 and these records are also in the Record Office.

Wills

In Ireland there were only two kinds of probates – the diocesan court and the prerogative court. There were no archdeaconry courts as in England and Wales.

Before 1858 the ecclesiastical courts of Ireland came under the jurisdiction of the Archbishop of Armagh, and within his province were some twenty-eight dioceses. All the records of these diocesan courts, and most of the records of their successors (after 1858) – the district probate registries – were destroyed in the June 1922 fire.

Fortunately, there are indexes to most of these records, including the following:

1. index to the prerogative wills of Ireland (1536-1810)
2. index to the wills of the Diocese of Dublin (to 1857)
3. index of wills from all Irish courts (1829-79)
4. index to abstracts of wills (Genealogical Office)
5. indexes to miscellaneous wills (in the record offices in Dublin and Belfast)
6. indexes to abstracts of wills relating to land (1708-85) in the Registry of Deeds, Henrietta St., Dublin.

Other district indexes exist and details of these can be found in the following books:

Anthony J. Camp, *Wills and Their Whereabouts* (London, 1974)

J. S. W. Gibson, *Wills and Where to Find Them* (Chichester, 1974)

Marriage Licence Bonds

There are a number of MS indexes to these from a number of different dioceses – some up to 1800 and others to 1857. These can be found in the Genealogical Office.

Quaker records

These are kept in the Friends Meeting House in Eustace Street, Dublin.

Church of Ireland records

There is a list of the surviving Protestant registers at the Church of Ireland Library, Braemore Park, Dublin 14. This list is by diocese and covers over six hundred registers. There is also the MS collection of the Rev. H. B. Swanzy, which contains hundreds of pedigrees of families in various parts of Ireland – particularly from Northern Ireland.

Libraries
There are also many records in the National Library of Ireland, Dublin, and the Trinity College Library, Dublin.

BELFAST

Civil registration
This commenced in 1845 for Protestants and in 1864 for Catholics. The original records are in the custody of the district registrars of the areas in which the events occurred. Since 1922 there are central records at the General Register Office, Oxford House, Chichester St., Belfast, and these are indexed. (The central records before 1922 are in the General Register Office in Dublin.)

Parish registers
As mentioned, most of the Protestant registers were destroyed in 1922, but two hundred of them are still in the local churches. Information about these can be obtained from the Public Record Office, Belfast.

Wills
For full information refer to the paragraphs under this heading in the section above about Eire. Indexes to the diocesan courts' probate of wills in Northern Ireland are in the Public Record Office, Belfast. The following dioceses cover the Northern Ireland counties:

ARMAGH: County Armagh and the south of County Londonderry
CLOGHER: the south of County Tyrone, County Louth, and County Fermanagh
CONNOR: County Antrim
DERRY AND RAPHOE: north and central County Londonderry and County Donegal and the north of County Tyrone.
DOWN: north of County Down
DROMORE: south of County Down

It is important to remember that although the original wills prior to 1858 were destroyed, some copies of them can often be found in other records. Such copies in the Belfast Public Record Office can be traced in the card index. In addition, small family trees are to be found in the Burke Collection. This is indexed.

There are also administrative bonds which relate to people

who died without making a will. These are indexed and can be found in the various Northern Ireland dioceses.

The Public Record Office, Belfast, contains the following records:

TITHE APPLOTMENT RECORDS
These are lists of people who paid tithes about 1830. A card index gives the personal names for the whole of Northern Ireland, and a catalogue gives the references for the books for the various parishes. The lists give the name of the tithe-payer, and the acreage of his farm. The tithe-payers are listed townland by townland within the parish (a townland covers the area of a farm).

VALUATION RECORDS
These are lists of people occupying lands and houses, and run from 1830 onwards. The 1830 valuation is not of much use because it does not give names. The valuation of 1860 has been printed and is in thirty volumes in the Record Office.

GRANTS INDEX
This gives all probate and intestate and marriage licence bonds from 1595 to 1857. Marriage licence bonds were issued by the bishop of the diocese of the Church of Ireland. The originals were destroyed in 1922 but the indexes are available.

HEARTH MONEY, SUBSIDY, AND POLL TAX RECORDS
These are lists of people paying taxes and go back to the seventeeth century. The hearth money rolls list people, parish by parish, who paid a tax of two shillings on every hearth or fireplace. The subsidy rolls list the people who paid a grant in aid to the King of England. The poll tax rolls list people who paid a tax on everyone in the family over twelve years of age. They give detailed facts about each person. Here again, the originals were destroyed, but several copies survive in the Record Office.

MILITIA, YEOMANRY, AND MUSTER RECORDS
These are lists of men liable for service in local defence forces.

CHURCH REGISTERS
There is a sectional list which shows which church registers are available for all the different denominations – Church of Ireland, Catholic, Presbyterian, Congregational, Methodist, and Quaker.

This list is arranged by what are known as civil parishes.

They differ slightly from ecclesiastical parishes and so some care is needed in checking these. The list indicates whether the original registers or copies of them are available in the Public Record Office and whether the registers are held by the local church. Almost all Church of Ireland and many Presbyterian registers are available on photocopies.

VOTERS', POLL, AND FREEHOLDERS' RECORDS
These are lists of people entitled to vote, or actually voting at an election. They are by no means complete. From 1727 to 1793 Protestants with a freehold worth forty shillings were entitled to vote. From 1793 both Protestants and Catholics could vote.

CENSUS RECORDS
Census records in Northern Ireland are scarce. Those for 1901 are in the Public Record Office, plus a few scattered returns for a few places in 1821, 1831, 1841, and 1851.

There were also religious censuses and a few of these are available for certain districts.

There are also some miscellaneous records such as:
1. Landed estate records
2. Poor law records
3. County and grand jury records
4. Business records
5. Emigration records (very few – not a good source)
6. Survey records

ULSTER HISTORICAL FOUNDATION, 66 Balmoral Avenue, Belfast BT9 6NY
This organization was set up to give assistance to descendants of Ulster people tracing their ancestors. It is conveniently located in the same building as the Public Record Office, Northern Ireland. Its services are available on a fee basis.

Before visiting Northern Ireland you should write to the Public Record Office, 66 Balmoral Avenue, Belfast BT9 6NY, and ask for a free copy of the Introductory Guide. Also, do not forget that many records are in Dublin.

THE CHANNEL ISLANDS

These are located in the English Channel off the coast of France and consist of five main islands and a number of small ones. The main islands are Jersey, Guernsey, Alderney, Sark, and Herm. The Channel Islands have been a possession of the

Crown since 1066 and are very largely self-governed. They consist of the Bailiwick of Jersey and the Bailiwick of Guernsey (this includes Alderney, Sark, and Herm).

Jersey

The civil registration of births, marriages, and deaths commenced in 1842. Before that date the only records were kept by the churches. For information you should write to the Dean of Jersey, The Deanery, David Place, Jersey (Church of England), and to the Roman Catholic Bishop of Portsmouth, Hampshire, England, for church records. (The Channel Islands are in the Anglican Diocese of Winchester, and the Catholic Diocese of Portsmouth.) Census returns are exactly the same as those of England (see Chapter Nine).

There is also the Société Jersiaise, 9 Pier Road, St. Helier, Jersey, which has a number of old records in its custody and can be very helpful to the ancestor-hunter.

Guernsey

The civil registration of births, marriages, and deaths commenced in 1840, with the exception of Anglican marriages, which were not registered until 1919. Central registration in Guernsey for Sark and Alderney began in 1925. All the records mentioned are in the custody of Her Majesty's Greffier, Royal Court, Guernsey.

CHURCH RECORDS

Anglican records of births and deaths prior to 1840 are in the original churches, as are records of marriages before 1919. Enquiries may be sent either to the Clerk of the Court, Alderney, or to the Greffier of Sark for those islands. Guernsey enquiries should go to the rector of the parish concerned, and these parishes are located at St. Peter Port, St. Sampson's, Vale, Castel, St. Saviour's, St. Peter-in-the-Wood, Torteval, Forest, St. Martin's, and St. Andrew's.

CENSUSES: see Chapter Nine – as in England.

WILLS

It first became possible to make wills of realty in Guernsey in 1841, and these are registered and deposited in the office of the Greffier after the death of the testator. Wills of personalty are registered in the Ecclesiastical Court, and enquiries regarding them should be sent to the registrar of that court at 12 New Street, St. Peter Port, Guernsey.

You may also be able to obtain assistance in your search from La Société Guernesiaise, Courtil à l'Herbe, St. Saviour, Guernsey.

THE ISLE OF MAN

The Isle of Man is located in the Irish Sea almost exactly equidistant from England, Ireland, and Scotland. It is not a part of the United Kingdom, but is a Crown possession with a considerable degree of self-government. It was first settled by the Vikings in 800, and during the next four hundred years they controlled the island and its original Celtic inhabitants. The King of Norway sold it to the King of Scots in 1266. It was later seized by Edward I of England, and then belonged to a succession of English noblemen until the Crown took it over in 1609. Its government is the Tynwald Court, which consists of an upper house called the Council and a lower house called the House of Keys. This is one of the oldest parliaments in the world.

CIVIL REGISTRATION
The registration of births started in 1878, marriages in 1884, and deaths in 1878. The records are in the custody of the Chief Registrar, General Registry, Douglas, Isle of Man. The office does not undertake genealogical searches but will supply certified copies of extracts, provided sufficient details are given by the enquirer.

CHURCH RECORDS
Most of these are also in the custody of the Chief Registrar and the same fees apply. Church of England baptismal records date from 1611 and are on file until 1878. Since that year they are in the original churches. Church of England marriages from 1629 to date, and dissenters' marriages from 1849 to date, are on file. Later marriage records are in the churches. Burial records in the office cover the period from 1610 to 1878 (Church of England).

The records held *before* civil registration are not indexed, and so a number of years may need to be searched if you cannot supply the exact year. Roman Catholic records date from 1817 and are in the Roman Catholic Church, Douglas, Isle of Man. Nonconformist registers from 1800 are in the various local chapels. No central list or index is available.

CENSUSES
These have been taken every ten years since 1821 (except in 1941). The first seven censuses are open for public search and are located both in the Public Record Office, London, and in the Manx Museum, Douglas, Isle of Man.

DIRECTORIES
Many of these date back to 1808 and are in the Manx Museum and local libraries.

NEWSPAPERS
These start from 1793 and are most useful for notices of births, marriages, and deaths. They are in the Manx Museum.

WILLS
These date from 1628. For the period from 1628 to 1847 they are in the Manx Museum, and from 1847 on they are in the General Registry, Douglas.

Other useful records are manorial records (1610-1922) in the General Registry; books of common pleas in the Manx Museum and the General Registry; mortgages from 1709 in the General Registry; and monumental inscriptions (tombstones) from 1611 to date, in the Manx Museum, Douglas.

SOCIETIES
There are two useful and helpful societies on the island:

The Manx Society, c/o The Manx Museum.

The Manx Family History Society (Mrs. I. J. Lyle, The Old Manse, Kirkmichael).

12. THE UNITED STATES

The area of the United States is so large, and its records are so scattered and varied, that it is impossible to go into every detail in the course of a single chapter. I will try to cover the main genealogical records in each of the states and give fuller information about federal sources. Fortunately, there is tremendous interest in genealogy there and many, many hundreds of books have been published about the early records. In the bibliography you will find a fairly comprehensive list of the most important of these books.

The first thing to remember is that the fifty states joined the Union at intervals from 1788 to 1959, and this affects both the quantity and the quality of the records, federal, state, and local. Let us deal with the federal records first.

CENSUS RETURNS
These are in the National Archives in Washington, but some extracts are available in various libraries. The census is taken every ten years and the first one occurred in 1790. It was ordered by Congress to determine the military potential of the country. The returns of this census were published in 1909 in twelve volumes by the Bureau of the Census. The states covered were Connecticut, Delaware, Georgia, Kentucky, Maine, Maryland, Massachusetts, New Hampshire, New Jersey, New York, North Carolina, Pennsylvania, Rhode Island, South Carolina, Tennessee, Vermont, and Virginia. Unfortunately, the returns for Delaware, Georgia, Kentucky, New Jersey, Tennessee, and Virginia were destroyed when the British burned the capitol in Washington in the War of 1812. It was found that partial returns for Virginia were available from the tax lists of the state, and these are included in the Virginia volume of the 1909 publication.

The 1790 census included five classifications:
1. free white males, sixteen years of age and over
2. free white males under sixteen
3. free white females
4. all other free persons
5. slaves

The 1800 census also has many missing sections:

All of Georgia, Indiana Territory, Kentucky, Mississippi Territory, New Jersey, North West Territory, Ohio River, Tennessee, and Virginia.
Parts of Maine (York County), Maryland (Baltimore County outside the city), Massachusetts (Suffolk County), New Hampshire (parts of Rockingham and Strafford counties), Pennsylvania (parts of Westmoreland County), and South Carolina (Richland County).

The 1820 census has the following gaps:
All of Alabama, Arkansas Territory, Missouri, and New Jersey. Parts of Georgia (Franklin, Rabun, and Twiggs counties), parts of Indiana (Daviess County), parts of Maine (Penobscot and Washington counties), New Hampshire (parts of Grafton, Rockingham, and Strafford counties), North Carolina (Currituck, Franklin, Montgomery, Randolph, and Wake counties), Ohio (Franklin and Wood counties), Pennsylvania (parts of Lancaster and Luzerne counties), Tennessee (Anderson, Bledsoe, Blount, Campbell, Carter, Claiborne, Cocke, Grainger, Greene, Hawkins, Hamilton, Jefferson, Knox, McMinn, Marion, Munroe, Morgan, Rhea, Roane, Sevier, Sullivan, and Washington counties).

Since the 1909 publication of the 1790 census returns, other early tax lists have come to light (as in the case of Virginia that is mentioned above), and so the 1790 census has been "reconstructed" for Delaware and Kentucky and the 1800 census has been "reconstructed" for Vermont and Kentucky. These were privately prepared, and copies will be found in the main libraries of these states.

The 1790 census is available in most major libraries. All the censuses from 1800 to 1880 have been reproduced on microfilm, and the reels containing the records for any particular area may be bought from the National Archives. (It is unlikely you will have your own microfilm viewer, but most libraries in large cities have them available.)

Other records in the National Archives include:
Bounty land warrants
Bounty land affidavits
Bounty land applications
Military records (various wars)
Pension files (various wars)
Shipping and passenger lists
Immigration records
Passport records and applications
Naturalization records

There are also a great many land records in the General Land Office, Washington.

The individual state (or territorial) records include vital statistics, appellate court proceedings, state archives and libraries, state censuses.

The county records include wills, guardianship and adoption proceedings, civil law actions, vital statistics, land records, tax rolls, registers of voters, maps and plats.

Town and municipal records often duplicate those of the county.

So far as church records are concerned it is impossible to be specific. There are very many denominations; many records have been lost or destroyed; many churches have been closed, abandoned, or amalgamated; custody of records varies from state to state and from church to church; and there is no common denominator. You will have to start with the local church or churches in the area in which you are interested and go on from there. You may find the original registers are still there in the original church, or they may have been lodged with the state headquarters of that particular denomination, or the early registers may be in the state library or archives. In other cases, a local historical or genealogical society may have taken custody on behalf of the state.

Where difficulty is experienced locally it is worth while going higher up the church hierarchy in the state or the nation.

In addition, some information about the location of early registers may be obtained from the following:

Baptist   The Librarian, Colgate University, Hamilton, N.Y.
Catholic   The Official Catholic Directory, published in 1943
Methodist   The Drew Theological Seminary, Madison, New Jersey
Jewish   American-Jewish Archives, Clifton Ave., Cincinnati, Ohio
Episcopalian Episcopalian Church Historical Society, 4205 Spruce Street, Philadelphia, Pennsylvania
Evangelical   The Evangelical United Brethren Church Historical Society, Knott Building, Dayton, Ohio
Quakers   Friends Historical Association, Swarthmore College, Swarthmore, Pennsylvania
Lutheran   Historical Society of the United Lutheran Church in America, Gettysburg, Pennsylvania
Presbyterian Presbyterian Historical Society, 520 Witherspoon Building, Philadelphia, Pennsylvania

Here are the basic details about each of the states – capital, date of entry into the Union, and the names of historical and genealogical societies (if known). Further information about the latter can always be obtained from the public library of the capital city. Details of vital statistics are also given.

Alabama

Capital: Montgomery. Organized as a Territory 1817; entered Union in 1819; seceded 1861; re-entered 1868.
Alabama Historical Association, Birmingham.
State Archives, Montgomery.
BIRTHS: Since 1908 in custody of State Registrar, Bureau of Vital Statistics, Montgomery. Before 1908 in the probate court of the county where birth took place.
MARRIAGES: Since 1936 with State Registrar. Before 1936 probate court of the county.
DEATHS: Since 1908 State Registrar. Before 1908 probate court of the county.

Alaska

Capital: Juneau. Organized as a Territory 1912; entered Union in 1959.
BIRTHS: In custody of Bureau of Vital Statistics, Juneau. Incomplete prior to 1913, complete since then.
MARRIAGES: see Births.
DEATHS: see Births.

Arizona

Capital: Phoenix. Organized as a Territory 1863; entered Union in 1912.
Arizona Pioneers' Historical Society, Tucson.
State Archives, Phoenix.
BIRTHS: In custody of Division of Vital Records, State Department of Health, Phoenix. Incomplete prior to 1909.
MARRIAGES: In custody of the Superior Court at the county seat.
DEATHS: see Births.

Arkansas

Capital: Little Rock. Organized as a Territory 1819; entered Union in 1836; seceded 1861; re-entered 1868.
State Archives, Little Rock.
BIRTHS: In custody of Bureau of Vital Statistics, State Department of Health, Little Rock. Complete since 1914, incomplete prior to that date.
MARRIAGES: In custody of Bureau of Vital Statistics since 1917. Before 1917 in custody of County Clerk.
DEATHS: see Births.

California

Capital: Sacramento. Entered Union in 1850.

California Genealogical Society, San Francisco.

California Historical Society, San Francisco.

Society of California Pioneers, San Francisco.

Southern California Historical Society, Los Angeles.

State Library, Sacramento.

BIRTHS: In custody of Bureau of Vital Statistics, State Department of Public Health, Sacramento, since 1905. Before that date with County Recorder, at seat of county where the birth took place. In case of cities, write to City Health Department.

MARRIAGES: *see* Births.

DEATHS: *see* Births.

Note: There was a state census in California in 1852. This shows name, age, sex, race, occupation, address, and state or country of birth. In the custody of the Secretary of State, Sacramento. Copies available in the State Library.

Colorado

Capital: Denver. Organized as a Territory 1861; entered Union in 1876.

State Historical Society of Colorado, State Museum, Denver.

State Archives, Denver.

BIRTHS: Records and Statistics Section, Department of Public Health, Denver, since 1907. Before that date with County Clerk.

MARRIAGES: Records kept by County Clerk since 1881 (before that date there was no civil registration of marriages).

DEATHS: Records and Statistics Section since 1900. Before that date with County Clerk.

Note: There was a state census in Colorado in 1885. This shows name, relationship to head of family, race, sex, age, marital status, and place of birth. Copies available in the National Archives, the State Archives, and the University of Colorado Library.

Connecticut

Capital: Hartford. Entered Union in 1788.

Connecticut Historical Society, Hartford.

Connecticut State Library, Hartford.

BIRTHS: State Registrar of Vital Statistics, State Department of Health, Hartford, since 1897. From 1850 to 1897 Town Clerk, and before 1850 the State Library.

MARRIAGES: *see* Births.

DEATHS: *see* Births.

Delaware

Capital: Dover. Entered Union in 1787.

Historical Society of Delaware, Wilmington.

Public Archives, Hall of Records, Dover.

BIRTHS: Bureau of Vital Statistics, State Board of Health, Dover, since 1881 (a few records back to 1861).

MARRIAGES: Bureau of Vital Statistics since 1847.

DEATHS: Bureau of Vital Statistics since 1881 (a few records back to 1861).

District of Columbia

Formed in 1800.

Columbia Historical Society, Washington.

BIRTHS: Bureau of Vital Statisics, Health Department, Washington, since 1872.

MARRIAGES: United States District Court, Washington, since 1811.

DEATHS: Bureau of Vital Statistics, incomplete 1855 to 1874, complete since 1874.

Florida

Capital: Tallahassee. Organized as a Territory 1822; entered Union in 1845; seceded 1861; re-entered 1868.

Florida Historical Society, University Station, Gainesville.

Florida State Library, Tallahassee.

BIRTHS: Bureau of Vital Statistics, State Board of Health, Jacksonville, since 1865.

MARRIAGES: County Judge of the county where the licence was issued, since 1887. Prior to that date, the circuit court at the county seat.

DEATHS: Bureau of Vital Statistics, since 1877.

Georgia

Capital: Atlanta. Entered Union in 1788; seceded 1861; re-entered 1870.

Georgia Historical Society, Savannah.

Georgia Historical Commission, Secretary of State's Annex, Atlanta.

State Archives, Rhodes Memorial Hall, Atlanta.

BIRTHS: Department of Public Health, Atlanta, since 1919.

MARRIAGES: The County Clerk of the county in which the licence was issued.

DEATHS: see Births.

Note: The State Archives have yearly property tax lists between 1790 and 1820 which, to some extent, take the place of the missing census returns for the state.

Hawaii

Capital: Honolulu. Organized as a Territory in 1900; entered Union in 1959.

BIRTHS: Department of Health, Research, and Statistics, Honolulu, has custody. Records are incomplete, but in some cases date back to the time of the monarchy in the mid nineteenth century.

MARRIAGES: Department of Health, since 1841.

DEATHS: *see* Births.

Idaho

Capital: Boise. Organized as a Territory in 1863; entered Union in 1890.

Historical Society of the State of Idaho, State House, Boise.

BIRTHS: Bureau of Vital Statistics, Department of Health, Boise, since 1911. Before that date, the County Recorder of the county in which the event occurred.

MARRIAGES: The County Recorder, since 1895.

DEATHS: *see* Births.

Illinois

Capital: Springfield. Organized as a Territory 1809; entered Union in 1818.

Archives Division, Illinois State Library, Springfield.

Illinois State Historical Society, address as above.

BIRTHS: Bureau of Statistics, Department of Public Health, Springfield, since 1916. Before that date, if in a city, write City Clerk. If in an unincorporated area write to the County Clerk, at the county seat.

MARRIAGES: The County Clerk.

DEATHS: *see* Births.

Note: There were state censuses in Illinois in 1810 and 1818, and indexed copies are at the State Historical Library, Springfield.

Indiana

Capital: Indianapolis. Organized as a Territory in 1800; entered Union in 1816.

Indiana Historical Society, Indianapolis.

Indiana State Library, Indianapolis.

Society of Indiana Pioneers, Indianapolis.

BIRTHS: Division of Vital Records, State Health Department, Indianapolis, since 1907. Before that date, the County Health Officer of the county in which the event occurred, or the City Health Officer in the case of a city.

MARRIAGES: County Clerk, at the county seat.

DEATHS: Division of Vital Records, since 1899. Before that date, county or city health officers.

Note: Some state census records have been preserved and will be found, if they exist, in the custody of the various county auditors.

Iowa

Capital: Des Moines. Organized as a Territory in 1838; entered Union in 1846.

State Department of History and Archives, Des Moines.

State Historical Society of Iowa, Iowa City.

BIRTHS: State Registrar, Records and Statistics Division, State Department of Health, Des Moines, since 1880. Before that date, County Clerk in the county where the event occurred.

MARRIAGES: *see* Births.

DEATHS: *see* Births.

Note: There were territorial censuses in 1836 (Des Moines and Dubuque counties only) and 1844 (Keokuk County only). These gave the name of the head of the family. There were state censuses at intervals between 1847 and 1925. All these records are in the custody of the State Department of History and Archives.

Kansas

Capital: Topeka. Organized as a Territory in 1854; entered Union in 1861.

Kansas State Historical Society, Topeka.

BIRTHS: State Registrar, Division of Vital Statistics, Topeka, since 1911. Before that date, city or county clerks.

MARRIAGES: Division of Vital Statistics since 1913. Before that date, Probate Judge at the county seat.

DEATHS: *see* Births.

Note: State censuses were held every ten years from 1855 onwards. Records in the custody of the State Historical Society (Census Division), Topeka.

Kentucky

Capital: Frankfort. Entered Union in 1792.

Kentucky Department of Library and Archives, Frankfort.

Kentucky Historical Society, Old State House, Frankfort.

Southern Historical Association, University of Kentucky, Lexington.

BIRTHS: Office of Vital Statistics, State Department of Health, since 1911. Before that date, no complete records.

MARRIAGES: County Clerk at the county seat.

DEATHS: *see* Births.

Louisiana

Capital: Baton Rouge. Organized as a Territory in 1804; entered Union in 1812; seceded 1861; re-entered 1865.

Louisiana Genealogical and Historical Society, Baton Rouge.
Louisiana Historical Society, New Orleans.
Louisiana State Museum Library, New Orleans.
Louisiana State University Department of Archives and Manuscripts, Baton Rouge.

BIRTHS. Division of Public Health Statistics, State Department of Health, Baton Rouge, since 1914. Before that date the Parish Clerk at the parish seat (the parish in Louisiana is the equivalent of the county in other states). The records for New Orleans, where the City Health Department has custody.

MARRIAGES: Clerk of the Court, at the parish seat (except for New Orleans, where the City Health Department has custody).

DEATHS: *see* Births.

Note: There has been no state census in Louisiana, but some local censuses are in parish courthouses. In addition, censuses during the Spanish and French control of the present area of Louisiana are in the Spanish National Archives, in Seville, Spain, and in the French National Archives, in Paris. There was a New Orleans census in 1805, and a copy of this is in the New Orleans Public Library.

Maine

Capital: Augusta. Entered Union in 1820.
Maine Historical Society, Portland.
Maine State Library, Augusta.
BIRTHS: Office of Vital Statistics, Department of Health and Welfare, Augusta, since 1892. Before that date, the city or town clerk of the area where the event occurred.
MARRIAGES: *see* Births.
DEATHS: *see* Births.

Maryland

Capital: Annapolis. Entered Union in 1788.
Hall of Records of Maryland, Annapolis.
Maryland Historical Society, Baltimore.
Maryland State Library, Annapolis.
BIRTHS: Maryland State Department of Health, Baltimore, since 1898 (except for the city of Baltimore, apply to Commissioner of Health, Baltimore). Before that date records are non-existent, except for Baltimore.
MARRIAGES: State Department of Health since 1914. Before that date the clerk of the circuit court in the county where the event occurred (except for the city of Baltimore, where the clerk of the Court of Common Pleas has custody).
DEATHS: *see* Births.
Note: There were state censuses in 1776 and 1777. Records,

which are not complete, are in the Hall of Records, Annapolis.

Massachusetts
Capital: Boston. Entered Union in 1788.

American Antiquarian Society, Worcester.
Massachusetts Historical Society, Boston.
Massachusetts State Library, Boston.
New England Historic and Genealogical Society, Newbury.
Pilgrim Society, Pilgrim Hall, Plymouth.
In addition, there are very many local historical societies and the Boston Public Library has information about their location.
BIRTHS: State Bureau of Vital Statistics since 1850. Before that date the Town Clerk of the municipality (for Boston, the City Registrar of Vital Statistics).
MARRIAGES: *see* Births.
DEATHS: *see* Births.
Note: State censuses were held in 1855 and 1865. The records are in the custody of the Archives Division, Office of the Secretary of the Commonwealth, State House, Boston.

Michigan
Capital: Lansing. Organized as a Territory in 1805; entered Union in 1837.
Michigan Historical Commission, Lansing.
Michigan State Library, Lansing.
University of Michigan Library, Ann Arbor.
Western Michigan Genealogical Society, Grand Rapids.
BIRTHS: Michigan Department of Public Health, Lansing, since 1867. For City of Detroit, the Department of Health; for Wayne County, the Clerk of the Circuit Court, Detroit. Before 1867 the clerk of the circuit court in the county where the event occurred.
MARRIAGES: *see* Births.
DEATHS: *see* Births.
Note: Some records exist of territorial and state censuses and these are in the custody of the Michigan State Library, Lansing.

Minnesota
Capital: St. Paul. Organized as a Territory in 1849; entered Union in 1858.
American Swedish Institute, Minneapolis.
Minnesota Historical Society, St. Paul.
BIRTHS: Division of Birth and Death Records, St. Paul, since 1900. Before that date Clerk of the District Court, at the seat of the county where the event occurred.
MARRIAGES: The Clerk of the District Court.

DEATHS: *see* Births.

Note: Territorial censuses were held in 1849 and 1857. State censuses were held every ten years from 1865 to 1905. These are in the custody of the Territorial and State Census Records, Minnesota State Archives, St. Paul.

Mississippi

Capital: Jackson. Organized as a Territory in 1798; entered Union in 1817; seceded 1861; re-entered in 1870.

Mississippi Genealogical Society, Jackson.

Mississippi State Library, Jackson.

State Department of Archives and History, Jackson.

BIRTHS: Division of Public Health Statistics, State Board of Health, Jackson, since 1912, and some incomplete records before that date for Jackson, Gulfport, and McComb.

MARRIAGES: In the custody of the clerk, the circuit court, at the county seat.

DEATHS: *see* Births.

Note: There were territorial and state censuses for some years and some counties between 1805 and 1845. These are in the custody of the Department of Archives and History.

Missouri

Capital: Jefferson City. Organized as a Territory in 1812; entered Union in 1821.

Missouri Historical Society, St. Louis.

Public Library and Historical Association, Lexington.

State Historical Society of Missouri, Columbia.

BIRTHS: Vital Records, Missouri Division of Health, Jefferson City, since 1910. Before that date, Recorder of Deeds, at the seat of the county where the event occurred. For the City of St. Louis, the Department of Health, St. Louis, and also for some records prior to 1910, the Department of Health, Kansas City.

MARRIAGES: The County Recorder at the seat of the county in which the event occurred.

DEATHS: *see* Births.

Note: All state census records were destroyed by fire in 1911.

Montana

Capital: Helena. Organized as a Territory in 1854; entered Union in 1867.

Historical Society of Montana, Helena.

State Historical Library, Helena.

BIRTHS: Registrar of Vital Statistics, State Board of Health, Helena, since 1907. Before that date for Bozeman, Great Falls, and Helena, write to the county clerks.

MARRIAGES: Registrar of Vital Statistics, since 1943. Before that date the clerk of the district court of the county.

DEATHS: *see* Births.

Nebraska

Capital: Lincoln. Organized as a Territory in 1854; entered Union in 1867.

Nebraska State Historical Society, Lincoln.

BIRTHS: Bureau of Vital Statistics, State Department of Health, Lincoln, since 1905. Before that date the Clerk of the county in which the event occurred.

MARRIAGES: Bureau of Vital Statistics since 1909. Before that date the clerk of the county.

DEATHS: *see* Births.

Note: There were territorial censuses in 1854, 1855, 1856, and 1865 (Otoe, Cuming, and Lancaster counties). There were state censuses for Lancaster County in 1870, 1874, 1875, 1878, 1879, 1880; for Butler County in 1869; for Stanton in 1869; and for Frontier in 1874 and 1876. All these records are in the custody of the State Historical Society.

Nevada

Capital: Carson City. Organized as a Territory in 1861; entered Union in 1864.

Nevada State Historical Society, State Building, Reno.

BIRTHS: Division of Vital Statistics, Carson City, since 1911. Before that date, the County Recorder of the county in which the event occurred

MARRIAGES: The County Recorder.

DEATHS: *see* Births.

New Hampshire

Capital: Concord. Entered Union in 1788.

New Hampshire Historical Society, Concord.

New Hampshire State Library, Concord.

BIRTHS: Department of Health and Welfare, Bureau of Vital Statistics, Concord, since 1640.

MARRIAGES: *see* Births.

DEATHS: *see* Births.

New Jersey

Capital: Trenton. Entered Union in 1787.

New Jersey Historical Society, Newark.

New Jersey State Library and Public Record Office, Trenton.

Note: There are also a number of local historical societies, and information can be obtained from the State Library.

BIRTHS: State Registrar of Vital Statistics, since 1848.

MARRIAGES: *see* Births.

DEATHS: *see* Births.

Note: State censuses took place in New Jersey every ten years from 1866 to 1915. The two earliest ones are incomplete. The records are in the custody of the New Jersey State Library.

New Mexico

Capital: Santa Fé, Organized as a Territory in 1850; entered Union in 1912.

Historical Society of New Mexico, Governor's Palace, Santa Fé.

Museum of New Mexico Library, Santa Fé.

BIRTHS: Vital Records Unit, Health and Social Service Department, Santa Fé, since 1920. Some incomplete earlier records are available.

MARRIAGES: The Clerk of the county where the event occurred.

DEATHS: *see* Births.

Note: There was a territorial census in 1885 and this is in the custody of the National Archives.

New York

Capital: Albany. Entered Union in 1788.

American-Scandinavian Foundation, New York.

New York Genealogical and Biographical Society, New York.

New York Historical Society, New York.

New York Public Library (Genealogy Dept.), New York.

New York State Historical Association, Cooperstown.

New York State Library, Albany.

Note: There are a very large number of local societies and associations and information about them can be obtained from the State Library.

There are also miscellaneous church records in the custody of the New York Genealogical and Biographical Society, and the New York Historical Society.

BIRTHS: The Division of Vital Statistics, State Department of Health, Albany, from 1880 to 1897 (except Albany, Buffalo, Brooklyn, Yonkers, and New York City); from 1898 to 1913 (except for Greater New York City, Albany, Buffalo, and Yonkers); from 1914 for the whole state (except for Greater New York). Pre-1914 records for Albany, Buffalo, and Yonkers in the custody of the City Registrar of Vital Statistics; for Greater New York in the custody of the various Borough Departments of Health.

MARRIAGES: From 1880 to 1897, marriage records were filed with the local Boards of Health, and with the State Department of Health (except for Albany, Buffalo, Brooklyn, Yonkers, and New York). From 1898 to 1907, the records are with the State Department of Health (except for Albany, Buffalo, Yonkers, and Greater New York). From

1908 to 1915 with the State Department of Health (except for Greater New York). From 1915 to date the same arrangement. Greater New York records are in the custody of the City Clerk.

DEATHS: *see* Births.

There are a few records before 1880 in various places, and these will be in the custody of the city and town clerks of the places concerned.

Note: Various state censuses took place in various parts of the state from 1825 onwards. However, these are so fragmented into various counties and towns that it is best to enquire about state census records for a particular place by writing to the Clerk of the county and to the New York State Library.

North Carolina

Capital: Raleigh. Entered Union in 1789; seceded 1861; re-entered 1868.

State Department of Archives and History, Raleigh.

North Carolina State Library, Raleigh.

BIRTHS: Office of Vital Statistics, State Board of Health, Raleigh, since 1913. Before that date the Registrar of Deeds at the county seat, or in a city, the Board of Health.

MARRIAGES: The Registrar of Deeds at the county seat.

DEATHS: *see* Births.

North Dakota

Capital: Bismarck. Organized as a Territory in 1861; entered Union in 1889.

North Dakota Historical Society, Bismarck.

BIRTHS: State Registrar of Vital Statistics, Bismarck, since 1907. Some earlier records are in the custody of the various county auditors.

MARRIAGES: State Registrar of Vital Statistics, since 1925. Some earlier records in the custody of the judges of the counties in which the event occurred.

DEATHS: *see* Births.

Note: A territorial census took place in 1855, and state censuses in 1905, 1915, and 1925. These are in the custody of the State Historical Society in Bismarck.

Ohio

Capital: Columbus. Entered Union in 1803.

Historical and Philosophical Society of Ohio, University of Cincinnati Library, Cincinnati.

Ohio Historical Society, Ohio State Museum, Columbus.

Western Reserve Historical Society, Cleveland.

BIRTHS: Division of Vital Statistics, Columbus, since 1908.

Before that date, the Board of Health in a city, and the Clerk of the Probate Court in a county.

MARRIAGES: The Clerk of the Probate Court.

DEATHS: *see* Births.

Oklahoma

Capital: Oklahoma City. Organized as a Territory in 1890; entered Union in 1907.

Oklahoma Historical Society, Oklahoma City.

BIRTHS: Division of Vital Statistics, Department of Public Health, Oklahoma City, since 1907.

MARRIAGES: Division of Vital Statistics, since 1890. Before that date, the County Clerk at the seat of the county where the event occurred.

DEATHS: *see* Births.

Oregon

Capital: Salem. Organized as a Territory in 1848; entered Union in 1859.

Oregon Historical Society, Portland.

Oregon State Library, Salem.

Oregon State Archives, Salem.

BIRTHS: Statistics Section, State Board of Health, Portland, since 1903. Incomplete records before that date in the custody of the various county clerks.

MARRIAGES: The County Clerk of the county where the event occurred from 1850.

DEATHS: *see* Births.

Note: Territorial and state censuses were held at fairly frequent intervals from 1848 to 1905, but all counties were not included in any one census. These are in the custody of the Oregon State Archives from whom more detailed information can be obtained.

Pennsylvania

Capital: Harrisburg. Entered Union in 1787.

American-Swedish Historical Foundation, Philadelphia.

Genealogical Society of Pennsylvania, Philadelphia.

Friends Historical Association, Swarthmore College, Swarthmore.

Historical Society of Pennsylvania, Philadelphia.

Pennsylvania Free Library (Genealogy Division), Philadelphia.

Pennsylvania Historical and Museum Commission, Harrisburg.

Pennsylvania State Library, Harrisburg.

Pennsylvania Historical Association, State College.

Pennsylvania Historical Commission, Harrisburg.

Note: There are many more local historical associations and societies and information can be obtained from the Pennsylvania Free Library.

BIRTHS: Division of Vital Statistics, Department of Health, Harrisburg, since 1906. Before that date, the records are scattered and incomplete. Some are in the custody of the clerk of the county, or the City Clerk, and for the years 1852 to 1854 the Registrar of Wills at each county seat. Some of the cities have birth records going back to 1860.

MARRIAGES: Division of Vital Statistics, since 1906. Very few earlier marriage records have survived.

DEATHS: *see* Births.

Note: Although official records are in bad shape prior to 1906, there are a tremendous number of local county histories in print; lists of settlers and immigrants, etc.

Rhode Island
Capital: Providence. Entered Union in 1790.
Rhode Island Historical Society, Providence.
Rhode Island State Library, Providence.
Rhode Island State Archives, Providence.

BIRTHS: Division of Vital Statistics, Department of Health, Providence, since 1853. Before that date the city or town clerks, or the City Registrar in the case of Providence.

MARRIAGES: *see* Births.

DEATHS: *see* Births.

Note: State censuses were held in 1774, 1776, 1777, 1875, and 1885. These are incomplete, but those that exist are in the custody of the State Archives.

South Carolina
Capital: Columbia. Entered Union in 1788; seceded 1860; re-entered in 1868.
South Carolina Archives Department, Columbia.
South Carolina Historical Society, Charleston.
South Carolina State Library, Columbia.

BIRTHS: Bureau of Vital Statistics, State Board of Health, Columbia, since 1915. Before that date Health Department, City of Charleston, or the various county clerks.

MARRIAGES: Bureau of Vital Statistics, since 1911. Before that date, the Clerk of the Probate Court at the county seat.

DEATHS: *see* Births.

South Dakota
Capital: Pierre. Organized as a Territory 1861; entered Union in 1889.
State Historical Society, Memorial Hall, Pierre.

BIRTHS: Division of Public Health Statistics, South Dakota Department of Health, Pierre, since 1905. Before 1905, the Director of Vital Statistics.

MARRIAGES: *see* Births.

DEATHS: *see* Births.

Note: Territorial censuses were held in 1860, 1880, 1885, 1905, and every ten years until 1945. Records in the custody of the South Dakota State Historical Society, Pierre.

Tennessee

Capital: Nashville. Entered Union in 1796; seceded in 1861; re-entered in 1866.

East Tennessee Historical Society, Knoxville.

Tennessee Historical Commission, State Library, Nashville.

Tennessee Historical Society, Nashville.

Tennessee State Library, Nashville.

West Tennessee Historical Society, Memphis.

BIRTHS: Department of Public Health, Nashville, since 1908. Before that date, incomplete, and in the custody of the Court Clerk for the county in which the event occurred. Records in the four main cities are more complete:

Chattanooga	1882-1914	City Health Department
Knoxville	1881-1914	Bureau of Health
Memphis	1874-1914	City Health Department
Nashville	1871-1914	City Health Department

MARRIAGES: State Registrar of Vital Statistics, Nashville, since 1945. Before that date the clerk of the particular county.

DEATHS: *see* Births, with the following date changes for the four cities:

Chattanooga	1872-1914	City Health Department
Knoxville	1881-1914	Bureau of Health
Memphis	1840-1914	City Health Department
Nashville	1874-1914	City Health Department

Texas

Capital: Austin. Entered Union in 1845; seceded in 1861; re-entered 1870.

Dallas History and Genealogy Society, Dallas.

Cody Memorial Library, Georgetown.

Texas State Historical Association, Austin.

West Texas Historical Association, Abilene.

Texas State Library, Austin.

BIRTHS: State Bureau of Vital Statistics, Austin, since 1903. Before that date, in the custody of the City Clerk, or the

County Clerk of the area where the event occurred.
MARRIAGES: The City Clerk or County Clerk concerned.
DEATHS: *see* Births.

Utah

Capital: Salt Lake City. Organized as a Territory in 1850; entered Union in 1896.
The Genealogical Society of Utah, Salt Lake City.
Utah State Historical Society, Salt Lake City.
BIRTHS: Division of Vital Statistics, Department of Health, Salt Lake City, since 1905. Before that date, the clerk of the county where the event occurred. (For Salt Lake City, 1890-1904, the City Board of Health.)
MARRIAGES: The County Clerk.
DEATHS: *see* Births.

Vermont

Capital: Montpelier. Entered Union in 1791.
Vermont Historical Society, Montpelier.
Vermont Historical Society, Library and Museum, Montpelier.
Vermont State Library, Montpelier.
BIRTHS: Secretary of State, Montpelier, since 1857. The same for marriages and deaths. (Civil registration became mandatory in 1890.)
Note: It should be noted that the Secretary of State will no longer deal with requests for genealogical information, but will refer enquiries to professional researchers.

Virginia

Capital: Richmond. Entered Union in 1788; seceded in 1861; re-entered in 1870.
Archives Division, Virginia State Library, Richmond.
Virginia Historical Society, Richmond.
BIRTHS: Bureau of Vital Records and Health Statistics, Department of Health, Richmond, since 1912. Also some incomplete records between 1853 and 1896.
MARRIAGES: Bureau of Vital Records, since 1853 (with missing years for some counties). Before that date, the clerk of the Hustings Court of the city, or the Circuit Court of the county where the event occurred.
DEATHS: *see* Births.
Note: Some cities and one county commenced civil registration of births and deaths much earlier, and details are given below:

	Births	Deaths
Elizabeth City County	1900	1900
Lynchburg	1910	1910
Newport News	1896	1896

Norfolk	1892	1892
Petersburg	1910	1900
Portsmouth	1900	1881
Richmond	1900	1900
Roanoke	1891	1891

The records are in the custody of the city and county clerks.

Washington
Capital: Olympia. Organized as a Territory in 1853; entered Union in 1889.
State Archives, Olympia.
State Historical Society, Tacoma.
State Library, Olympia.
BIRTHS: Bureau of Vital Statistics, Department of Health, Olympia, since 1907. Before that date, the County Auditor at the county seat (the City Health Department for Seattle, Spokane, and Tacoma).
MARRIAGES: The clerk of the county where the event occurred.
DEATHS: *see* Births.
Note: State censuses were held in 1871, 1883, 1885, 1887, 1889, 1892, and the records are in the custody of the State Library.

West Virginia
Capital: Charleston. Entered Union in 1863.
West Virginia Department of Archives and History, Charleston.
West Virginia Historical Society, Charleston.
BIRTHS: Division of Vital Statistics, Department of Health, Charleston, since 1917. Before that date, the County Clerk.
MARRIAGES: As for Births, except that the operative date was 1921.
DEATHS: *see* Births.

Wisconsin
Capital: Madison. Organized as a Territory in 1836; entered Union in 1848.
State Historical Society of Wisconsin, Madison.
BIRTHS: Section of Vital Statistics, Department of Health and Social Service, Madison, since 1860 (some counties incomplete).
MARRIAGES: *see* Births.
DEATHS: *see* Births.
Note: Territorial censuses were held in 1836, 1838, 1842, 1846, and 1847. There were state censuses every ten years from 1855 to 1905. All of these records are in the custody of the State Historical Society in Madison.

Wyoming

Capital: Cheyenne. Organized as a Territory in 1868; entered Union in 1890.

Wyoming State Archives, Cheyenne.

Wyoming State Library, Cheyenne.

BIRTHS: Department of Public Health, Cheyenne, since 1909. Before that date, the clerk of the county in which the event occurred.

MARRIAGES: Department of Public Health, Cheyenne, since 1941. Before that date, the County Clerk.

DEATHS: *see* Births.

Note: There was a state census in 1905. It is in the custody of the Secretary of State, Cheyenne, and is in poor condition. The records of later state censuses in 1915 and 1925 are lost.

The details given about the various states are very basic, because there are limits on space. However, you will find there are very many other records available: wills; military records; divorce, court, and land records; *and* a very great number of books on genealogical subjects – particularly in the older states like Massachusetts, New York, and Pennsylvania.

THE NATIONAL ARCHIVES

The National Archives, in Washington, have custody of millions of records relating to persons who have had dealings with the federal government. The National Archives will not make very extensive searches but, given enough identifying information, will try to find a record about a specific person. Most of the records may be freely consulted at the Archives or in the Washington National Records Center in Suitland, Maryland. Photocopies of most of the records can be supplied for a moderate cost per page. A list of persons who do research for a fee can be obtained from the Board for Certification of Genealogists, 1307 New Hampshire Avenue N.W., Washington, D.C. 20036. A more detailed description of records of genealogical interest is contained in *Guide to Genealogical Records in the National Archives*, which can be bought for $5 from the Superintendent of Documents, United States Government Printing Office, Washington, D.C. 20402.

Briefly, the National Archives contain the following records:

BIRTH, MARRIAGE, AND DEATH RECORDS

These cover these events at United States Army facilities between 1884 and 1912, with some records as late as 1928.

CENSUSES

The Archives have the schedules from 1790 to 1870, a copy of the 1880 schedules, and fragments of the 1890 schedules. (Nearly all the 1890 schedules were destroyed by fire in 1921.)

LAND RECORDS

These cover the period from 1800 to 1950 and include bounty land warrant files, homestead application files, and private land-claim files relating to individual settlers. There are no land records for the thirteen original states for they are still in the individual state capitals. This also applies to Maine, Vermont, West Virginia, Kentucky, Tennessee, Texas, and Hawaii.

NATURALIZATION RECORDS

These cover the period from 1802 to 1926 for the District of Columbia, and for the period from 1787 to 1906 for Maine, Massachusetts, New Hampshire, and Rhode Island. The Immigration and Naturalization Service, Washington, D.C. 20536, has records of all naturalizations after 1906.

PASSENGER LISTS

There are incomplete records of passenger lists of ships arriving from abroad at Atlantic and Gulf of Mexico ports:
    Baltimore from 1820
    Boston from 1820
    New York from 1820
    Philadelphia from 1800
    New Orleans from 1820
    A few minor ports from 1820

CLAIMS FOR PENSIONS AND BOUNTY LAND

These cover the years from 1775.

SERVICE RECORDS – ARMY

These date from 1789.

SERVICE RECORDS – NAVY AND MARINE

These are from 1775 on and also include the Confederate Navy and Marine Corps from 1861 to 1865.

There are eleven regional Archives branches, established in 1969. Their records include those of District Courts, Courts of Appeal, Bureau of Indian Affairs, Bureau of Customs, etc. The addresses are:

    Boston: 380 Trapelo Road, Waltham, Mass. 02154.
    New York: Building 22-MOT Bayonne, Bayonne, N.J. 07002
    Philadelphia: 5000 Wissahickon Ave., Philadelphia, Pa. 19144.
    Atlanta: 1557 St. Joseph Ave., East Point, Ga. 30344.
    Chicago: 7358 South Pulaski Road, Chicago, Ill. 60629.
    Kansas City: 2306 East Bannister Road, Kansas City, Mo.
       64131.

Fort Worth: 4900 Hemphill St., Box 6216, Fort Worth, Tex. 76115.
Denver: Building 48, Denver Federal Center, Denver, Colo. 80225.

San Francisco: 1000 Commodore Drive, San Bruno, Ca. 94066.
Los Angeles: 24000 Avila Road, Laguna Niguel, Ca. 90377.
Seattle: 6125 Sand Point Way N.E., Seattle, Wash. 98115.

GENEALOGICAL PUBLISHERS

The major publishers of genealogical material in the United States are listed below. It will be well worth while writing for their lists of books before starting a search in any particular state:

Genealogical Publishing Co., Inc., 111 Water Street, Baltimore, Maryland 21202.
Gale Research Co., Book Tower, Detroit, Michigan 48226.
The Everton Publishers, Inc., P.O. Box 368, Logan, Utah 84321.
Deseret Book, 44 East South Temple, Salt Lake City, Utah 84110.
Heritage House, Rt. 1, Box 211, Thomson, Illinois 61285.
Daughters of the American Revolution, 1776 D Street N.W., Washington, D.C. 20006.

GENEALOGICAL AND HISTORICAL SOCIETIES

There are far too many of these to list in this book, but 982 of them can be found in the *Directory of Historical Societies and Agencies in the United States and Canada* ($20 from the American Association for State and Local History, 1400 Eighth Avenue South, Nashville, Tennessee 37203). It may also be in your local library. This association also publishes a great number of technical leaflets, some fourteen of which are about genealogical research.

INTRODUCTORY NOTE TO CHAPTERS 13 TO 15

EUROPEAN COUNTRIES

In dealing with European records it must be remembered that many countries came into existence only in recent times (Czechoslovakia, Yugoslavia); others were conquered by powerful neighbours and disappeared (Estonia, Latvia, Lithuania); others were under Turkish rule for centuries (Albania, Bulgaria, Greece, Romania, Yugoslavia); older countries and principalities (like Bosnia, Herzegovina, and Montenegro) have merged to form new countries; many have changed their boundaries several times (Austria, Hungary, Poland, Romania, Bulgaria, Greece); and, to make matters worse, there is no real centralization of records so far as civil registration is concerned.

Early records do exist in most countries through many hundreds and thousands of local municipalities – the problem is to find where they are located. It is impossible to list all these records but the main sources of information in the various countries are set out in the following chapters. For some countries I have been able to go into great detail; in others the information is very basic – it has depended on the co-operation of the governments concerned, the existence of genealogical societies, the number of available books, and the time I have been able to spend in each country.

13. FRANCE

The system of record-keeping in France differs from most other countries and so I think it best to explain the system first, before going into details. Because so many Canadians trace their ancestry back to France it is particularly important to explain French genealogical sources.

Vital records are the civil-status documents showing proof of a person's legal status. They are used to prove birth, marriage, death, divorce, etc. These records originated in France with two customs begun by the Catholic clergy:

1. Baptismal records, which enabled the priests to discover a person's genealogy and so make sure they would not be marrying two people related to a degree prohibited by church law.

2. Marriage and death records were kept so that the priests could record the gifts and offerings received by the church on these occasions.

Speaking generally, it can be said that baptismal records date back to the early thirteenth century, and marriage and death records to the fourteenth century.

The parish records maintained by the clergy became increasingly useful to the state, and the royal government started to regulate them. In 1539 it became law to keep baptismal records, and a similar ordinance in 1563 covered marriage records. Finally, in 1579 the same regulations applied to deaths. Of course, these laws applied only to the Catholic clergy and their Catholic parishioners. It was not until the French Revolution that the records were placed under governmental control and applied to everyone in the country. In spite of this, the Catholic Church continued to keep its own records as well as the official ones.

Civil-status documents, as they are called, are kept in the Town Hall of the commune. They are recorded by the Registrars and each document is signed by all those present. French law requires that any change in status of the individual must be recorded in the margin of the original birth certificate and this change in status will include marriage, divorce, death, movement out of the commune, and the birth of an illegitimate child.

In the smaller communes, instead of having three different

records for birth, marriage, and death there may be only a single record covering all three events. At the end of each year the original is retained in the Town Hall and a copy is sent to the Registrar of the Court of the First Instance. The Mayor acts as the Registrar in his commune and his other duties include verifying the fact of death, performing marriages, publishing the banns, etc.

The Vital Records are public documents – unlike the case in most other countries – and any person may obtain a copy of any document without having to prove the reason for his request. However, so far as birth records are concerned, this open access does not apply – only relatives or descendants may obtain copies. This is done to prevent disclosure of illegitimacy.

French subjects living in other countries may register births, marriages and deaths by using the forms of the country in which they are living, and then lodging a copy with the nearest French embassy or consulate. Alternatively, they may register the event at either of these latter offices and, in that case, the normal French forms are used, and the French representative acts as the Registrar.

CIVIL REGISTRATION
As a result of the system described above, there is no centralization of records in France. This means you must know the particular department from which your family came. There are ninety of these departments in France, and they are the equivalent of a county.

I mentioned above that the second copy is in the custody of the Court of the First Instance (either called Le Greffe or Le Tribunal de Première Instance). This applies to the period from 1860 up to and including the present day. Those for the period from 1792 to 1860 are now in the archives of each department – each of the departments has its own archives and these are listed at the end of this chapter.

Both the copies (in the commune and in the archives) are indexed. So, to obtain a copy of an entry for the period from 1792 to 1860, you must write to the Archivist of the department, or to the Mairie (Town Hall) of the commune for the years since 1860. In the case of a request for a birth certificate you must remember to include details of your relationship.

If your ancestor was a French citizen who lived in another country but retained his citizenship, you can obtain information about him from Le Service Central de l'État-Civil, Ministère des Affaires Étrangères, Nantes, France. You must be able to send the basic information about the person concerned – name, approximate dates, and name of country.

CHURCH RECORDS

Early registers – up to 1792 – are in the department archives or the Mairie. Later ones are still in the churches. This is a general statement – there are exceptions. In addition, a further copy is always sent to the diocesan archives, i.e., to the office of the bishop of the district.

PROTESTANT RECORDS

Lutheran registers exist since 1525, and Calvinist since 1559. However, remember these records were not recognized as legal before 1787 and many Protestants were included in Catholic registers before then. Here again, records are very scattered and I can only make a general statement – you will find them in Mairies, departmental archives, in the original churches, and, in some cases, in private hands. Many registers from the south of the country are in the custody of Le Centre de Documentation d'Histoire Protestante, Archives Départementales du Gard, Nîmes, France. Others are lodged with the Protestant Historical Society (La Société d'Histoire du Protestantisme Français, rue des Saints-Pères, Paris).

HUGUENOT RECORDS

These particular Protestants were persecuted and killed on a large scale between 1560 and 1660, and those who survived fled to other countries. If you are descended from a Huguenot family you should consult the following sources:

Various publications of the Huguenot Society, London, England (you may be able to obtain some of these through the regional library system).

The Walloon Library, Leyden, Holland.

The French National Archives, Paris.

The Protestant organizations in Nîmes and Paris mentioned above.

The City Archives of Frankfurt-am-Main, Germany.

The City Archives of Bern, Switzerland.

WILLS

In some cases these go back to the fourteenth century and are to be found in the National Archives, departmental archives, Mairies, and notaries' offices. This makes life a little difficult. However, efforts are being made to centralize wills *within* a department, and the archives of the department can give you up-to-date information about this development. The Archives de la Seine now have their wills indexed, and others are attempting the same.

CENSUSES

The first censuses were held in 1590, but the early ones are generally of little interest to the ancestor-hunter because few family details are given. Those since 1836 are of great value, although a number have been destroyed in the various wars. All are in the departmental archives.

EMIGRATION RECORDS
These cover the period from 1788 to the present day and include name, date and place of birth, and intended destination. They are in the departmental archives, generally speaking, but some are in the National Archives. They are called *Registres d'émigrés*.

INTERNAL PASSPORTS
These were issued between 1800 and 1870 for travel *within* France and give name, date and place of birth, address, and destination. They can be found in the departmental archives.

VOTERS' LISTS
These give similar information over the period from 1820 to the present day and are in the departmental archives.

CONSCRIPTION LISTS
These date from 1800 and list every male drafted into the Services, together with his personal details. These, also, you will find in the departmental archives.

MILITARY AND NAVAL RECORDS
Dating from the seventeenth century these record the personal details of all officers and their families. They are in the usual scattered locations — National Archives in Paris; departmental archives; and the Service Historique de l'Armée, Château de Vincennes, Vincennes, France. Some of them are on microfilm in the Library of Congress in Washington, D.C.

PASSENGER LISTS (Rôles des passagers)
Some of these go back to the middle seventeenth century, but most are from about 1820 to the present day. The records give name, age, and town of origin of emigrants (adult males), occupation, date and place of embarkation, and intended destination. They are even more scattered than other records. You can find them in the National Archives, the Admiralty records (liasses des Amirautés), departmental archives, port archives of the merchant marine (inscriptions maritimes), or of the naval port archives (marines nationales) at the ports of Brest, Bordeaux, Lorient, Rochefort, and Toulon.

INDENTURES (Registres d'engagements)
These records can often be of great help since they list all

indentured passengers sailing to French colonies – giving name, place of origin, and destination. The records are either in the departmental archives or in the port archives of such coastal cities as St. Malo, Dieppe, Rouen, Nantes, La Rochelle, and Bordeaux. The period covered is from 1634 to about 1730.

LEGAL RECORDS

Dating from the fifteenth century to the present day, they are to be found in the National Archives and in city and town archives. Records in this general area include:
    Inventories after death (Inventaires après décès)
    Donations to heirs (Donations entre vifs)
    Land and property records (Ventes des terres et bâtiments)
    Administrations of estates (Portages de succession)
    Marriage contracts (contrats de mariage)
    Cartularies (Cartularies). Basically, these are records of property disposal of persons living in religious houses.

TAX RECORDS

These date from the fourteenth century to 1792 and give details of taxpayers and their place of residence and death. They can be found in the usual places – National Archives, departmental archives, city and town archives.

CEMETERY INSCRIPTIONS

Many of these from the twelfth century are listed and the records kept by Le Bureau des Cimetières in the larger cities. Some departmental archives have indexes of these.

MISCELLANEOUS RECORDS

These include military pensions dating from 1817 (Service Historique de l'Armée, Château de Vincennes, Vincennes, France); and school and hospital records (in the usual archives listed so frequently above).

SURNAMES

The following indexes are useful in locating places in France where certain surnames are prominent:
    Archives de la Guerre, Vincennes, France. Pensions of 1817 in alphabetical order. It is indexed and has the names of forty-eight thousand soldiers and sailors with their places of birth.
    Archives Nationales, rue des Francs-Bourgeois, Paris.
    Archives de la Ville de Paris, Quai Henri VI, Paris. Lists of voters and conscripts in alphabetical order, giving places of birth.
    The Genealogical Society of the Church of Jesus Christ of

Latter-Day Saints, Salt Lake City, Utah, also has a great many of the above records on microfilm.

GENEALOGICAL RESEARCH

Professional French genealogists now have their own organization and can supply the names of researchers who will search for you on a fee basis. The address is:

Chambre Syndicale des Généalogistes,
74 rue des Saints-Pères,
Paris 75007

DEPARTMENTAL ARCHIVES (Archives départementales)

Department and City in which records are located

Ain, 01000 Bourg
Aisne, 02000 Laon
Allier, 03400 Yzeure
Alpes de Haute-Provence, 04000 Digne
Alpes (Hautes-), 05000 Gap
Alpes-Maritimes, 06000 Nice
Ardèche, 07000 Privas
Ardennes, 08000 Charleville Mézières
Arlège, 09000 Foix
Aube, 10000 Troyes
Aude, 11000 Carcassonne
Aveyron, 12000 Rodez
Bouches-du-Rhône, 13006 Marseilles
Calvados, 14000 Caen
Cantal, 15000 Aurillac
Charente, 16000 Angoulême
Charente-Maritime, 17000 La Rochelle
Cher, 18000 Bourges
Corrèze, 19000 Tulle
Corse, 20000 Ajaccio
Côte-d'Or, 21000 Dijon
Côtes-du-Nord, 22000 St. Brieuc
Creuse, 23000 Guéret
Dordogne, 24000 Périgueux
Doubs, 25000 Besançon
Drôme, 26000 Valence
Eure, 27000 Évreux
Finistère, 29000 Quimper

Gard, 30000 Nîmes
Garonne (Haute-), 31000 Toulouse
Gers, 32000 Auch
Gironde, 33000 Bordeaux
Hérault, 34000 Montpellier
Ille et-Vilaine, 35000 Rennes
Indre, 36000 Châteauroux
Indre-et-Loire, 37000 Tours
Isère, 38000 Grenoble
Jura, 39000 Lons-le-Saunier
Landes, 40000 Mont-de-Marsan
Loir-et-Cher, 41000 Blois
Loire, 42000 St-Etienne
Loire (Haute-), 43000 Le Puy
Loire-Atlantique, 44000 Nantes
Loiret, 45000 Orléans
Lot, 46000 Cahors
Lot-et-Garonne, 47000 Agen
Lozère, 48000 Mende
Maine-et-Loire, 49000 Angers
Manche, 50000 St-Lô
Marne, 51000 Châlons-sur-Marne
Marne (Haute-), 52000 Chaumont
Mayenne, 53000 Laval
Meurthe-et-Moselle, 54000 Nancy
Meuse, 55000 Bar-le-Duc
Morbihan, 56000 Vannes

Moselle, 57000 Metz
Nièvre, 58000 Nevers
Nord, 59000 Lille
Oise, 60000 Beauvais
Orne, 61000 Alençon
Pas-de-Calais, 62000 Arras
Puy-de-Dôme, 63000 Clermont-
    Ferrand
Pyrénées-Atlantique, 64000
    Pau
Pyrénées (Hautes-), 65000
    Tarbes
Pyrénées-Orientales, 66000
    Perpignan
Rhin (Bas-), 67000 Strasbourg
Rhin (Haut-), 68000 Colmar
Rhône, 69000 Lyon
Saône (Haute-), 70000 Vesoul
Saône-et-Loire, 71000 Mâcon
Sarthe, 72000 Le Mans
Savoie, 73000 Chambéry
Paris, 30 Quai Henri IV, 75004
    Paris
Seine-Maritime, 76100 Rouen
Seine-et-Marne, 77000 Melun
Sèvres, 79000 Niort
Somme, 80000 Amiens

Tarn, 81000 Albi
Tarn-et-Garonne, 82000
    Montauban
Var, 83000 Draguignan
Vaucluse, 84000 Avignon
Vendée, 85000 La Roche-sur-
    Yon
Vienne, 86000 Poitiers
Vienne (Haute-), 87000
    Limoges
Vosges, 88000 Épinal
Yonne, 89000 Auxerre
Territoire-de-Belfort, 90000
    Belfort
Yvelines, 73000 Versailles
Essonne, 91100 Corbeil
Hts-de-Seine, 92500 Rueil-
    Malmaison
Seine-Saint-Denis, 93000
    Bobigny
Val-de-Marne, 94100 Saint-
    Maur
Val-d'Oise, 95300 Pontoise
Martinique, 97200 Fort-de-
    France
Réunion, 97400 St. Denis
Guadeloupe, 97100 Basse-Terre

Note: The last three names on the list are of departments located in the West Indies, and off the coast of Africa.

CALENDAR
When searching older records, bear in mind the revolutionary calendar in use from 1793 to 1805. It is too complicated to set out in detail, but the months were Vendémiaire, Brumaire, Frimaire, Nivôse, Pluviôse, Ventôse, Germinal, Floréal, Prairial, Messidor, Thermidor, and Fructidor. These months did not coincide with the normal calendar.

14. SCANDINAVIA

Many Canadians have their family roots in one of the Scandinavian countries – Denmark, Iceland, Finland, Norway, and Sweden. Fortunately the records in all these countries (with the possible exception of Finland) have been well kept, go back a long way, and are easily accessible. In addition, the governments of these countries are very helpful to genealogists.

Here again, let me remind you to assemble every last bit of information you have before you take off for Scandinavia. You will be much more successful if you do as much of your research as possible here before you go.

DENMARK

Denmark, Norway, and England were united under one king for a short period in the eleventh century. After the Norman Conquest in 1066, England came under the control of the Normans, and Denmark and Norway remained united. In 1397 the two countries joined with Sweden under one king, and this union was to last until 1523, when Sweden broke away. From then until 1814 the Danes and Norwegians were united under one king. In that year Norway joined Sweden, and Denmark became a separate country. It also controlled Iceland until the latter country became an independent nation in 1944.

PARISH REGISTERS (Kirkebøger)
The State Church is Lutheran and the registers date from 1645 until the present day. There are also a few scattered ones which go back to 1573. These registers include birth and baptism (with names of witnesses and their relationship to the child), marriage, death, and burial. In addition, confirmations are listed from 1736, and arrivals and removals in the parish between 1814 and 1875. These are in the Provincial Archives covering each particular district.

There are also Nonconformist records in the various city archives. The *recognized* Nonconformists were Reformed French and German churches, Roman Catholics, Jews, and Methodists. They kept their own registers. Other sects and groups were not recognized and had to have their records entered in the registers of the local Lutheran church.

Up to 1891 parish registers are collected in the Provincial Archives (Landsarkiver). There are four of these in Åbenrå (South Jutland), Copenhagen (Zealand, Bornholm, and Lolland-Falster), Odense (Funen), and Viborg (North Jutland). Since 1891 one copy of the parish registers is lodged with the regional archives thirty years after it is completed. There is an index of all the registers in the archives.

CIVIL REGISTRATION
This does not exist in the form which applies in most other countries. The State Church is still responsible for the registration of vital statistics, and the normal information about births or baptisms, marriages, and deaths is to be found in the individual churches. There are some exceptions to this:

1. The civil registration of births, marriages, and deaths for the counties of Åbenrå-Sønderborg, Haderslev, and Tønder exist from 1874 and are located in the Provincial Archives at Åbenrå.
2. Death certificates for Zealand, Fyn, Bornholm, and Lolland-Falster from 1857 onwards are in the Archives in Copenhagen.
3. Some civil marriages were recorded from 1851 and these can be found in provincial or city archives.
4. Records of marriage licences for Copenhagen only (1735-1868) are in the City Archives in Copenhagen. These are called Kopulations-protokoller.

THE PUBLIC RECORD OFFICE (Rigsarkivet)
This was set up in 1889 and consists of an office in Copenhagen and four provincial archives (for locations see above). The head office has always been called the Public Record Office and the records there include all the central archives of the government. The provincial archives act as depositories for local government archives.

WILLS
Old wills are kept in the Public Record Office and more recent ones are in the possession of local notaries. A central index exists for all wills since 1932. Some wills go back to the fourteenth century.

CENSUSES
The census lists for 1787 to 1911 are in the Public Record Office in Copenhagen.

OTHER RECORDS

These include military rolls from 1788, county and town account books, land and tax registers. They are all in the Public Record Office in Copenhagen, and can be a great help to the ancestor-hunter.

EMIGRATION

Full records exist of emigrants from Denmark from 1868 to 1920. These include name and address, occupation, date and place of birth, date of embarkation, and intended destination. They are in the Provincial Archives in Copenhagen. There are also records of passports issued from 1780 and these are in the various provincial archives.

If you are descended from a noble or landed family, you should consult an annual publication called *Danmarks Adels Aarbog*. It is published by J. H. Schultz of Copenhagen and lists coats-of-arms and several hundred individual family trees.

A final word of warning about early Danish records: the old Gothic script was used and this takes a great deal of deciphering.

FINLAND

Until 1809 Finland was part of Sweden. In that year it became part of Russia under the name of the Grand Duchy of Finland (the Tsar of Russia became the Grand Duke of Finland). Finland declared its independence at the time of the Russian Revolution in 1917.

Over ninety per cent of the population of Finland belongs to either the Lutheran or the Greek Orthodox church and the records of birth, marriage, and death are to be found in the church registers. Civil registration applies only in the cases of people who do not belong to either of these churches. The latter records are in the various municipal offices.

The Lutheran church registers date back to 1648 in some cases, the Greek Orthodox to 1779, and the Roman Catholic to about 1800. (One exception is that the Lutheran records from the former province of Viipuri (Viborg) are in the provincial archives at Vaasa.)

ARCHIVES

The name and address of the Central Archives in Finnish and Swedish is:

Valtionarkisto, Helsinki (Finnish)
Riksarkivet, Helsingførs (Swedish)

It should be mentioned here that both languages are official in Finland. The Archives contain a great many records of great value in ancestor-hunting but, unfortunately, cataloguing of the collection is by no means complete. The Genealogical Society can help with up-to-date details, but the records do include many early church records, such as chronological lists (historiebocker) which recorded movement in and out of the parish and lists of members (kommunionbocker). In order to trace an individual in these records it is necessary to know the parish or commune in which he lived.

WILLS
These are uncommon in Finland because of the use of estate inventories (bouppteckningar). These are located in the National Archives.

CENSUSES
These have been held at irregular intervals since 1635 and records are in the National Archives.

LAND AND COURT RECORDS
These date from the early seventeenth century and are also in the National Archives. There is also a Register of the Inhabitants of Finland (1539-1809) in the same place.

TOMBSTONES
Copies of tombstone inscriptions from 1745 onwards are in the library of the Genealogical Society of Finland, in Helsinki (Genealogiska Samfundet i Finland).

ICELAND

The country was settled by Scandinavian immigrants between 870 and 930 C.E. Massive emigration to North America started in 1870. *Icelandic Families*, a recently published (1974) book by Eric Jonassen of the Icelandic Society in Winnipeg, gives details of Icelandic families and how to trace them. It is published by Wheatfield Press, Box 205, St. James P.O., Winnipeg, Manitoba.

The Statistical Bureau of Iceland (Hagstofa Islands) has been in charge of civil registration since 1953. Before that, vital statistics were the responsibility of the churches, beginning in 1735.

CENSUSES
These go back two centuries and are in the Archives.

WILLS

All wills are in the National Archives, except for the most recent ones, which are with the notary public in each district.

The early Registers are now with the National Archives of Iceland in Reykjavik, and the recent ones are still with the individual churches. Ninety-seven per cent of the population belongs to the established Lutheran Church, and three Lutheran Free Churches. Censuses commenced in 1703 and are now taken regularly every ten years. Returns are lodged with the Statistical Bureau, Reykjavik, for recent years and earlier ones with the National Archives of Iceland (Thjodskjalasafn), which is housed in the National Library Building in Reykjavik.

NORWAY

Originally, this was a very divided country, ruled by a number of petty kings. During the reign of Magnus II of Sweden (1319-63) he succeeded to the crown of Norway through his mother. He was succeeded by his son, Haakon VI, who married Princess Margaret of Denmark. When Haakon died in 1380 he was succeeded by King Olaf of Denmark and the original Norwegian royal line ended. In 1387 Olaf died and his mother, Margaret, was elected to the Norwegian throne. She was then ruler of Denmark, Norway, and Sweden. Each country was semi-independent but a kind of loose federation joined them together.

In 1523 Sweden broke away, but Norway remained under Danish control. In 1814 Sweden acquired Norway from Denmark in exchange for Pomerania. Norway was given a new constitution and attempted to elect a Danish prince as its king, but Sweden prevented this. Later in the year Norway declared itself a free and independent kingdom under the Swedish king and, in 1815, Sweden accepted this and the union was ratified by treaty. In 1905 Norway declared the union with Sweden dissolved, and a treaty of separation was signed. Oscar II of Sweden renounced the Norwegian throne and the Norwegians elected as their king Prince Charles of Denmark, who became Haakon VII. From this time Norway has been completely independent.

In Norway it is difficult to trace your ancestors further back than the second half of the seventeenth century. A lot depends, of course, on the occupation of your ancestors. If they were farmers you may be lucky because, by and large, they stayed in one area.

When ancestor-hunting in Norway, names should be given a great deal of attention. In olden days Norwegians were identified by their first name and the name of their father (e.g., Olav

Haakonsen, the son of Haakon; Sigrid Haakonsdotter, the daughter of Haakon). In addition, a third name – usually that of a farm – was used. When the farmer Ole Olsen Li moved from Li to Dal he became known as Ole Olsen Dal. Sometimes the preposition "pa" could be placed between the surname and the farm name. This showed the holder of the name worked at the farm, and did not necessarily own it or lease it. Similarly, a tenant farmer was often recorded under the name of the farm to which his house belonged. Thus, someone living at Dal and previously recorded as Ole Olsen Dal, on becoming a tenant of a farm or house owned by the bigger farm of Lunde, could become known as Ole Olsen Lunde.

When emigrating to Canada a Norwegian often took the name of his farm in Norway as his surname and so Ole Olsen could become Ole Lunde upon arrival in Canada. Sometimes, too, the spelling of the name was quite arbitrarily changed by the immigration officer at the port of entry, who would often write down an English-language version of a Norwegian name.

There are a number of organizations you can contact in North America before you leave to hunt for ancestors or relatives in Norway:

The Supreme Lodge of the Sons of Norway, 1312 West Lake Street, Minneapolis, Minnesota 55408.

The Norwegian-American Historical Association, St. Olaf College, Northfield, Minnesota 55057.

The Library of the Lutheran Theological Seminary, St. Paul, Minnesota (microfilms of parish records of the Norwegian Evangelical Lutheran Church in America).

In addition, Professor Gerhard Naeseth, 4909 Sherwood Road, Madison, Wisconsin 53711, is a leading researcher into early Norwegian emigration to North America. He is willing to give advice (reply-paid envelope, of course).

It is also well worth while checking to see if any history of your family has been written. You can do this by checking with the following places and people in Norway:

Universitetsbiblioteket i Oslo (The University Library), Oslo 2

Universitetsbiblioteket i Bergen, N-5000 Bergen.

Videnskabsselskabets bibliotek, N-7000 Trondheim.

Deichmanske bibliotek, Oslo 1.

Norsk Slektshistorisk Forening (Norwegian Genealogical Society), Øvre Slottsgate 17, Oslo 1. This society also publishes the chief genealogical magazine in Norway (*Norsk Slektshistorisk Tidsskrift*).

Norway is divided into counties like Britain. These districts were called *amt* until 1919 but are now called *fylke*, and many of the old names have been changed. There are nineteen *fylker* and the names are given below (with the old *amt* name in parentheses):

Østfold (Smaalenene)

Akershus

Oslo (called Kristiania before 1925

Hedmark

Oppland (Kristian)

Buskerud

Vestfold (Jarlsberg og Larvik)

Telemark (Bratsberg)

Aust-Agder (Nedenes)

Vest-Agder (Lister og Mandal)

Rogaland (Ryfylke, also Stavanger)

Hordaland (Söndre Bergenhus, also Bergen)

Sogn og Fjordane (Nordre Bergenhus)

More og Romsdal

Sör-Tröndelag (Söndre Trondheim)

Nord-Tröndelag (Nordre Trondheim)

Nordland

Troms (Tromsö)

Finnmark

There are, of course, much smaller administrative areas – such as *kommuner* (townships) and *prestegjeld* and *sokn* (parishes). The best account of farm names in Norway is in a very large series of books *Norsk Gaardnavne* by O. Rygh. There is one volume for each *fylke* and a separate index volume. There is also *Norsk Stedsfortegnelse* published by the Postdirektoratet in 1972. Making use of these books can often lead to the identification of the parish in which a particular family lived. You should get a good map of Norway, and these can be bought from the Amundsen Book Center, Decorah, Iowa 52101.

PARISH REGISTERS (Kirkeböker)
These records are usually kept by the pastor or parish minister. They give information about baptisms, confirmations, marriages, and deaths. They also give some information about movements of individuals in and out of the parish; but these records are by no means complete.

Some parish registers date from the early seventeenth century, but most are from after 1700. The registers are transferred to the regional archives eighty years after the last entry, so that only the more recent ones are in the custody of the parish minister. However, in the rural districts (and in some towns and cities) a duplicate of the registers is made by the deacons and sent to the regional archives as soon as it is completed. Registers less than sixty years old are not available to ancestor-hunters without special permission from the regional archivist.

Abstracts of the parish registers from 1873 to 1877, and from 1921 onwards, are held by the Central Bureau of Statistics (Statistisk Sentralbyrå, Oslo). Abstracts for the periods from 1866 to 1872 and from 1889 to 1920 are in the National Archives.

Registers of the Nonconformist churches are still in the individual churches; but this is not too important as up until the later years of the last century practically all Norwegians were members of the Lutheran State Church.

CENSUS RETURNS (Folketellinger)

Official censuses were held in 1769, 1801, and then every tenth year from 1815 up to and including 1875. Since 1890 a census has been taken every tenth year. All the returns up to and including 1900 are open for inspection in the National Archives (except for 1875 and 1900, which are kept in the regional archives). The best census from the ancestor-hunter's point of view is that of 1801, as this gave name, age, occupation, and family status. From 1865 onwards the place of birth of each individual was also included. The earlier records gave statistical data only (i.e., numbers of people).

There are some earlier records which are of value. Before the official censuses commenced, population rolls (*manntall*) were kept for the rural districts. They list men and boys, and also women if they were engaged in farming. Many of these rolls are missing, but those that do survive are in the National Archives.

PROBATE REGISTERS (Skifteprotokoller)

These show the registration, valuation, and division of real estate and property left by the deceased person, and also give the names of heirs. The registers started in 1660. They were kept by the probate court in the rural districts and by the magistrates in the cities and towns. They are kept in the regional archives and are only partially indexed. They do not cover all the estates of deceased persons, i.e., when the heir or heirs were under age.

Other less important records are:

Court records (*tingböker*)
Registers of mortgages (*panteregister*)
Real-estate books (*matrikier*)
Citizenship registers (*borger-skapsprotokoller*)
All of these are in the regional archives.

REGISTERS OF VITAL STATISTICS (Folkeregister)

This started in 1945 and is to be found in all municipalities.

As you will have realized, the main Norwegian records are split between the National Archives and the regional archives, and to make use of the latter you will need to have some idea as to exactly where in Norway your ancestor came from. The locations of these various archives are as follows:

The National Archives (Rikssarkivet), Folke Bernadottes v 21, Oslo 8.

The Regional Archives (Statsarkivet):

Statsarkivet i Oslo, Folke Bernadottes v 21, Oslo 8 (for Østfold, Akershus, Oslo, Buskerud, Vestfold, and Telemark fylker)

Statsarkivet i Hamar, Strandgata 71, N-2300 Hamar (for Hedmark and Oppland fylker)

Statsarkivet i Kristiansand, Vesterveien 4, N-4600 Kristiansand (for Aust-Agder and Vest-Agder fylker)

Statsarkivet i Stavanger, Domkirke-plassen 3, N-4000 Stavanger (for Rogaland fylker)

Statsarkivet i Bergen, Arstadveien 22, N-5000 Bergen (for Bergen, Hordaland, and Sogn og Fjordane fylker)

Statsarkivet i Trondheim, Högskoleveien 12, N-7000 Trondheim (for Moreog Romsdal, Sör-Tröndelag, Nord-Tröndelag, Nordland, Troms, and Finnmark fylker). (However, the principal records for Troms and Finnmark are kept at the Statsarkivkontoret i Tromsö, at Petersborggata 21-29, N-9000 Tromsö – just to make life difficult!)

You will find the archives in the various centres very helpful to you – provided that you can supply some specific information at the start. They will not construct family trees for you, but if you do want some long and detailed research done they will put you in touch with a private individual who will work for you for a fee. They will supply a copy of a baptismal, marriage, or death certificate if you give the approximate date and the name of the parish in which the event occurred. It is not sufficient to say that your ancestor was born in, say, Finnmark or Nordland.

So far as Norway is concerned there are two very important sources of information which should be checked on this side of the Atlantic. The library of the Genealogical Society of the Church of Jesus Christ of Latter-Day Saints, Salt Lake City, Utah, possesses microfilm copies of many of the early Norwegian records (see the Appendix about the Mormon records on p. 283). There is also a book called *Nordmaendene i Amerika* (Vol. 1, 1907, and Vol. 2, 1913) by Martin Ulvestad. He gives brief information about many thousands of Norwegians who emigrated to North America. A set of these books is in the library of the Lutheran Theological Seminary, Saskatoon, Saskatchewan.

SWEDEN

The Swedes, like the Danes and Norwegians, are descended from the Vikings, but, unlike the Danes and Norwegians, who went west to conquer the British Isles, France, and the Low Countries, the Swedes turned east and penetrated deeply into Russia. The first Christian ruler of Sweden was Olaf Skutkonung in 993 C.E. After this there was a century of fighting between the Swedes and the neighbouring Goths until the two races joined in one country in 1150. Finland was conquered at this time. From 1650 to 1808 there were almost constant wars against Russia, Poland, and Prussia. The original Swedish royal family died out in 1818 and the throne was offered to Jean Bernadotte, one of Napoleon's marshals – his descendants are the nominal rulers of Sweden today.

Ancestor-hunting in Sweden, like any other country, needs the usual research in North America before you attempt a trip to Stockholm. Find out all you can about your Swedish ancestor, particularly the name of the parish from which he came – there are more than two thousand of them in Sweden. If you can, find out his *name in Sweden*. He may have changed it or anglicized it on arrival in North America – many thousands did so. Olsson became Oliver, Persson became Perkins, Stalhammar became Steel.

Check your family papers. You may find a *flyttningsbetyg* – an official exit permit from Sweden, issued by the pastor of the parish from which the emigrant left. It will give his full name, date and place of birth, and a character reference.

In Sweden the keeping of vital statistics is the responsibility of the established church. Every parish maintains the record of its inhabitants – whether they attended the church or not. This system has been in effect since the latter part of the seventeenth century.

Before giving details of Swedish records and their locations I should mention the system of administration. The country is divided into twenty-four districts or divisions (*lan*). Sometimes these *lan* are identical with the province (*landskap*), although there may be more than one *lan* in a *landskap*.

Each *lan* is divided into smaller units, known as *fogderi*. These, as well as the cities and towns, have their own separate administrations. From a judicial point of view, each *lan* is divided into other units, known as *harad*. Each *lan* is still further divided into smaller ecclesiastical units known as parishes. These were originally known in Swedish as *socknar*, but are now called *forsamlingar*.

Records from the parishes which are over a century old are kept in the provincial archives – known as *landsarkiv*. In addition, a few of the larger cities maintain their own city archives, called *stadsarkiv*.

The following archives are now in existence in Sweden:

Landsarkivet in Uppsala, S-751 04, Uppsala (for the *lan* of Stockholm, Uppsala, Sodermanland, Orebro, Vastmanland, and Kopparberg).

Landsarkivet in Vadstena, S-592 00, Vadstena (for the *lan* of Ostergotland, Jonkoping, Kronoberg, and Kalmar).

Landsarkivet in Visby, P.O. Box 142, S-621 00, Visby (for the *lan* of Gotland).

Landsarkivet in Lund, Fack 2016, S-220 02, Lund (for the *lan* of Blekinge, Kristianstad, Malmohus, and Halland).

Landsarkivet in Goteborg, P.O. Box 3009, Geijersgatan 1, S-400 10, Goteborg (for the *lan* of Goteborg and Bohus, Alvsborg, Skaraborg, and Varmland).

Landsarkivet in Harnosand, Nybrogatan 17, S-871 01, Harnosand (for the *lan* of Gavleborg, Vasternorrland, Vasterbotten, and Norrbotten).

Landsarkivet in Ostersund, S-831 01, Ostersund (for the *lan* of Jamtland).

Stadsarkivet in Stockholm, P.O. Box 22063, Kungsklippan 6, S-104 22, Stockholm (for the city of Stockholm).

Stadsarkivet in Malmo, St. Petrigangen 7a, S-211-22, Malmo (for the city of Malmo).

Stadsarkivet in Boras, P.O. Box 851, S-501 15, Boras (for the city of Boras — except for church records, which are at the Landsarkivet in Goteborg).

Stadsarkivet in Vasteras, S-721 87, Vasteras (for the city of Vasteras — except for church records, which are at the Landsarkivet in Uppsala).

Stadsarkivet in Orebro, Fack, S-701 01, Orebro (for the city of Orebro).

Stadsarkivet in Uppsala, P.O. Box 216, S-751 04, Uppsala (for the city of Uppsala).

Stadsarkivet in Gavle, Stapeltorgsgatan 5B, S-802 24, Gavle (for the city of Gavle).

Stadsarkivet in Karlstad, Drottninggatan 32, S-652 25, Karlstad (for the city of Karlstad).

Stadsarkivet in Eskilstuna, Carcliigatan 8, S-632 20, Eskilstuna (for the city of Eskilstuna).

Stadsarkivet in Norrkoping, S-601 81, Norrkoping (for the city of Norrkoping).

The following archives are also important for genealogical research:

Riksarkivet (The National Swedish Record Office), Fack,
 Fyrverkarbacken 13-17, S-100 26, Stockholm.
Kammararkivet (The Cameral Archives), address as for Record
 Office.
Emigrantinstitutet (The Emigrant Institute), P.O. Box 201,
 S-351 04, Vaxjo.
Statistiska centralbyran (The National Bureau of Statistics),
 Fack, Karlavagen 100, S-102 50, Stockholm.

PARISH REGISTERS

In these registers you will find a quite extraordinary collection
of information – they bear little resemblance to our parish
registers in Canada. In addition to records of birth, marriage,
and death, you will also find details of everyone leaving the
parish and everyone arriving in it; and the uniquely Swedish
husforhorslangder – household examination rolls set up by
the minister as a record of his visits to his flock (in the days
when clergymen, like doctors, made house calls!). These rolls
tell us about the educational status of people, their character,
their physical condition, their journeys away from the parish,
and the names of their boarders or visitors. They give a complete picture of a family and its position in its own native area.
Some of these rolls go back to the early seventeenth century
(Diocese of Våsterås), but generally speaking they begin about
1750. In 1895 some changes were made in these records and
they were renamed *forsamlingsbocker*.

Although, in general, all the old parish registers are in the
custody of the local *landsarkiv*, about forty parishes (mostly
in the *landskap* of Dalarna) have been allowed to keep all their
early records. So, check with the *landsarkiv* as to whether
your parish is one of these.

In addition to the parish records, the various archives also
hold many other documents – inventories of the estates of
deceased persons, court records, real-estate transfers, mortgages, marriage settlements, property lists, and census records.
Copies of the latter two items are also in the Kammararkivet
(Cameral Archives) in Stockholm and date back to 1540.

Another source of information in Sweden is the police
records of Malmo and Goteborg (Gothenburg). Almost all
emigrants left from these ports and had to register with the
police before their departure. These records show name, age,
sex, and home parish, *plus* the actual destination in the United
States or Canada. These records began in 1867.

Finally, I should mention that the National Central Bureau
of Statistics in Stockholm has a collection of extracts from the
registers of births, marriages, and deaths from 1860 to 1947.
From 1860 you can also find summaries of Swedes who emi-

grated, listed by parishes. Each person who emigrated is listed here with his age, occupation, and destination.

There are two genealogical societies in Sweden:

> *Personhistoriska samfundet*, Riksarkivet, Fack, S-100 26, Stockholm,
> *Genealogiska foreningen*, Arkivgatan 3, Box 2029, S-103-11, Stockholm.

Speaking in general terms, *if* you know the parish of origin of your Swedish ancestor, you should be able to get back some two hundred or three hundred years, unless some disaster has destroyed records in that particular area.

15. THE REST OF EUROPE

Albania
Austria
Belgium
Bulgaria
Czechoslovakia
Estonia, Latvia
    Lithuania
Germany
Greece
Hungary

Italy
Liechtenstein
Luxembourg
Malta
Netherlands
Poland
Portugal
Spain
Switzerland

It is regretted that the following countries ignored repeated requests for information: Cyprus, Romania, Turkey, U.S.S.R., Yugoslavia.

ALBANIA

Albania obtained its independence from Turkey in 1912. Civil registration started in 1929 and, before that, records of births, marriages, and deaths were kept in the churches so far as the Roman Catholic and Greek Orthodox churches were concerned. Records of death only were recorded in the mosques for Moslems. A census was first held in 1921 and records are in the custody of the Ministry of the Interior.

In each municipality an office keeps records of births, marriages, and deaths and all civil marriages take place in the same office. Church and mosque records for the district are also lodged here now. Religious marriages are not recognized by the state, although they are not actually banned. A couple may be married in a church or a mosque, but this must be followed by a civil marriage.

It has not been possible to obtain fuller information from the Albanian government in Tirana, the capital. Probably, of all the communist countries, this is the most suspicious of foreign genealogical enquiries. Some early records, prior to 1912, are in the Turkish National Archives in Istanbul, and an enquiry there may be worthwhile. Otherwise, if you are of Albanian descent, you can simply hope for political conditions to improve so that the government there will be prepared to be more forthcoming with its information.

AUSTRIA

Austria was originally a major part of the Holy Roman Empire, and under the rule of the Hapsburgs it expanded into a great power and joined with the Kingdom of Hungary to form the Austro-Hungarian Empire. This empire included a great many small principalities and a dozen different nationalities. After the Treaty of Versailles in 1919 these various small sections were separated from the old empire and became parts of other countries – some new, some old. Hungary became an independent country, and only Austria itself was left – basically consisting of Vienna and the surrounding provinces. In 1938 the Anschluss took place. This was the union of Germany and Austria into the Third Reich of Adolf Hitler. This union lasted until the end of the Second World War in 1945, when Austria again became an independent country.

When considering Austria as a source of genealogical information, always remember its history, because this affects the location of the records. They may still be in Austria, or in the new countries concerned. Records which you might expect to find in Czechoslovakia, for example, may still be in Austria. There was some handing over of records from one country to another, but this was often influenced by local conditions and political and religious differences.

Brief details of the areas of change are given below. Refer to the new country under its alphabetical listing in this chapter:

Banat	northeast part to Romania, southwest to Yugoslavia
Bohemia and Moravia	now part of Czechoslovakia
Bosnia and Herzegovina	now part of Yugoslavia
Bucovina	now part of Romania
Croatia	now part of Yugoslavia
Dalmatia	now part of Yugoslavia
Galicia	east part to U.S.S.R., west part to Poland
Serbia	now part of Yugoslavia
Slavonia	now part of Yugoslavia
Slovakia	now part of Czechoslovakia
Slovenia	now part of Yugoslavia
Transylvania	now part of Romania
Tyrol	north part in Austria, south part to Italy

In addition, the Romanian Province of Bessarabia was seized by the U.S.S.R. in 1945 and incorporated in the Soviet Union.

CIVIL REGISTRATIONS

This started in 1939 and before that date records were kept in the various churches. Since civil registration started so recently, you can see it is almost vital that you know the place of origin of your family in Austria. There is a break in your favour if your ancestors came from the Province of Burgenland – civil registration started there in 1895 and the records are in the Registrar's office at Eisenstadt.

CHURCH RECORDS

Registers are in existence as far back as 1523, but generally speaking you should not count on too much before 1700. Since Austria is predominantly Roman Catholic, the records of this church are the most important. The Protestant records – although recognized separately – were actually merged into the Catholic records for the period from 1648 to 1849. Each of the provinces into which modern Austria is divided has its own archives and their locations are listed below:

Burgenland	7001 Eisenstadt
Carinthia	9020 Klagenfurt
Lower Austria	1014 Wien
Upper Austria	4020 Linz
Salzburg	5020 Salzburg
Styria	8010 Graz
Tyrol	6010 Innsbruck
Vorarlberg	6901 Bregenz
Wien	1082 Wien

In addition, many early records are in the Vienna City Archives, including a partially indexed record of deaths in that city from 1648 onwards. (There are a few gaps between 1657 and 1677.)

The main Protestant denomination is the Evangelical Church. This is in two sections – the Augsburg Confession and the Geneva Confession, but both are responsible to the High Church Council, located at Schellingasse, Vienna, and the records of the Church since 1878 are located there.

There are also some records existing of the Old Catholic Church, which broke away from the main Catholic Church in 1870; and of the Greek Orthodox Church, which commenced keeping records in 1790. Information about these churches can be obtained from your nearest Austrian embassy or consulate.

At one time the earliest Jewish records in existence were those of the Viennese Jews, but after the Anschluss these records were removed to Germany and destroyed. Further information about Jewish records in general can be found in Chapter Seventeen.

WILLS
These date back to about 1600 and are kept in the various district court offices for the period 1900 to the present day. Before that period they are in the various provincial archives.

MILITARY RECORDS
Since military service was compulsory for all male citizens, valuable information about ancestors can often be found in these records. For information, write to the Federal Ministry of the Interior, Vienna.

BELGIUM

Note: For historical information about Belgium please refer to the Netherlands.

Since French and Flemish are both official languages in Belgium, I have tried as far as possible to give names and addresses in the language used in that particular part of the country. In bilingual areas I have given names in both languages.

CIVIL REGISTRATION
This started in Belgium in 1795 under the French occupation. Two copies of the record are made – one is kept in the town or commune hall of the municipality and the other is in the custody of the Courts of Justice of the First Resort. However, up to 1870 these have been transferred to the State Archives of the province concerned, where they may be examined free of charge. The registers are indexed from 1802 onwards. (Names with the prefix "de" are under the letter D, and those with "van" are under the letter V.) Any letters to the local municipality should be addressed to M. l'Officier de l'État Civil (M. Officier van de Burgerlyke Stand).

There are population registers dating from 1850 and these are also in the local municipal offices. They are not open to the public for inspection, but information from them can be obtained from the local official mentioned above.

CHURCH RECORDS
The older registers are now in the custody of the State Archives in the various provinces, or the local municipal offices, or (in a

few cases) in the original churches. The location of the various State Archives is given below. In the nineteenth century an index of names in the registers was made and copies are in the archives and the local municipal offices. You can find out where a particular parish register is located by writing to the Antwerp Society for Family Research (Antwerpsche Kring voor Familiekunde), Moonstraat 25, Antwerpen. Another useful source is Office Généalogique et Héraldique de Belgique, Parc de Cinquantenaire, B 1040, Bruxelles. The earliest registers date back to the sixteenth century.

WILLS

The early wills dating back to the seventeenth century are in the State Archives. Later ones are in the possession of the official notaries in each district. The Chamber of Notaries maintains a list of the notarial records and further information can be obtained by writing to the State Archives of the particular province.

ARCHIVES (Archives du Royaume or Ryksarchief) are located in the following cities:

Anvers (Antwerpen)
Arlon (Aarlen)
Bruges (Brugge)
Ghent (Gent)
Hasselt
Liège (Luik)
Mons (Bergen)
Namur (Namen)

The General Archives in Brussels (Archives Générales du Royaume, or Het Algemeen Rijksarchief) contain the Governmental Archives, records of contested lands or moneys, and parish registers from the Province of Brabant dating back to 1612. There are also family archives and genealogial collections.

BULGARIA

Bulgaria became semi-independent from Turkey in 1878 and fully independent after 1908.

CIVIL REGISTRATION

This started in 1893, and records are kept in the offices of the People's Councils for each district.

CHURCH RECORDS
Generally speaking, these only started in 1860 and are still in the local churches.

WILLS

These are deposited with the Notary Public of the State. Early ones are at the Ministry of Justice and current ones at the Court of Justice – both located in the capital, Sofia.

It is not easy to obtain information from Bulgaria and I think the best methods of approach are either through the Department of External Affairs in Ottawa; the Canadian Embassy in Sofia; or the Bulgarian Embassy in Ottawa – probably all three!

CZECHOSLOVAKIA

Czechoslovakia was formed in 1918 from Bohemia, Moravia, and Slovakia – previously parts of the Austro-Hungarian Empire.

CIVIL REGISTRATION
This started with the formation of the country, but was only compulsory for those people who were not members of any church. The children of such people were not baptized, the marriages were civil ones, and they were buried in state ceme-teries and not in church graveyards. In 1950 all the registers were taken over by the state and all entries are now "official". Even so, those who wish may have their children baptized, and may be married in a church after the civil ceremony has taken place. The civil registers are kept in the offices of the local municipality. Copies of certificates of all births, marriages, and deaths before 1950 may be obtained for a fee through the Czecho-Slovak Embassy, 3900 Linnean Avenue N.W., Wash-ington, D.C. 20008. The Embassy is also willing to arrange for extensive searches through all genealogical records in the country.

CHURCH RECORDS
Church registers go back to the early seventeenth century and are now in the National Archives (Archivni Sprava, Praha, for Bohemia and Moravia, and Archivni Sprava, Bratislava, for Slovakia). Protestant registers did not commence until about 1770. The early registers – both Catholic and Protestant – were kept in German and Latin. Czech was used after 1848.

The more recent registers, dating from 1870, are kept in the local Register Offices (Matricni Urad) in each district. The National Archives mentioned above are not exclusively centred in Praha and Bratislava, but the officials will tell you where the particular register in which you are interested is located.

WILLS
These are not centralized, but are kept in each district by the state notary. There are nearly three hundred of these districts. If you know the particular district from which your ancestor came, you can write to Statni Notarstvi of the main town.

ESTONIA, LATVIA, LITHUANIA

It has not been possible to obtain any information about the records of these three Baltic states, now part of the U.S.S.R. They had a short-lived period of independence between 1918 and 1944. During that time each country introduced civil registration. Early church records did exist but there seems to be a possibility these were removed to Moscow.

GERMANY

No ancestor-hunting can be successful in Germany unless you are familiar with the division of the country after the Second World War. Germany was not only divided into East and West, but, in addition, various parts of the country were taken by Poland and the U.S.S.R. Details are given below:

German Democratic Republic, or *D.D.R.*
This contains the former German States of Anhalt, Mecklenburg-Schwerin, Mecklenburg-Strelitz, Reuss, Sachsen, Sachsen-Altenburg, Sachsen-Gotha, Sachsen-Meiningen, Sachsen-Weimar, Schwarzburg-Rudolstadt, and Schwarzburg-Sondershausen; also four provinces of the State of Prussia (the western part of Brandenburg, Pommern, Sachsen, and Schleisen).

Federal Republic of Germany or *B.D.*
This contains Baden, Bayern, Braunschweig, Hessen-Darmstadt, Lippe, Oldenburg, Sachsen-Coburg (including the city of Coburg), Schaumburg-Lippe, Waldeck, Württemberg; the Free Cities of Bremen, Hamburg, and Lübeck; and five provinces of Prussia (Hannover, Hessen-Nassau, Rheinland,

Schleswig-Holstein, Westfalen) and the district of Sigmar-
ingen.

The following parts of Prussia went to Poland and the
U.S.S.R.:

Poland: The eastern part of Brandenburg, the eastern part
of Pommern, the southern part of Ost Preussen, Posen,
Schleisen, West Preussen.
U.S.S.R.: The northern part of Ost Preussen.

Note: At the end of the Second World War a large number of
records were removed from the churches in Prussia and taken
to safety before the Polish and Russian occupation. Some of
these are in the West Berlin Archives and open to the public.
The rest are in the Genealogische Zentralstelle at Leipzig in
East Germany, and not open. The church records of Mecklenburg-Schwerin are in the Cathedral Archives at Ratzeburg,
Schleswig-Holstein.

Germany provides many problems for the ancestor-hunter –
partly because of the present division of the country and partly because, until 1875, Germany consisted of a great number
of kingdoms, principalities, and duchies, each with its own
laws. However, do not be put off – the records are there, they
go back a long way, and there is a great deal of information
available – be patient and persistent.

CIVIL REGISTRATION (Reichspersonenstandsgesetz)
This started for the newly united country in 1875, when every
city, town, or municipality set up its own Register Office
(*Standesamt*). Since then all records have been kept in these
local offices. They are made out in duplicate – one copy is
retained in the Standesamt and the other is sent to the Kreis-
verband in the state capital. Before 1875, records were the
responsibility of the various parish churches.

If your ancestors came from that part of Germany under
French control from 1798 (i.e., Alsace-Lorraine and other
areas west of the Rhine) you are lucky because civil registration started there in that year. (It has also been in effect in
Baden since 1810, Frankfurt since 1850, and Prussia since
1874.)

The death registers are particularly useful because very
often they give the place and date of birth of the deceased, the
names of parents, and the surviving children of the deceased.

CHURCH RECORDS
First, you must try and find out the religion of your German

ancestor. Speaking very generally, Bavaria and the Rhineland are Catholic; Brandenburg is Lutheran; Hesse is Protestant, but not necessarily Lutheran. Catholic registers date back to the mid sixteenth century and are in the local churches. Protestant ones date from a hundred years later and are also in the local churches. The various state and local archives often contain copies of the early registers (*Kirchenbücher*).

ARCHIVES

Every province (that is a former state like Bavaria) has its own archives (*Staatsarchiv*) and in turn these are often divided into smaller archives located in the main cities of the province. Details of actual addresses can be obtained from the nearest embassy of the Federal Republic of Germany (West Germany) or of the People's Republic of Germany (East Germany).

WILLS

These are not centralized and are to be found in local courthouses (*Amtsgerichte*) or with the State Archives.

There are many other sources of information and basic details are given below.

PASSENGER LISTS

Lists of emigrants leaving the port of Hamburg from 1837 onwards are in the Hamburg State Archives (Staatsarchiv Hamburg). *Note:* Those for Bremen were destroyed by Allied bombing during the Second World War.

CITY DIRECTORIES

These date back to 1810 for a number of the major cities and are in city archives and local libraries.

EMIGRATION

Some records from about 1830 are to be found in the various state archives.

POLICE REGISTERS

These date from 1830 and give full details of population movement from town to town. Apply for information to Einwohnermeldeamt in the district concerned.

CENSUSES

These have been held at irregular intervals for the past three centuries in many areas and are in the various state archives.

The local and state archives also have such items as funeral sermons (which give details of the family of the deceased); lists of school and university students from the sixteenth century; house books (details of houses and their owners); burgher rolls from the thirteenth century; and apprentice and guild rolls. There are also records of transactions in land to be found in state and local courts.

As I mentioned at the start, the records are there, but because they are not centralized, it is a slow business tracking them all down. So far as the Federal Republic is concerned there are genealogical societies in the various states and their addresses can be obtained from the nearest embassy.

At the moment, the People's Republic is not very co-operative, but there are signs of an improvement, and now that there is an embassy in Ottawa and Canadian representation in East Berlin the problems of communication may be solved.

Further information about German sources can be obtained from Deutsche Arbeitsgemeinschaft Genealogischer Verbände, Stolzingerstrasse 4/13, 8000 München 81. I have not found them very helpful, but it is worth trying. Be sure you write in German and enclose an international reply coupon for return postage.

GREECE

Greece became an independent country in 1821. Before that, the country had been under the control of the Ottoman Empire for many centuries.

Civil registration of births, marriages, and deaths commenced in 1831. These records are in the custody of the Ministry of the Interior, Athens. There are, however, many gaps. In addition, records are kept in the individual churches of the Greek Orthodox Church, but here again, due to invasion, occupation, and civil war, these records are intermittent. Very few church registers date back before 1840.

Copies of wills are lodged with the Secretary of the Court of the First Instance, Panepistimiou St. 47, Athens.

HUNGARY

Hungary became completely independent in 1918 – after the break-up of the old Austro-Hungarian Empire.

CIVIL REGISTRATION
The state registration of births, marriages, and deaths started in 1895. The originals are in the local registry offices in each municipality or administrative district. There are copies in the various regional archives and also in the National Archives Centre (Leveltarak Orzagos Kozpontja) in Budapest. Copies of the certificates will be issued for a small fee, provided you

know the approximate date of the event. Extended searches cannot be made at present, but there is a possibility more help will be given to genealogists in the near future.

CHURCH REGISTERS

Baptisms were first recorded in 1515, but the law of recording such events was not widely observed before 1629. Registration of marriages started in 1545 when the Council of Trent ordained such registration throughout the Catholic world. Deaths were recorded from 1614. The original churches retain custody of the registers, but the State Archives have microfilm copies of all Hungarian church registers before 1895. A catalogue of these copies is now being prepared, and should be available by the time you read this.

WILLS

There is no central registry of wills and they are in the custody of the various notaries public in the various judicial districts. There are copies in the regional and local archives and these are found among such files as Proceedings of the Orphans Court and reports of notaries public, and in family papers.

CENSUSES

All the main libraries in Hungary have summaries of the national censuses. There have been a number since the seventeenth century and these are in the State Archives in Budapest. There were also local censuses, and these records are in the regional archives.

STATE ARCHIVES

These consist of the State Archives in Budapest, containing the government archives, and other State Archives from each of the twenty-two counties. The staff is anxious to be helpful within limits and any enquiry (in Hungarian) will be answered. If you do not speak the language of your ancestors, you should write to the Canadian Embassy in Budapest and ask them to contact the State Archives on your behalf. Be sure you have all the facts set out clearly in your letter — whether it is to the Archives or the Canadian Embassy.

There are a number of books available in the State Archives about Hungarian genealogy. I do not know if it is possible to obtain copies in Canada. Probably not, because the books are not recent and may be out of print now:

Ivan Nagy, *Magyarorszag csaladai czimerekkel és nemzed-
ékrendi tablakkal* (Hungarian families with their coats-
of-arms and genealogical charts) (1857)
Béla Kempelen, *Magyar names* (Budapest 1911-32)

Béla Kempelen, *Magyar forangu csaladok* (Hungarian families of upper status) (1931)

Béla Kempelen, *Magyarorszagi zsido és zsido eredetu csaladok* (Jewish families and families of Jewish origin) (1937)

Some of the above may be among the holdings of the Genealogical Research Library, London, Ontario (see page 3).

There are also a number of manuscripts about genealogy in the Manuscript Collection of the National Hungarian Library in Budapest. Also on the shelves of the library you will find copies of *Turul*, the journal of the Hungarian Heraldic and Genealogic Society, 1883-1945 (this Society no longer exists). There are also various genealogical bulletins and booklets published in Budapest and Kolozsvar between 1899 and 1910. The copies of *Turul* between 1883 and 1936 have been indexed under family name, and this will be worth checking in Budapest.

ITALY

It was only a century ago – in 1870 – that Italy became a country. Before that, for many centuries it had been a quite extraordinary conglomeration of tiny principalities, large states, city states, duchies, kingdoms, republics – you name it, Italy had it! As a result the early Italian records are widely scattered and in varying stages of completion and accuracy.

CIVIL REGISTRATION

This started in 1870 for the whole country and is known as *stato civile*. The records are in the registry offices (Ufficio di Stato Civile) of the cities, towns, or municipalities where the event occurred. The birth records also include date and place of the parents' marriage. When writing to the Ufficio di Stato Civile for a copy of a birth certificate, be sure you say "Favorisca inviare estratti con nomi dei genitori". This means you want names of the parents included. If you do not request this you will only receive a short form of the birth certificate.

The marriage records also include the addresses and the occupations of the parents on both sides, including the maiden names of the mothers – all very useful information for the ancestor-hunter. The death records include the date and place of birth of the deceased, names of parents, and occupation and address.

Now, having said that civil registration started in 1870, I must also mention it started earlier in some parts of the country – 1820 in Sicily and the Province of Calabria, 1803 to 1815 in those parts of northern Italy occupied by Napoleon, and from the sixteenth century in the district of South Tyrol (Trentino). More information about civil registration can be obtained from Instituto Centrale di Statistica, Via Cesare Balbo 16, Roma.

CHURCH RECORDS

So far as the Roman Catholic Church is concerned (and that means about everybody in Italy) the parish registers started in 1545, but very few exist before the seventeenth century. They are to be found either in the original church or in the diocesan archives (archivio vescovile della diocesi). If you know the general area from which your ancestor came, but are not sure of the particular diocese or the name of the church, I suggest you write to the Secret Archives of the Vatican (Archivio Segreto del Vaticano, Roma). They have nearly all the early Rome parish registers in their custody, and have details of the location of others throughout the country. You will find this office very helpful.

The baptism records give great detail – names of the grandparents, the godparents (and their parents), and their relationship to the child. The marriage registers also include names of other parishes where the banns were proclaimed, and the names of any previous spouses.

Other church records include (from 1545) confirmations, dispensations, excommunications, and church property records. These are all in either the diocesan archives or the state archives. In addition, the Vatican Archives mentioned above also have the tax and census registers of the old Papal states from the mid fourteenth century. These included the modern provinces of Ancona, Ascoli Piceno, Macerata, Pesaro-Urbino, Perugia, Terni, Frosinone, Latina, Rieti, Roma, and Viterbo.

There are a few Waldensian Protestant registers dating back to 1685, and these are in the local churches.

Other records of value to the ancestor-hunter include conscription records (Registri degli Uffici Leva) from 1869. These are retained in the Military District for the area in which the conscript lived. For information write to the Ministry of War, Rome, asking for the name and address of the Military District (Distretto Militare). Many parish records also include a record of *status animarum* – this was kept from 1700 to 1860 and lists all people in each parish. Very many of these are no longer in existence, but it is worth checking to see if one exists for the particular district in which you are interested.

The state archives also have registers of names of young men eligible for conscription, and these cover the period from 1792 to 1917. There are tax assessment registers for the former

Grand Duchy of Tuscany and these are in the state archives at Florence (Firenze). They date from about 1740 and cover the present provinces of Massa Carrara, Arezzo, Firenze, Grosseto, Livorno, Lucca, Pisa, Pistoia, and Sienna.

The state archives at Naples (Napoli) have similar records and census returns for the former Kingdom of Naples, dating back to 1747. The various state archives through the provinces also have indexed copies of notarial records dating back, in some cases, for six hundred years. These include marriage settlements, sales of land, mortgages, and wills. There are also many hundreds of genealogical collections in the various archives, but these have not been listed, and all you can do is to enquire at a particular archive whether your family name is mentioned.

LIECHTENSTEIN

The Principality of Liechtenstein is an independent state located on the north bank of the Rhine between Austria and Switzerland. Originally part of the Holy Roman Empire, it became independent in 1806. It is represented abroad by Switzerland.

Civil registration commenced in 1878 and the registry books were kept by the local Catholic priests, acting as representatives of the government. In 1874 a Civil Registry Bureau was established in Vaduz, the capital, and all records since that date have been kept there. Before 1878 the records are in the local churches and in many cases go back to 1640. The earliest available will is dated 1690 and the wills are in the custody of the local courts in each district.

Copies of records can be obtained from the Civil Registry Bureau or the local council – either for a small fee, or free, depending on the amount of work to be done and the staff available. If the records have been indexed, a search is simple, but if not, some considerable searching may be involved. Enquiries on any matter concerning records or documents should be sent to the Chancellery of the Government of Liechtenstein (Kanzlei der Regierung des Fürstentums Liechtenstein, FL-9490, Vaduz).

LUXEMBOURG

This has been a Grand Duchy since 1814 and independent since 1867. Before that it belonged, in turn, to Burgundy, Spain, Austria, and France.

CIVIL REGISTRATION
This started in 1793 and the registers are in the offices of the various communes and municipalities – of which there are over a hundred. A copy remains there and a second copy is lodged with the Courts of Justice in Luxembourg or Diekirch. Every ten years all names are indexed, and the indexes are in the Public Record Office in Luxembourg.

CHURCH RECORDS
Some of these date back to the seventeenth century and are either in the original churches or in the Courts of Justice. In addition, microfilm copies are in the state archives (Archives de l'État), Plateau du Saint-Esprit, Luxembourg. (A detailed inventory of the church records is being prepared and will be available shortly.)

WILLS
These date back to 1606 and are in the state archives, with settlements and transfers of property.

MALTA

Originally a British colony, Malta is now independent.

CIVIL REGISTRATION
This started in 1863 and the records are in the Public Registry Office, Merchants Street, Valletta, Malta.

CHURCH REGISTERS
In some cases these date back to the early eighteenth century, but many records were destroyed during the bombing of Malta during the Second World War. Full information about existing registers can be obtained from the Archbishop's Curia, Archbishop Street, Valletta.

CENSUSES
The first census was taken in 1842, and the second in 1851. From then on the censuses were taken every ten years (except in 1941). They restarted in 1947, 1957, and 1967. They are available for inspection in the Public Library, Valletta. The staff will not make extended searches but the names of local genealogists who will work for a fee are given later in this section.

WILLS
These records started in 1859 when registration became official. However, there are a number of wills which date back to

1691. The original wills are in the Notarial Archives, 3 Scots Street, Valletta, and there is a complete index and register at the Public Registry Office, Merchants Street, Valletta. This refers to public wills – for information on secret wills you must apply to the Registrar of the Superior Courts, Valletta.

COURT RECORDS
These are kept in the Courts of Justice, Republic Street, Valletta, and date back to 1814. All documents before that date and back to 1532 are in the Central Archives, Valletta.

NOTARIAL RECORDS
For Malta, these are registered at 24 St. Christopher Street, Valletta, and for the island of Gozo, St. Domenica Street, Rabat.

GENEALOGICAL SOCIETY
There is no society in the islands, but the following genealogists will undertake searches of records for an agreed fee:

Francis Cassar Parnis, 97 Marina Street, Pieta.
Chev. Carmelo Meli, O.S.J., F.R.C.P., 328 St. Paul's Street,
    Valletta.
Miss Mary Anne Muscat, St. Philip Square, Zebbug.

THE NETHERLANDS

The Low Countries (what is now the Netherlands and Belgium) have had a very chequered history. Because of their strategic position they were almost constantly in a state of war for many centuries. Originally they belonged to the empire of Charlemagne, and later the major part of them came under the control of one of the minor German kings. After 1384 the various provinces were ruled by the Dukes of Burgundy, who acquired them by purchase, marriage, and cession by neighbouring rulers. In 1548 they passed by marriage into the possession of Spain.

From 1568 to 1648 there were a succession of risings in the northern provinces (what is now called the Netherlands or Holland) and these were followed by similar rebellions in the southern provinces (now Belgium). In 1581 the northern provinces proclaimed their independence and William of Orange became the *statthalter*. Spain did not recognize this independence until the Treaty of Westphalia in 1648. From 1810 to 1814 the Netherlands were incorporated into France by Napoleon. In 1815, at the Congress of Vienna, the Netherlands and Belgium (now known as the Austrian Netherlands) were united in one country. In 1831 Belgium seceded and became an independent country.

There is no central registration of births, marriages, and deaths in the Netherlands. Civil registration was commenced by the French in 1811 and each of the thousand-odd municipalities keeps its own records. From 1811 to 1892 duplicate records were kept in the various provincial archives, but these are not indexed, and so, without knowledge of the town or village from which your ancestor came, it is almost impossible to trace him. To make matters still more complicated, before the nineteenth century births, marriages, and deaths were registered according to religious denomination, and there were a number of these. So, even if you know the village you will also have to check the records of each church, unless you know for sure the religion of your ancestor.

CIVIL REGISTRATION (Burgerlijke Stand)

As I have mentioned above, this commenced in 1811 for the whole country, but in some areas in the south it started in 1796.

The records were made in duplicate. One copy was kept by the registrar of the municipality and the other was sent to the clerk of the county court and kept in his archives. These duplicates, for the period from 1811 to 1892, have now been deposited in the various provincial archives. They are indexed. One very useful bonus is that the records include all the original documents submitted at the time of a marriage – copies of birth or baptism records, death records of parents on both sides (if deceased), and details of a man's army service. After 1892 copies of the records can be obtained only from the Registrar of each municipality (Ambtenaar van de Burgerlijke Stand).

POPULATION REGISTERS (Bevolkingsregisters)

Since about 1830 population registers have been kept by the various municipalities in their archives. These records are not generally available until one hundred years have passed since the registration, except at the discretion of the Registrar. If a person dies, his card is sent to the Central Bureau of Statistics, and then once a year the cards from the previous year are sent to the Central Bureau for Genealogy for safe-keeping (Centraal Bureau voor Genealogie, The Hague). This means that this bureau has a complete card index of everyone who has died in the Netherlands since 1939. The cards are arranged alphabetically for the whole country. They are particularly valuable because, apart from the details about the deceased person, they also contain the birthdates of his parents. So, a man who died in 1940, aged eighty, may well have on his card the birth dates of his parents, going as far back as 1820 or earlier.

CHURCH RECORDS

The registers of births (or baptisms), marriages, and deaths are kept by the ministers of the various denominations. During the period from 1588 to 1795 the Dutch Reformed Church was the official State Church and non-members had to marry in that church, or before a magistrate, as well as in the church of their own religion. So the marriage records of Catholics, Jews, etc., are to be found in the registers of the Dutch Reformed Church for that period. Most of the registers were handed over to the civil authorities during the French occupation (1795-1813) and are now in the various archives. Where the registers are kept and which periods they cover can be found in *Repertorium DTB*, a booklet published in 1969 by the Central Bureau for Genealogy. Many copies of original registers are in the library of the bureau.

There are other records of use to the ancestor-hunter in the archives – such as wills, court records, divisions of property, land transfers, tax rolls, etc. Details of these records can be found in *De Rijksarchieven in Nederland*, published in 1953 and now being reprinted.

The state archives in the various provinces are located as follows:

Rijksarchief in Drenthe, Brink 4, Assen.
Rijksarchief in Friesland, Turfmarkt 13, Leeuwarden.
Rijksarchief in Gelderland, Markt 1, Arnhem.
Rijksarchief in Groningen, St. Jansstraat, Groningen.
Rijksarchief in Limburg, St. Pietersstraat 7, Maastricht.
Rijksarchief in Noord-Brabant, Waterstraat 20, 's-Hertogenbosch.
Rijksarchief in Noord-Holland, Ceciliasteeg 12, Haarlem.
Rijksarchief in Overijssel, Sassenpoort, Zwolle.
Rijksarchief in Utrecht, Alexander Numankade 201, Utrecht.
Rijksarchief in Zeeland, St. Pietersstraat 38, Middleburg.
Algemeen Rijksarchief (for Zuid-Holland, Colonial Archives, etc.)
   Prins Willem-Alexanderhof 20, 's-Gravenhage (The Hague).

There are three organizations of value to the genealogist in the Netherlands:

The Central Bureau for Genealogy (Centraal Bureau voor Genea-
   logie, Prins Willem-Alexanderhof 22, The Hague)
The Netherlands Genealogical Association (Nederlandse Genea-
   logische Vereniging, Postbus 976, Amsterdam)
The Royal Netherlands Association for Genealogy and Heraldry
   (Koninklijke Nederlandse Genootschap voor Geslachten
   Wapenkunde, Prins Willem-Alexanderhof 24, The Hague)

Of these, the first is by far the most important. It was set up in 1945 as a semi-official non-profit organization, and is under the control of the Minister of Culture, Recreation, and Social Welfare. Its main function is to maintain the genealogical collections of the state and to be a documentation centre for family history. It has a staff of about forty who are civil servants and whose salaries are paid by the state. All other expenses are provided by a circle of Friends of the Bureau and by fees charged to visitors for genealogical research.

There is a very large library which, apart from printed works on genealogy, also has a large manuscript collection of family histories. So be sure you check with the Bureau to find out if someone has traced your ancestors already. Over fifteen hundred Dutch families are included, so you may be lucky!

A unique feature is a collection of millions of family announcements (births, marriages, deaths) copied from newspapers from 1795 up to the present day.

There are also one and a half million cards on baptisms, marriages, and deaths, and membership of the Walloon churches in the Netherlands, France, and Germany. These are on microfilm and there is a viewer in the library.

The Bureau will undertake research for you, if it is not possible for you to visit the Netherlands, and will give you an estimate of the cost based on the knowledge you have to start. By and large, the Bureau will not start a search for you unless it is thought there is a good chance of success. Remember, you are paying for the services of a fully qualified genealogical researcher who will work conscientiously for you.

When you have succeeded in tracing your family in the Netherlands you can also check with the Bureau to find out if they ever had a coat-of-arms. If they did not, the Bureau will also arrange for you to have a coat-of-arms designed for you and duly registered, and the cost is not out of line for the work involved.

Finally, it should be mentioned that, in addition to the provincial archives listed above, there are some seventy-five smaller archives throughout Holland. I have not listed these because they are strictly local in scope, but you can get a list of them from the Central Bureau for Genealogy.

The following books and booklets are published by the Bureau and obtainable from it:

Op zoek naar onze voorouders 1972 (Een algemene handleiding voor stamboomonderzoek voor beginners en gevorderden, met lijst van Nederlandse archieven, genealogische verenigingen enz)
Overzicht van de verzamelingen 1972 (berustende bij het Centraal Bureau voor Genealogie en het Iconographische Bureau)
Wenken en adressen voor Genealogisch onderzoek in het Buitenland 1973 (Bevat behalve een inleiding en een hoofdstuk "Hoe

gaan wij te werk?" gegevens over 36 landen, steeds met adressen, meestal met literatuuropgaven. De Westeuropese landen zijn uitvoerig behandeld)

Searching for your ancestors in the Netherlands 1972 (Een beknopte handleiding voor buitenlanders)

Genealogisch Repertorium 1972 deel 1 A-I , deel 2 M Z (Op familienamen gerangschikte verwijzingen naar gedrukte genealogische en andere werken en periodieken, bijgewerkt tot 1 Januari 1970)

Repertorium DTB 1969 (Geeft een beknopt overzicht van de Nederlandse doop-, trouwen begraafregisters enz. van voor de invoering van de Burgerlijke Stand met opgave van tijdvakken en bewaarplaatsen)

POLAND

Poland is a very ancient country that disappeared from the map of Europe in 1795 when it was partitioned between Russia, Germany, and Austria. It became independent again in 1918, but following the Second World War it lost considerable eastern territory to Russia, although it incorporated German territory east of the Oder. This constant rearrangement of boundaries and long periods of foreign domination and occupation, plus heavy fighting, has had its effect on Polish records. Ancestor-hunting is possible, but it needs much patience, a knowledge of Polish, and a visit to Poland.

CIVIL REGISTRATION
This started only in 1946, except that some ecclesiastical registration did exist for some years before that in Biolystok Voivodship, and in the Silesia area. Civil registration was in force in the Katowice area, and all these records are in the local archives. (A Voivodship is roughly the equivalent of our county.)

Before the First World War parish priests kept the civil registration records in the Russian-occupied areas; the same applied to the Austrian-controlled part; while civil authorities were responsible for registration in the German section.

CHURCH RECORDS
Basically, these are from the Roman Catholic Church and date back to the mid seventeenth century, except where destroyed or missing.

WILLS
These are in the custody of the local Courts of Justice.

ARCHIVES

The State Archives in Warsaw are Archiwum Glowne Akt Dawnych, Dluga 7, Varsova. There is a separate section for modern records at the same address, called Archiwum Akt Nowych.

In addition, there are local Archives in the main centres – Brzeg, Bialystok, Bydgoszcz, Cieszyn, Czestochowa, Gliwice, Gdansk, Jelenia Gora, Katowice, Kielce, Krakow, Lodz, Lublin, Olsztyn, Opole, Polck, Poznan, Piotrkow, Pszczyna, Ratusz, Rzeszow, Radom, Szczecin, Wroclaw, Warsaw, Zamek. The best collections appear to be in Cieszyn, Krakow, Lodz, Poznan, Radom, Ratusz, Szczecin, Warsaw, Wroclaw, and Zamek.

Once you know the district in Poland in which you are interested, the best thing is to write to the local archives, explaining *very clearly* what you want to find out. It will be much wiser to get your letter translated into Polish – there is a Polish Translation Agency at 67 Yonge Street, Toronto. The following words may help you to address the envelope:

Oddzial Terenowy (Local Record Office)

or Wojewodzkie Archiwum (Archives)

PORTUGAL

Portugal has been an independent country since 1185. It shares the Iberian Peninsula with Spain and the country is predominantly Roman Catholic.

CIVIL REGISTRATION (Registo Civil)

This was started *on an optional basis* on 16 May 1832. The Civil Code (Codigo Civil) of 1867 was the real beginning of compulsory civil registration, and this was further confirmed on 28 November 1878. Basically, civil registration existed side by side with Church registration, and the former was only used by non-Catholics. In spite of the law, Catholics continued to use the registration facilities of the Church. It was not until 1911 that civil registration was applied to both Catholics and non-Catholics and was enforced.

The books of civil registration and some parish registers are to be found in the Registry Office (Conservatorias do Registo Civil) in the various districts. After one hundred years these records are transferred to the National Archives of Torre do Tombo.

The parish priest had authority to make entries of births and christenings, marriages, and deaths. After 1911 his registers were transferred to the civil registry offices. For further information you should write to Direccao-Geral do Registe e Notoriado, Do Ministério da Justiça, Lisbon, Portugal.

CHURCH REGISTERS
Generally speaking, these date from the late sixteenth century, but come dating back to 1390 are in the National Archives of Torre do Tombo.

WILLS
The General Registry of Wills (Testamento) was established in 1950 with the creation of the Central Registry (Conservatoria dos Registo Centrais). Wills dating before that are either in the Public Archives or in the Registry of the Commissioners for Oaths (Cartorios Notariais).

ARCHIVES
Apart from civil and church registers, the National Archives in Lisbon (Arquivo Nacionale da Torre do Tombo) have records of grants of arms and some details of land transactions.

There are also some legal records of birth and descent, of marriage contracts and pre-nuptial settlements, and of guardianship in the custody of the Direccao-Geral do Registo e Notoriado mentioned above.

SPAIN

Spain, like Italy, was once a collection of small independent kingdoms and principalities, plus a large area in the southern part of the country that was under the occupation of the Moors from North Africa. Fortunately for you – if you are of Spanish descent – the country became united in 1492 and the invaders were expelled.

CIVIL REGISTRATION
This commenced in 1870. Records are in the offices of local municipalities with copies in the Ministry of Justice in Madrid.

CHURCH RECORDS
These, of course, are Roman Catholic records, since no other religion ever established itself in Spain. Church registers came into existence in Spain earlier than in any other country in the world, and in some districts they date back to 1394, but the practice did not become general before 1570. Many registers were destroyed in the war against Napoleon (1808-15) and in the more recent Civil War (1936-9). There is no central listing

available so all you can do is to write to the parish priest (Rev. Sr. Cura Parroco) of the place in which you are interested. However, many church registers are now located in the Parochial Archives (Los Archivos Parroquiles) or the Diocesan Archives (Los Archivos Diocesanos).

WILLS

These often go back for three centuries and are preserved in the archives of the Notarial Protocols (Probate Offices). These are set up in each notarial or high court district – Albacete, Barcelona, Burgos, Caceres, La Coruna, Granada, Madrid, Palma de Mallorca, Las Palmas de Gran Canaria, Pamplona, Oviedo, Seville, Valencia, Valladolid y Zaragoza. (Write Los Archivos Historicos de Protocolos in the city nearest to your family's place of origin.)

OTHER ARCHIVES

Each ministry of the government has its own archives but, in the main, these are of no great interest to ancestor-hunters. There is one exception – in the Military Archives in Segovia you can find the complete personal records of every Spanish soldier from the early 1600s to the present day. The lists have been published and indexed and information can be obtained by writing to the Military Archives, Segovia.

You can also get help and advice from the Spanish Genealogical Society (Instituto Internacional de Genealogica y Heraldica) in Madrid.

SWITZERLAND

A Swiss Confederacy was formed in 1291 from three cantons that previously owed allegiance to Austria. Other cantons joined the Confederacy over the next two centuries, and there are now twenty-six of them. A canton is a semi-independent district responsible for the affairs within the canton. In 1648 the independence of the Swiss Confederation was recognized in the Treaty of Westphalia. In 1815 the perpetual neutrality of the country was endorsed at the Congress of Vienna. The majority of Swiss are German-speaking, but there are sizeable French and Italian minorities, and a very small number speak Romansch. All four languages are officially recognized.

CIVIL REGISTRATION

This was introduced for the whole of the country in 1876, but there is no central indexed registry. The records are kept in the commune (municipality) where the event took place. For copies of entries write to the Civil Registrar (Zivilstandesamt) of the district and ask for a family certificate (Familienschein). Before 1876 registration was included in the various church records. All records for the pre-civil-registration period (1834-75) are also in the custody of the Civil Registrar. The general principle governing civil registration in Switzerland is that all vital records including birth, marriage, death, divorce, and nullity are kept in the place where the citizen was born.

CHURCH RECORDS
Protestant records date back to 1550 and Catholic records to 1580. The Catholic registers are in the local church, the Protestant registers are either in the state archives, the city or town archives, or the Civil Registrar's office. The problem with Swiss records is caused by the autonomous character of the cantons – each one has its own ideas about the best system of keeping records.

WILLS
This problem of varying systems applies particularly to wills. Until 1912 the probating, or proving, of wills was the responsibility of the cantons; then it became a federal matter. In the case of death, the will has to be submitted to the judge, or other authority, who is dealing with matters of succession for proof of probate – regardless of whether the will has been kept in private hands or has been deposited with a notary. Searching for wills, therefore, involves both probate courts and notaries. Copies can be found in the local courthouse, but some older ones are also in state and city archives, depending on the law of the canton. You can see that dogged determination and quite a lot of detective work are needed in Switzerland. However, the search can be successful, and I know of several cases in which ancestors have been traced back to the mid 1600s.

CENSUSES
A city census was taken in Berne in 1764, but federal censuses started in the period from 1836 to 1838. From 1860 onwards the records are complete and are lodged in the state archives in the capital, Berne.

There are a number of other records scattered about the country which will be of great value, and some examples are given below:

FAMILY REGISTERS (Familien-Register)
These give details of births, marriages, and deaths, religion,

occupation, age, and parents, and cover the period from 1820 to the present day. They are in the offices of the local registrars in each district.

MILITARY RECORDS
Each male citizen must spend a certain time in the Army and then go on the Reserve. These records date from 1800 and are in the Military Department of the federal government in Berne (Eidgenössisches Militär, Bundeshaus, Bern).

EMIGRATION
There are complete records of each emigrant from the early seventeenth century to the present day. Those dating before 1848 are in the state archives of the canton; after that date they are in the Schweizer Bundesregierung, Bundeshaus, Bern.

UNIVERSITY REGISTERS
Many of these lists of students date back to 1550 (varying from place to place) and give place of birth and names of parents. Early records are in the various state archives, and later ones in the various university archives.

OTHER RECORDS
There are also books recording tithes paid (Zehntbücher); genealogical registers (Genealogische-Stadt-Register); and donations for masses for the dead (Jahrzeitbücher). All these date from 1640 onwards and are to be found in Catholic churches or state archives. Many land records, marriage settlements, inventories, and mortgages are in the local courthouses (Kantonal-und-Amtsgerichte). Finally, the local Registrar sometimes has burgher rolls dating back to the eleventh century. (They are called Bevölkerungsverzeichnisse.)

The cantons and the chief city in each are listed below, and also details of the appropriate language to use when writing:

German-speaking cantons	Chief city	Remarks
Aargau	Aargau	
Appenzell Outer Rhoden	Herisau	
Appenzell Inner Rhoden	Appenzell	
Basel (town)	Basel	
Basel (country)	Liestal	
Bern	Bern	also French
Glarus	Glarus	
Graubünden	Chur	also Italian and Romansch
Luzern	Luzern	also French

German-speaking cantons	Chief city	Remarks
Nidwalden	Stans	
Obwalden	Sarnen	
St. Gallen	St. Gallen	
Schaffhausen	Schaffhausen	
Schwyz	Schwyz	
Solothurn	Solothurn	
Thurgau	Frauenfeld	
Uri	Altdorf	
Zug	Zug	
Zürich	Zürich	

French-speaking cantons

Fribourg	Fribourg	also German
Genève	Genève	
Jura	Delémont	
Neuchâtel	Neuchâtel	
Valais	Sion	also German
Vaud	Lausanne	

Italian-speaking cantons

Ticino	Bellinzona	also German

16. OTHER COUNTRIES

Australia	Lebanon
Barbados	New Zealand
India	Pakistan
Japan	South Africa
Jordan	

It is regretted that the following countries ignored repeated requests for information: Algeria, China, Cuba, Egypt, Hong Kong, Iran, Iraq, Israel, Jamaica, Korea, Mexico, Morocco, Philippines, Syria, Trinidad, Tunisia.

AUSTRALIA

Australia was first discovered by the Dutch and later colonized by the British, who used New South Wales as a penal settlement. Previously, convicts had been sent to the American colonies, but after the War of Independence this was no longer possible. The first convicts arrived in Australia in 1788 and the last in about 1853. When the convict had served his sentence he was given a grant of thirty to fifty acres of land. The various states and the Northern Territory were established between 1800 and 1860. The Commonwealth of Australia, incorporating the various states, was established in 1900.

Each state and territory of Australia has an independent system of civil registration of births, marriages, and deaths. Provisions for compulsory registration have been in force in Tasmania from 1839, in Western Australia from 1841, in South Australia from 1842, in Victoria from 1853, and in New South Wales and Queensland (originally part of New South Wales) from 1856. Registration in the territories is administered by the federal government, the registration having been taken over from South Australia in 1911 in respect of the Northern Territory, and from New South Wales in 1930 in respect of the Australian Capital Territory.

Prior to these dates, some records were kept by the churches, but these records are scattered and many are missing. Information about early church records can be obtained from the various registration offices listed below.

Wills are recorded with the probate divisions of the Supreme Courts of the states and territories and a list of these is also given below.

There are the following genealogical organizations in Australia:

Australian Institute of Genealogical Studies,
P.O. Box 68,
Oakleigh, Victoria 3166.

Society of Australian Genealogists,
120 Kent Street,
Sydney, New South Wales 2000.

Heraldry and Genealogical Society of Canberra,
P.O. Box E185,
Canberra, ACT 2600.

New South Wales
Broken Hill Genealogy Group,
8 Brooks Street,
Broken Hill, New South Wales 2880.

Nepean Family History Society,
784 York Road,
South Penrith, New South Wales 2750

Queensland
Queensland Family History Society,
P.O. Box 171,
Indooroopilly, Queensland 4068,
(The above society has affiliated groups but will not divulge names).

Genealogical Society of Queensland,
329 Logan Road,
Stones Corner, Queensland 4120.

Townsville Genealogical Society,
66 Kings Road,
Hermit Park, Queensland 4812.

South Australia
South Australia Genealogical Society,
P.O. Box 13,
Marden, South Australia 5070.

South East Family History Group,
P.O. Box 758,
Millicent, South Australia 5280.

Northern Yorke Peninsula Family History Group,
4 Fourth Street,
Kadina, South Australia 5554.

Tasmania

Genealogical Society of Tasmania
G.P.O. Box 640G
Hobart, Tasmania 70001.

Genealogical Society of Tasmania,
Burnie Branch,
P.O. Box 748,
Burnie, Tasmania 7320.

Genealogical Society of Tasmania,
Devonport Branch,
5 Victory Avenue,
Devonport, Tasmania 7310.

Genealogical Society of Tasmania,
Launceston Branch,
17 Outram Street,
Summerhill,
Launceston, Tasmania 7250.

Victoria

The Genealogical Society of Victoria,
98 Elizabeth Street,
Melbourne, Victoria 3000.

Western Australia

Western Australia Genealogical Society,
P.O. Box 7,
West Perth, Western Australia 6005.

Western Australia Genealogical Society,
Albany Branch,
P.O. Box 709,
Albany, Western Australia 6330.

Northern Territory

Genealogy Society of Northern Territory,
P.O. Box 37212,
Winnellie, Northern Territory 5789.

There are also a number of state and local historical societies, many of which are also concerned with genealogy:

Canberra and District Historical Society,
P.O. Box 40,
Civic Square,
Canberra, ACT 2608.

Royal Historical Society of Victoria,
459 Collins Street,
Melbourne, Victoria 3000.

Royal Western Australia Historical Society,
49 Broadway,
Nedlands, Western Australia.

WILLS
Australian Capital Territory:
  Probates Office,
  Law Courts,
  Knowles Place,
  Canberra, 2600.

New South Wales:
  Probate Division,
  Supreme Court, Queen's Square,
  Sydney, N.S.W. 2000.

Northern Territory:
  Public Trustee Office, Registration Offices,
  Attorney General's Dept.
  P.O. Box 3094,
  Darwin, N.T. 5794.

Queensland:
  Registrar of Probate,
  Supreme Court, George Street,
  Brisbane, Q. 4000.

South Australia:
  Probate Office,
  345 King William St.,
  Adelaide, S.A. 5000.

Tasmania:
  Probate Registry, Public Buildings,
  Macquarie Street,
  Hobart, Tasmania 7000.

Victoria:
  Probate and Administration Office,
  221 Queen Street,
  Melbourne, Victoria 3000.

Western Australia:
    Probate Duties,
    State Taxation Dept.,
    St. George Tce. and Barrack St.,
    Perth, W.A. 6000.

BARBADOS

Barbados was founded as a British colony in 1627 and established a parliament in 1639. The first native citizen was elected to office in 1843, and complete independence from Great Britain was achieved in 1966. The country is predominantly Protestant.

CIVIL REGISTRATION
Civil registration of births started in 1891, of marriages in 1904, and of deaths in 1924. The records are located in the Registration Office, The Law Courts, Bridgetown.

CHURCH RECORDS
Some of the parochial registers – as they are called – date back to 1644. They are located in the individual churches and in the Department of the Archives, Bridgetown.

WILLS
These go back to 1647 and are also in the Department of Archives.

INDIA

Before 1947, the sub-continent of India was under the control of the British. In 1947 it was divided between India and Pakistan and both countries became independent.

Births, marriages, and deaths were not generally recorded before 1900. However, among Hindus, whenever a person went on a pilgrimage it was, and is, the custom to register the names of the members of the family and other relatives with the *Panda*, or family priest. This register is carefully maintained by the priest and is admissible in a court of law as evidence of ancestry. These records are maintained in the local temples.

At sporadic intervals during the twentieth century – and with great reluctance – people started to register births, marriages, and deaths with the civil authorities. These authorities are the municipal committees, municipal corporations, notified areas committees, police stations, and district registrars of births and deaths. There is no central registration in force.

JAPAN

CIVIL REGISTRATION
Koseki – the Japanese system of registration – is unique. Theoretically, all Japanese, without exception, are registered. To be a *muse-kimono*, or unregistered person, is a great disgrace. No birth, marriage, or death is legally or officially recognized until the facts are entered in the register. A copy of the entry is issued on demand and serves as identification.

The registry is maintained for each household, and when a new household is established a new entry is made. The system started in 646 C.E. and in the temple at Nara you can see the register of Harube village with the first entry in 702! If you are of Japanese descent and your family lived in Harube you may be blessed above all other people!

Having said all the above, it must be stated that real, modern, systematic civil registrations started in 1870. Registration offices exist at all municipal levels – from cities to small villages. Your best plan is to write to the registration office in the district in which you are interested and find out how far back their records go and what they can tell you about your family.

CENSUSES
A census is held every five years and the modern system began in 1920. It is conducted by the Bureau of Statistics, Office of the Prime Minister, Tokyo, and all records are located there.

WILLS
Wills have existed since the Middle Ages and details of the various locations where they are held can be obtained from the Ministry of Justice, Tokyo.

It is regretted it has not been possible to obtain further information from the government of Japan.

THE HASHEMITE KINGDOM OF JORDAN

The country of Trans-Jordan was carved out of the old Ottoman Empire and was created, in 1923, under a British mandate. It became independent in 1946. In 1949 it was renamed the Hashemite Kingdom of Jordan.

The civil registration of births, marriages, and deaths started in 1927 and the records are in the custody of the Ministry of the Interior, Amman. Before civil registration the records for

Christians were kept in the local church, and for Moslems in the High Islamic Court. Wills are located in the Ministry of Justice, Amman.

LEBANON

Until the end of the First World War the country now known as Lebanon was part of the old Ottoman Empire. After 1919 the League of Nations awarded a mandate to govern Lebanon and Syria to France, which had already established a major influence in that area. This situation continued until the end of the Second World War, when Lebanon became an independent country. The population is almost equally divided between Moslems and Maronite Christians.

The civil registration of births, marriages, and deaths started in 1920. The records are kept in the Office of Vital Statistics in each district, or *Caza*. Larger districts, such as Beirut, have more than one such office. Before civil registration began, the religious authorities in each village – either Moslem or Christian – were responsible for keeping such records. However, these records do not go back far in time and they were not kept with any great degree of accuracy.

Wills for Christians have been recorded only since 1929 and are located in the district offices of the notaries public. No records of Moslem wills are available.

I am afraid this is a country where research can only really be undertaken in person, and your chances of success are no higher than fifty-fifty – particularly after the recent civil war, which has resulted in a considerable destruction of records.

NEW ZEALAND

New Zealand was discovered by the Dutch in 1642, but they did not land, and the islands were rediscovered by Captain James Cook in 1769. Permanent settlements were established by British whalers in the early nineteenth century. The first colonists arrived soon after, and the British claimed sovereignty. In 1907 New Zealand became a Dominion of the British Empire.

Before civil registration the churches were responsible for recording the various events, most of which took place in the North Auckland area – which was the earliest settled. The Methodist records are in the custody of the Methodist Church, P.O. Box 931, Christchurch, and the Anglican and Catholic records are held by the diocesan secretaries at Auckland.

Registration of European births and deaths became compulsory in 1848, and that of marriages in 1854. (The word "European" is used because registration was not required for the native population – the Maoris.) Registration of Maori births and deaths became law in 1913. In 1955 (marriages) and 1962 (births and deaths) the European and Maori laws and regulations became the same and all records were amalgamated

CIVIL REGISTRATION

The Act of 1848 required the following information for births: date and place of birth, name and sex, parents' names, occupation of father, maiden name of mother; and (from 1875) date and place of marriage, and age and birthplace of each parent.

For marriages, under the Act of 1854, the particulars required were: date and place of marriage, full names and ages of bride and groom, occupation of the groom; and (from 1880) birthplace, residence, and full names of bride and groom, and maiden name of bride.

For deaths, the Act of 1848 requires the following: date of death, full name, sex and age, occupation, cause of death; and (after 1875) names of parents, father's occupation, mother's maiden name, place of birth, and length of time in New Zealand.

If the deceased had been married, the following was required: place of marriage, age at time of marriage, name of husband or wife, sex and age of children, and date and place of burial.

MAORI REGISTRATION

This system applied to people with half or more Maori blood for the period from 1913 to 1961 for births and deaths, and from 1911 to 1954 for marriages:

BIRTHS: Date and place; first names of child and sex; full name and address of parents; tribe and degree of Maori blood in each parent.

DEATHS: Date and place; full name, address, and tribe; sex and age; name of husband or wife; number and sex of living children; cause of death; names of parents of deceased with their address, tribe, and degree of Maori blood.

MARRIAGES: These were the same as for Europeans except that the details of the parents of the bride and groom are restricted to names only.

The Office of the Registrar General in Wellington has certain regulations regarding information given to enquirers:
1. The records may only be searched by the staff.
2. A copy of a birth certificate will not give the names of the

parents. This is to prevent disclosure of illegitimate birth, but *bona fide* genealogical researchers who are relatives may be given this information at the discretion of the Registrar General.

3. Normally a marriage certificate does not show particulars of the parents unless this information is specially requested.

4. The scale of fees depends on the information requested and given. If the year of the event is not known, a search fee is payable at the rate of one dollar for every ten years.

Probates of wills are granted by the Supreme Court and there are some eighteen registries in New Zealand. Each registry keeps custody of the wills probated there. The registries are in Whangarei, Auckland, Hamilton, Rotorua, Gisborne, Napier, New Plymouth, Wanganui, Palmerston North, Masterton, Wellington, Blenheim, Nelson, Greymouth, Christchurch, Timaru, Dunedin, and Invercargill.

GENEALOGICAL SOCIETIES
New Zealand Society of Genealogists (Mrs. K. Guthrie, P.O. Box 8795, Auckland, New Zealand 3).

New Zealand Family History Society,
P.O. Box 13301,
Armagh,
Christchurch, New Zealand.

The following addresses will be useful:

The National Archives,
P.O. Box 6162,
Te Aro,
Wellington, New Zealand.

The Alexander Turnbull Library,
P.O. Box 12349,
Wellington, New Zealand.

PAKISTAN

Before 1947, the sub-continent of India was under the control of the British. In 1947 it was divided between India and Pakistan and both countries became independent. East Pakistan seceded in 1971 and became Bangla Desh.

Births, marriages, and deaths were not generally recorded before 1900. They were registered in the local mosque or temple, according to whether the people concerned were Moslem, Hindu, or Sikh. Since independence, registration now takes place with the local Union Council (the smallest administrative unit in a municipality). There is no central registration.

In 1973 civil registration was made compulsory, but before that date recording was very much "hit-and-miss", and no one should have high hopes of success.

SOUTH AFRICA

South Africa was formed in 1910 by the union of four former British colonies – Cape Colony, Natal, Orange Free State, and Transvaal. After the First World War the League of Nations awarded South Africa the mandate to govern the former German colony of South-West Africa and this territory has now been incorporated into South Africa for administrative purposes.

CIVIL REGISTRATION
The first uniform law relating to civil registration of births, marriages, and deaths was enacted in 1923, but before that time each province had its own system, of which details are given below:

CAPE COLONY: Civil registration of births and deaths started in 1894, but *voluntary* registration of births had commenced in 1880. Registration of marriages was made compulsory in 1838, but the law was not always observed. As far back as 1711 church authorities were asked to submit names of persons whose funerals were conducted by the Board of Orphan Masters, and these records exist from 1758.

NATAL: Registration of births and deaths started in 1867, and that of marriages in 1846.

ORANGE FREE STATE: Registration of births commenced in 1902, but *voluntary* registration dates from 1879. Marriages had to be recorded by the church or the magistrate from 1859, and deaths from 1871. (The nearest relative had to send the death certificate and the will to the Master of the Supreme Court in the province.)

TRANSVAAL: Registration of births and deaths started in 1900, that of marriages of Europeans in 1871, and that of marriages of non-Europeans in 1897.

SOUTH-WEST AFRICA: Registration of births, marriages, and deaths started in 1893 under the German administration.

Since the registers of the Registrar of Births, Marriages, and Deaths are closed to the public, they obviously do not constitute a valuable research source. Complete birth, marriage, and death certificates are issued on payment of a prescribed fee, but in order to obtain a birth certificate, for instance, the

following information on the person concerned must be given
to the Registrar: the child's full name, place and date of birth
(the year at least), and the names of the parents. The value of a
birth certificate to the researcher is that it can establish whether
or not the information he already possesses is correct. If the
information supplied by the researcher is incorrect, the correct
entry cannot be traced.

The indexes of the birth, marriage, and death records are in
the custody of the Registrar of Births, Marriages, and Deaths,
Department of the Interior, Private Bag X123, Pretoria 0001.
The Transvaal and Central Archives depots have the following
registers:

Cape Colony births	1842-96
Cape Colony marriages	1820-99
Natal marriages	1868-99
Orange F. S. marriages	1872-99
Transvaal marriages	1861-99

The following death registers are in the custody of the Intermediate Archives Depot:

Cape Colony	1895-1954
Natal	1863-1954
Orange F. S. marriages	1916-54
Transvaal	1888-1954
South-West Africa	1893-1954
South Africa	1955-63

Other existing birth, marriage, and death registers are in the
custody of the Registrar of Births, Marriages, and Deaths in
each province.

The addresses of the various archives are as follows:

Government Archives Depots
Cape Archives, Parliament St., Cape Town 8000.
Natal Archives, 231 Pietermaritz St., Pietermaritzburg 3200.
Orange F.S. Archives, 37 Elizabeth St., Bloemfontein 9300.
Transvaal Archives, Government Bldgs., Pretoria 0001.
Archives Depot of S.-W. Africa, P.B. 13250, Windhoek 9100.
Intermediate Archives Depot, P.B. X236, Pretoria 0001.
Central Archives Depot, P.B. X236, Pretoria 0001.

CHURCH RECORDS
Before civil registration the records of vital events were kept
by the churches. During the seventeenth and eighteenth centuries the Dutch Reformed Church (Nederduitsch Gerefor-
meerde Kerk) was the only officially recognized church
denomination in South Africa and practically all the Whites
in the Cape were members of it. The earliest baptismal, mar-

riage, and death registers in the keeping of the Church Archives (P.O. Box 3171, Cape Town 8000) date from 1665. Photocopies of the original registers until 1842 are in the custody of the Transvaal Archives.

In 1778, freedom of public religious worship was granted to the Lutherans at the Cape. The original registers of the Evangelical Lutheran Church (1780-1864) are in the vaults of the church building in Cape Town. Microfilm copies of these, as well as of the registers of the Dutch Reformed Church in Cape Province (until 1899), the Orange Free State, and Natal, are kept by the Human Sciences Research Council (Section for Genealogy). In South-West Africa the early registers are in the office of the Evangelical Lutheran Church, Windhoek 9100.

WILLS

In South Africa the custody of wills and estate records is grouped on a provincial basis. They are to be found either in the State Archives or in the offices of the various Masters of the Supreme Court. There is considerable variation as to dates of registers available between the different provinces, so you should check the two possible locations in the area in which you are interested.

For the genealogist the death notices in the estate files are of great importance. A death notice form, properly completed, usually contains the following information: the deceased's full name, place of birth, date of birth or age at time of death, place and date of death, last residential address, occupation, names of surviving and/or predeceased spouse, place of last marriage, names of the deceased's surviving children, names of the deceased's parents, the signature of the person who completed the form and in what capacity he signed it. In the case of minor children, their dates of birth are supplied. The names of the deceased's heirs and details of his or her possessions can be obtained from the will and the estate accounts. Information which was not available when the death notice was completed, such as that giving the dates of birth of minor children, is sometimes sent in later on and can then be found in the estate accounts.

The Master of the Supreme Court (or Orphan Master) has offices in Pretoria, Cape Town, Kimberley, Grahamstown, Bloemfontein, Pietermaritzburg, and Windhoek. In Pretoria all estates from 1873 to 1954 are kept in the Government Archives in the Union Buildings. All estates dating from 1955 are kept in the Master's Office in Pretoria. In Cape Town the estates up to 1916 and the indices to the estates up to 1912 are to be found in the State Archives. Estates after 1916 and the index after 1912 must be consulted at the office of the Master. Kimberley estates from 1871 to 1933 have been transferred to the State Archives in Cape Town. Those after 1933 are still in the office of the Master in Kimberley. Estates preserved by the Master in Grahamstown date from 1957. Before this all estates of the Eastern Province were sent to Cape Town.

The oldest estates in Bloemfontein date from approximately 1850 onwards and are still to be found in the office of the Master of the Supreme Court. In Pietermaritzburg the oldest estates up to 1941 have been transferred to the State Archives. The remainder are still in the office of the Master. In Windhoek all estates from 1920 onwards are kept in the office of the Master. Some of these estates are those of persons who died before 1920, but the estates were only administered after 1920. The estates from the German colonial period (Nachlassakten) up to 1915 are stored in the Government Archives in Windhoek.

GENEALOGICAL SOCIETIES
The Genealogical Society, P.O. Box 3566, Cape Town 8000, publishes a quarterly journal called *Familia* (in English and Afrikaans). The Society will also do genealogical research at a fee which will be negotiated.

BIBLIOGRAPHY
Useful books published in South Africa are:

C. C. de Villiers and C. Pama, *Genealogies of Old South African Families* (Cape Town, 1982).

J. Hoge, *Bydraes tot die genealogie van ou Kaapse families* (Amsterdam, 1958).

R. T. J. Lombard, *Handbook for Genealogical Research in South Africa* (Pretoria, 1977).

D. F. Malherbe, *Family Register of the South African Nation (Stamregister van die Suid-Afrikaanse volk)* (Stellenbosch, 1966).

E. Morse-Jones, *Roll of the British Settlers in South Africa* (Cape Town, 1969).

C. Pama, *Heraldry of South African Families* (Cape Town, 1972).

Eric Rosenthal, *South African Surnames* (Cape Town, 1965).

17. JEWISH RECORDS

The tracing of one's Jewish ancestors is a very difficult, in fact an almost impossible, task – for reasons which are obvious. All the centuries since the diaspora have seen the persecution of the Jews in almost every country in which they have settled, culminating in the pogroms of Tsarist Russia and the death camps of Germany.

Over the years the Jewish people have moved from country to country, sometimes keeping their own records, sometimes registering their vital events according to government decree. In addition, the families of a great majority of Jews in the world today – wherever they now live – originated in central Europe and Russia, and the many boundary changes and wars have changed their nationalities several times and have destroyed original records.

There is also the question of name changes – Kanofsky became Kane, Moses became Moss, Friedmann became Fried or Freed, and so on. All of these compounded problems are almost insoluble.

The first Jewish emigration to North America occurred in 1654 when twenty-three Jews from Portugal arrived, and this flow has continued ever since, with the greatest numbers arriving at the end of the last century and again after the Nazis took power in Germany in 1933.

Unfortunately, not many synagogues have kept careful records over the years, but this is the first place to try. Of course, you should follow all the steps explained in Chapters One and Three – never forgetting your own family as a source of information.

The American Jewish Archives, Hebrew Union College, Cincinnati, have collected every available record of Jews in America for the period before 1900, including synagogue records, personal letters, diaries, wills, etc. They will not undertake individual searches, but they will tell you if they have records for a particular community. So, if your Jewish ancestors came to Canada via the United States, be sure you get in touch with them.

The American Jewish Historical Society, 2 Thornton Road, Waltham, Massachusetts 02154, also has a large collection of books, biographies, manuscripts, and personal papers.

In Israel, much information about Jewish communities in Europe has been gathered together by the Jewish Historical General Archives in Jerusalem. The Archives were set up in 1949 and there are a great many documents connected with Jewish history and also some of the German Jewish archives which survived the Nazi regime. In Germany there were several lists and registers – the circumcision books (Mohel-books), the marriage contracts (Ketuboth), the memor books, the records of the burial societies (Chewra Kadischa), and cemetery lists.

The age of the German Jewish records varies according to the German state in which they were located. It is impossible to be very specific, but many records do exist from about 1800. The Archives will sell you microfilms of the records of a community for $50. Be prepared to read Hebrew or Yiddish and possibly German Gothic script!

If your ancestors did come from Germany you may get some assistance by writing to the Leo Baeck Institute, 129 East 73rd Street, New York, N.Y. 10021. If they came from eastern Europe, then try the YIVO Institute for Jewish Research, 1048 Fifth Avenue, New York, N.Y. 10028.

One other possible source of information, if your emigrant ancestor arrived in the United States, is the Index of Naturalization for New York City prior to 1906. This is in the Federal Records Archive, Army Pier, Bayonne, New Jersey.

So far as Canada is concerned the following organizations and institutions may be useful:

Montreal: Jewish Immigrant Aid Services, 5151 Côte Ste. Catherine.
Jewish Public Library, 5151 Côte Ste. Catherine.
Canadian Jewish Congress Archives, 1590 Dr. Penfield Ave.
Ottawa: Ottawa Jewish Historical Society, 151 Chapel St.
Toronto: Canadian Jewish Congress (Central Region Archives), 4600 Bathurst Street, Willowdale, Ont.
Jewish Immigrant Aid Services, 4600 Bathurst Street, Willowdale, Ont.
Winnipeg: Jewish Historical Society of Western Canada, Suite 403, 322 Donald Street.
Canadian Jewish Congress (Western Region), 370 Hargrave Street.
Vancouver: Jewish Historical Society of British Columbia, 2867 Granville Street.

In England, the records of the older families go back for three hundred years and are well documented. The original Jewish families were Sephardim or Ashkenazim (the first from Portugal and Spain, and the latter from eastern Europe).

The Sephardic Jews are fairly easy to trace because the majority stayed in or around London, and their surnames are distinctive. However, many of these names have become anglicized — Martinez to Martins, Rodriguez to Rogers, etc.

The English Jewish historian W. S. Samuel has recorded many examples of name changes, some of which are a little complicated to follow. Jews called Zevi, which in Hebrew means "stag", became Hirsch or Hirschel in Germany, and then, in England, changed the name into Hart or Harris.

For further information about Jewish records in England you should write to the Jewish Museum, Woburn House, London. Among other records, the museum contains an alphabetical index of Jewish wills dating back for some hundred and fifty years.

The Genealogical Society of the Church of Jesus Christ of Latter-Day Saints (the Mormons) has microfilmed Jewish records in over 900 communities in Poland, Hungary, and Germany. *Toledot: The Journal of Jewish Genealogy* has listed these records country by country, and town by town. (Published quarterly, 808 West End Ave., Suite 1006, New York, N.Y. 10025.)

18. PREPARING A FAMILY HISTORY

Once you have completed your family tree you should write up the history of the family. You will find it will bring the whole story of the family together and be much more interesting than just the family tree itself. When you have done it, you can send photocopies to relatives who have helped you, and, *most important*, you can lodge copies with the local library in the place where your family originated, and also with the Genealogical Society of your country – if such an organization exists. This will be of help and interest to the generations which come after you.

A family history sets out in easy-to-read language the family story from your earliest ancestor; but it should also include some general history, information about conditions in the Old Country, and possible reasons for the emigration of your ancestor. At this point you will find your genealogical research leads you into new fields – into social history, so you can find out *how* your ancestors lived, as well as where they lived.

Perhaps an example will help to show you what I mean. Below, with the names and addresses changed to preserve privacy, you will find a family history I wrote some years ago for a Canadian family whose ancestors I had traced.

THE HISTORY OF THE DENNIS FAMILY OF IRELAND AND CANADA

The earliest known mention of a Dennis in Ireland is in 1693 (James Dennis of Drumore, County Down, leased some property).

It seems probable that the Dennis family arrived in Ulster as part of the Ulster Plantation, or Settlement, which was at its height between 1600 and 1700. At this time many thousands of Protestants from Scotland and northern England were given grants of land in Ireland, and the native Irish were killed or dispossessed. Dennis is a North Country name and is certainly not native to Ireland.

By the middle 1700s the members of the family were merchants or small farmers. In 1735 a person by the name of Dennis appears as the owner of the farm of Carra, near Ballyaran, County Down, and that farm remained in the family for just over two hundred years. The original house is still in existence, but has been modernized and is not easily recognizable as an old house.

From Carra, the family spread into the rich farmland of the surrounding area. Over the years the family farmed in Hillbridge (where it still is), Rathburn, Drumoyne, Edenbridge, and a dozen other small villages or townlands.

All seems to have gone well with the family until the early 1800s when the first of the great potato famines came, and the mass emigration to North America commenced. In the early part of the nineteenth century (between 1830 and 1850) the situation in Ireland could not have been worse. There was little or no industry and ninety per cent of the population depended on casual work on the farms. At that time seventy-five per cent of the working population was unemployed — victim to absentee English landlords and a complete lack of economic planning.

The small part of the land in Irish hands had been divided and subdivided so that the average small-holding was less than one acre. The Irish peasant never ate meat and was dependent on potatoes grown on his small patch and eked out with meal. Starvation came in the summer when the old crop was eaten and the new crop was not yet ready. June, July, and August were known as the "meal months".

The meal was imported from overseas and had to be bought for cash. The Irish worker — with no money to his name — had to borrow against his pay in the fall when the potatoes were harvested on the lands of the big landlords. Every village had its "gombeen man", or money-lender, who would lend at twenty-five per cent interest and then collect his repayments directly from the landlord. Few workers ever saw the money they earned in a fifteen-hour day in the fields at a wage of one shilling a day!

In those days the population of Ireland was eight million — double what it is today. In the early 1800s one million Irish emigrated, mostly to the United States and Canada.

The fare to New York or Quebec was £7. In 1845, 103,000 people sailed from Ireland in the first three months of the year. They sailed in "coffin ships" — ancient, leaking, overcrowded, and badly provisioned. Passengers were supposed to get seven pounds of provisions per person per week, but rarely saw any of it. A ship licensed to carry two hundred passengers would squeeze four hundred aboard. Passengers slept on floors, and there were no sanitary arrangements. The voyage across the Atlantic took from six to eight weeks and hundreds died of cholera, dysentry, exposure, and malnutrition.

Even this appalling voyage, with all its death and suffering, was better than conditions back in Ireland. The potato crop failed in

1832, 1836, 1837, 1839, 1841, and 1844, and utter starvation was widespread in the country.

James Dennis, who was born at Carra in 1809, arrived in Toronto in 1841. He married Mary Ryan at Trinity Church soon after he came here. They first settled at 212 King Street, and their names appear in the *Toronto Directory* for 1842. Their first child, John, was born there in 1843. He was baptized at Trinity Church, and John Ryan, Mary's brother, was one of the godparents. Presumably the child was named after him.

James worked as a brickmaker, and during the next few years his wife gave birth to two more children – Mary, in 1844, and James, in 1846. Mary died at the age of six, but her brother James grew up, married, and had several children; but so far as can be found, he has only one living descendant – William Dennis of Brampton, now aged eighty-four and unmarried.

James died in 1848 and is buried in the cemetery on Parliament Street. His widow continued to live at the address on King Street and in the 1849 *Toronto Directory* her occupation is given as milliner. A widow with three young children below the age of seven must have had quite a struggle to make a living. She did not appear in the *Directory* after 1854 – she may have remarried, or left the city. There is no record of her death (or remarriage) in the local church.

Her first son, John, appears in the *Directory* in 1866 as a brick-maker in Leslieville. He had married Ann Thomas in the previous year – when he was twenty.

Leslieville was located at what is now King Street and Leslie Street and was a separate village with a population of four hundred. A coach ran twice daily to Toronto. The village was named after the first settler in the area, George Leslie, who owned a large nursery. It was also the main centre for brick manufacture in the area. John's brother, James, also lived in the village with his five sons – all six of them were fishermen. It must be remembered that there were salmon in the River Don in those days!

Following John's progress through the *Toronto Directory* it is clear that he must have prospered as a brickmaker, as he followed that trade in Leslieville until his death in 1914. One son, also a John, was in the business with him, and the second son, Robert, became an engineer in Hamilton.

Note: At this point the family history concerned itself with the present generation and this is not of great interest. I hope I have shown you enough to demonstrate how you can turn your family tree into an interesting story for yourself and your family.

You could, of course, expand the story further by including more details about the various characters – how much they were paid; what their houses cost; where they bought their clothes; what amusements existed at that time; what they ate and how much it cost; what taxes they paid; and so on. All this information can be found in street directories, local history books at the library, and municipal records.

19. HERALDRY AND COATS-OF-ARMS

Heraldry is quite a different subject from genealogy, but occasionally there is some contact, and for this reason any book on ancestor-hunting should include a section on heraldry. First, let me say there is little chance you or your family have any right to a coat-of-arms. You may have had a circular letter from some company offering you a copy of your family coat-of-arms for $10 — you may even have had the offer of a whole dinner service with your coat-of-arms, or even a tastefully designed shield to hang in your toilet, or wherever. There are coat-of-arms book matches, and lampshades, and notepaper, and wine glasses, and book plates and bookmarks, and silverware and tankards, and decals for the car and boat, and flags and pennants. It is big business, but it has no basis in fact.

How it works is simple. Let us say your name is Adams and you are foolish enough to mail your money. You will receive an Adams coat-of-arms all right, but it will not be *your* coat-of-arms. So far as England or any European country is concerned, the right to a coat-of-arms was granted by the Head of State to a particular individual "and his heirs in the male line". This means that this person and his son and his grandson and so on are the only ones with a right to use a particular coat-of-arms.

So far as you are concerned, you have received a copy of a coat-of-arms granted at some time to a man with the same name as yourself. He could have been a man who owned vast estates in England in the Middle Ages, or he could have been a man who sold inferior uniforms to the British Army in the First World War and was knighted for his services. In any case, he was no ancestor of yours.

Although grants of arms are still made in Britain, it was in the Middle Ages that most coats-of-arms were registered. How did it all start?

The historian Herodotus, writing four hundred years before Christ, said, "The Carians seem to be the first who put crests upon their helmets and sculptured devices upon their shields." Caria was in Asia Minor, on what is now the Mediterranean coast of Turkey. From that time on there were many references to shields and ornamentation and devices. Once a man had a shield to use in battle it was a natural development for him to decorate it so it was recognizable and other men would be able to identify the mighty warrior from afar.

In the Middle Ages, everyone fought – the knight because knights were expected to fight or because he owed allegiance to his king or because he wanted the estates of his next-door neighbour, or even his next-door neighbour's lovely daughter. The ordinary man fought because the knight owned him and told him what to do. The knight's men-at-arms then started to wear a linen surcoat over their chain-mail armour. Originally it was to stop the armour getting wet and rusty in damp climates or too hot in hot climates. The next step was to decorate the surcoat with a symbol so that each man knew who was for him and who was against him. Usually the symbol was taken from the arms of the knight or earl or king who owned the soldiers. Thus the surcoat became known as the coat-of-arms.

Remember, only a comparatively few people were given the right to have their own coat-of-arms. It was the king of the country who made the gift, and naturally it went to someone who was a member of the small circle around the throne. It was not until the early seventeenth century that grants of arms were given more generously and wealthy businessmen received them, plus a title. Because such a small percentage of the population had the right to a coat-of-arms, it follows that only a few people alive today, in proportion to the total population, have inherited that right.

However, it may be that you will discover a genuine family coat-of-arms, and this chapter will tell you what it is, how you find it, and what you do with it.

In England, the approval of coats-of-arms, and, if necessary, the proving of the right to them, is the responsibility of the College of Arms in London. This is headed by the Earl Marshal of England – a hereditary title always borne by the Duke of Norfolk.

He and his staff are responsible for all the great state pageantries of England and Wales – funerals of kings and queens and princes and princesses; their marriages and christenings; the coronations, and so on. In the hierarchy of the College of Arms, the Earl Marshal is followed by the Kings-of-Arms, the Heralds-of-Arms, and the Pursuivants-of-Arms. The various titles have evolved over the centuries, and the origin of some of the names is unknown. In the early Middle Ages each ruler had a personal herald whose job it was to sing the praises of the king, to announce the events at a tournament, and to issue formal challenges from the king to his opponent in battle.

Employment at the College is in great demand among those

interested in heraldry, although the rate of pay is nominal. Of course, members of the staff also obtain income from the tracing and proving of the right of your ancestors to bear arms – proving your descent from an armigerous family as it is called.

There are three Kings-of-Arms – Garter, Clarenceux, and Norroy. Garter is the principal King-of-Arms, and the deputy of the Earl Marshal. The other two are provincial Kings-of-Arms. Clarenceux is responsible for that part of the country south of the River Trent, and Norroy for everything to the north of the river.

The Heralds number six – Chester, Windsor, Lancaster, and York, originally instituted by Edward III (1327-77), Richmond, instituted by Edward IV (1461-83), and Somerset instituted by Henry VIII (1509-47).

The Pursuivants are Rouge-Croix, Blue-Mantle, Rouge-Dragon, and Portcullis. Rouge-Croix is named from the red cross of St. George in the Arms of England, Blue-Mantle from the blue mantle of France assumed by Edward III, Rouge-Dragon from the Arms of Wales, and Portcullis from the badge of Henry VII.

In Scotland, the equivalent of the Earl Marshal is the Lyon King-of-Arms, known as the Lord Lyon, or simply as "The Lyon". (I visited him not too long ago, and when his secretary said, "The Lyon is waiting for you now," I felt like an early Christian!) His office is not hereditary and the appointment is made by the Crown. There are three Heralds in Scotland – Ross, Rothesay, and Albany – and three Pursuivants – Unicorn, Falkland, and Carrick.

The Office of Arms in Ireland is headed by the Ulster King-of-Arms. Under him is a Pursuivant named Athlone. There are also two Heralds, attached to the Order of St. Patrick and called Dublin and Cork.

Garter, Lyon, and Ulster are respectively Kings-of-Arms of the Orders of the Garter, the Thistle, and St. Patrick. In England the Kings-of-Arms, Heralds, and Pursuivants are appointed by the Crown. In Scotland the Heralds and Pursuivants are appointed by the Lord Lyon.

In Europe, although coats-of-arms go back as far or further than in the United Kingdom, no institution similar to the College-of-Arms exists. However, in Germany, Austria, Belgium, the Netherlands, Norway, Sweden, and Spain there are various non-governmental offices which regulate the use of coats-of-arms.

A coat-of-arms consists of a shield bearing the heraldic device of the family. It can be divided into quarters, and still further sub-divided to include the arms of families whose daughters married into the family. All these divisions are called quarterings, and there is at least one family in England whose shield bears no less than 356 quarterings (the Lloyds of Stockton-on-Cherbury, Salop).

Heraldic terms need a book of their own, and are not really understandable without some study; for example, two lions on a shield, each facing in opposite directions, are described as "Or, two lions passant counter-passant gules, the uppermost facing the sinister side of the escutcheon, both collared sable, garnished argent." This tells us the shield is gold, the lions red, one is facing left, both are wearing a black collar decorated with silver.

Above the shield is the Helmet, or Helm, and that is surmounted by a Wreath (or Torse) and a Crest. The latter is often something like a mailed fist clutching a sword, or a boar's head. There is a kind of drapery, which comes out from the helmet and hangs down each side of the shield, and this is called the mantling. Below the shield is the motto – usually in Latin. This can be a play upon words which includes the name of the family, or some worthy expression of opinion, like *In Recto Acer* (Vigorous in pursuit of the right).

If, as you trace back in your family, you find they were what is called "landed gentry", i.e., gentlemen owning land, or there was a title somewhere, or they held officer rank in the Army or Navy, then there is a good chance they did have a coat-of-arms. In that case, there are several books to check, and also several books about heraldry if you wish to study this exotic and erudite subject:

HERALDRY

Sir Anthony Wagner, *Heraldry in England* (London, 1946).
Francis Grant, *The Manual of Heraldry* (London, 1924).
A. C. Fox-Davies, *Complete Guide to Heraldry* (London, 1969).

FAMILY COATS-OF-ARMS

Bernard Burke, *The General Armoury of England, Scotland, Ireland, and Wales* (London, 1883).
James Fairbairn, *Crests of the families of Great Britain* (London, 1905).
Burke's Peerage

There are many more books on the subject to be found in English libraries. One very good source of information is a book (and there are several) listing the Heralds' visitations. They had trouble back in the sixteenth century with people using arms to which they were not entitled, and so the Heralds were sent out across the land in periodic visitations. People using arms had to prove their right to do so, and several books are available which list alphabetically those people who proved their right, county by county.

If you can find no mention of a family coat-of-arms, but still want to make sure, you can write to one of the Heralds and ask them what it would cost for them to check their records for you (the College of Arms is not open to the public, and you may not search for yourself). You will be charged a fairly large fee. You can also arrange for a grant of a coat-of-arms to *you* and your heirs, and this will cost about a thousand dollars. In Scotland and Ulster the charges are a little less.

When you have traced your ancestors, you may want an elegant edition of the family tree, prepared by a heraldic artist. One I can suggest, recommended by the Heraldry Society, is Miss Karen E. Bailey, Apt. 3, 130 Maclaren Street, Ottawa, Ontario K2P 0L1. If you have a description of your official coat-of-arms, she can also include a painting of the shield, motto, and crest with your family tree.

There is a Heraldry Society of Canada and you can get details of membership by writing to F. D'Alton Gooderham, 125 Lakeway Drive, Ottawa, Ont. K1L 5A9.

Finally, let me revert to the subject of the various so-called family coats-of-arms being offered in the mail at the moment. The following may amuse you.

A friend of mine publishes a magazine for the dental profession. It is called *Oral Health* and is listed under that name in the Toronto telephone directory. Last year he received the following letter in the mail:

> Sovereign Heraldry,
> A Division of Sovereign
> Seat Cover Mfg. Ltd.,
> 563 Boundary Road,
> Cornwall, Ont., K6H 6B4

Dear Mr. Oral,
Did you know that the family name Oral now has an exclusive and particularly beautiful Coat of Arms? This may surprise you, since Oral is an extremely rare name. Of the 7 million households in Canada, fewer than 50 carry the Oral name. We discovered this while doing some research on family names.

We have had one of our trained heraldic artists interpret the Oral Coat of Arms as the heralds in medieval times did it for the knights and noblemen. This drawing, along with other information about the name, has been printed up into an attractive one-page report which you may want to have.

Not all family names, of course, have a coat-of-arms. But your name has one now and I thought you might like a copy. The entire report is personal and individually prepared on parchment paper suitable for framing.

The right hand side of the report tells the unique story of the Oral Coat of Arms. The left half has a large beautiful reproduction of the artist's drawing.

These reports make distinctive wall decorations and they are great gifts for relatives. It should be remembered that we have not traced anyone's individual family tree, but have done extensive research to prepare the Oral report.

The price for the Oral report is surprisingly low. Since our biggest expense was in researching and writing the original report, extra copies don't cost us nearly as much as the original. So we're not charging very much (See below).

If you are interested, please let us know right away. Just fill in the enclosed order form and send the correct amount in cash or check for the number of reports you want. You may use the self-addressed reply envelope. It needs no stamp. We'll send your reports by first class mail.

Sincerely,

SHIRLEY I. MCDONALD

P.S. If you are ordering one report, send $3. Additional reports ordered at the same time and sent to the same address are $2 each.

I think that should be the final comment on the family coats-of-arms business – though I do wonder what coat-of-arms Shirley came up with for Mr. Health Oral. Maybe a set of artificial dentures, garnished argent, quartered with a face gules?

20. A PERSONAL EXPERIENCE

I think it may be interesting to you to talk about a personal experience of mine that happened twenty-seven years ago in England when I was starting to trace my wife's ancestors. It is a good example of the difficulties one experiences in ancestor-hunting and how the whole problem can eventually be solved by a combination of hard work and good luck.

My wife was born in Scotland and her maiden name was Pearson. She could already trace back to her great-great-grandfather and during all that time the family had been located in the border country of Scotland – in Dumfriesshire. Her grandparents on both sides were dead and so there was no aged relative available to consult about any family stories. However, her uncle told us that as a child he had heard – probably from his grandfather – that the family had originally come from England some two hundred years before. We kept this in mind but did not let it affect our initial search.

We did three things to start:

1. We wrote to every Pearson in the telephone directories for the whole border area of Scotland. (There were about thirty of these – the majority of people in Great Britain do not have telephones.) We gave details of what we knew about the family and asked them to get in touch with us.

2. We did the same thing for Pearsons in the various county directories and asked them the same questions.

3. We wrote letters to the editors of three local newspapers and asked the co-operation of their readers. (This was aimed mainly at any Pearson women who had married and changed their name – or their descendants, of course.)

All this brought in about a hundred letters and, as a result, we were able to link nearly all of them up with our existing family tree. Of course, there was a lot of duplication, since we heard from several members of the same section of the family, but this served as a double or triple check on dates and places. As a result we were able to zero in on a particular area.

My wife's great-grandfather was John Pearson, of Leadhills, Dumfriesshire (1818-97). We found details of his birth in the parish registers of that parish, and also, of course, details of his brothers and his sister — Thomas, Susannah, and William. We found that his father was William Pearson (who married Helen Hamilton in 1810).

William Pearson was born in 1781 and died in 1837. His father was David Pearson (who married Nellie Fleming in 1774). We found that David was born at Leadhills in 1741 and died in 1812. This, in turn, led us to his father, another David, who died in a neighbouring village (Sanquhar) in 1754. He was born in 1705.

During the course of all this we were able to link up the various Pearsons who had written to us because, of course, apart from tracing the direct line of my wife's ancestors, we also found the various brothers and sisters and their children. Fortunately, in those days people did not move around very much, and if we did not find them in one parish we found them in the neighbouring one.

David's father was Christopher Pearson, who died in the village of Sanquhar in 1710, aged forty-one. (At that time we could not find the name of his wife or details of his marriage because there were gaps in the church register.) In addition, although we knew he was forty-one when he died, and that meant he was born in 1669, we could find no mention of his birth.

So we then searched the registers of every parish within fifty miles, and not only was there no mention of Christopher's birth, but there were no other Pearsons anywhere — not a single one!

We checked and rechecked and then we remembered the fact that the family was supposed to have come from England two hundred years ago! This must have been the man who came from England! Two facts supported this supposition: no other Pearsons had been born in the whole area except for his children; and the name Christopher is an English name and not a Scottish one.

Now, we knew one more fact about Christopher. In the entry of death in the church register he was described as "overseer of the lead-mines in Wanlockhead". This is a village which lies midway between Leadhills and Sanquhar. The lead mines were the main local industry, apart from farming.

Well, it was one thing to believe Christopher came from England, but it was quite another thing to find the exact place. How on earth could we find this out? We thought about his occupation — overseer of the lead mines. This was a skilled job that needed training and experience. It was not the kind of occupation that anyone could do. He must have had a similar job in the place from which he came.

So I wrote to the Ministry of Mines, in London, and asked if they could tell me where lead was mined in the period from

1689 to 1705 – this covered the years from when he was aged twenty to the date of birth of his eldest child (David) in Scotland. I specified the area close to the Scottish border, again working on the principle that people did not travel too far. This enquiry covered the English counties of Cumberland and Northumberland.

I soon heard back from the Ministry. They were most helpful and gave me a list of nearly a hundred and fifty places where lead had been mined! I had been expecting maybe twenty, but a hundred and fifty! However, I started writing to the local minister of each of the places mentioned, starting with those the nearest to our home. After negative replies from twenty of them, all telling me there was no birth entry for Christopher in 1669, we said, "There must be an easier way than this." Once again, we sat and meditated about the whole problem. Then my wife said, "Who owned the lead mines in Wanlockhead when Christopher was overseer? Perhaps there are employment records somewhere?"

This was a brilliant idea; and so we started on this line of investigation and eventually found that the mines (which had been closed for seventy years) were owned by the Duke of Buccleuch. So I wrote to the Duke and told him our problem. He wrote back and said he was very sorry, but there were no records of the mines before 1814 when there had been a strike and a riot and the mine office had been set on fire.

That seemed to be that, but a couple of months later, the Duke wrote to me again and said he had been thinking about the problem since my first letter and had remembered that there was a Miners' Welfare Library, and although the mines had been closed for so many years, he knew the books were in the custody of a Mrs. Weir, in Leadhills, and perhaps there might be a book there which could be a help.

So, not long after this, my wife and I paid a visit to Mrs. Weir – a very pleasant old lady. We told her about what we now called – in capital letters – THE PROBLEM. She said the books, about two hundred of them, were stored in the attic, but she was sure there was nothing there of any use. They were all religious books designed "to elevate the moral and spiritual tone" of the miners. So there we were, back to square one!

Two months later, Mrs. Weir wrote to us and said she had been looking through the books in the attic and had found one called *God's Treasure House of Scotland* – an account by an old minister of visits he had paid to various country churchyards in the Sanquhar area of Scotland. In it, he described the church at Sanquhar and its kirkyard and tombstones and throughstones (throughstones were horizontal tombstones which rested on four legs at a height of about eighteen inches above the grave). He did not stop there, and in his own words wrote, "There is the resplendent tombstone of Christopher Pearson, overseer of the leadmines. The top of the through-stone, with a beautiful border of ivy leaves, bears this inscription:

Here lyes Christopher Pearson, overseer of the Lead Works in Wanlockhead. He was born at Bishopfield, in the parish of Allendale, in the County of Northumberland, and dyed July 27th, 1710, aged 41.

This, of course, was the most wonderful stroke of luck – not only because it told us where Christopher came from but also because the book (written in 1876) described a tombstone which no longer exists. Many months before we had checked all the local graveyards, including Sanquhar. Somewhere about 1880 the road by the kirkyard had been widened, and a number of tombstones had been moved and lost – including that of Christopher Pearson.

Our next move was to rush to our local library and look up the *County History of Northumberland*. We found the right volume for the Allendale area of the county, and looked up the index. There we found an entry which read "Pearson of the Spital, family tree", and also another entry entitled "Christopher Pearson". We turned to the pages that were indicated and there we found not only the Pearson family tree taking us back to the fifteenth century, but also included in the tree was Christopher Pearson, born 1669. About Christopher there was "No further information".

In other words, Christopher had left home and the local historians who had compiled the family tree did not know where he had gone. The Pearson family were the great land-owners of the district, Lords of the Manors of Haltwhistle and Allendale, owners of many farms, *and* owners of the local lead mines in Allendale. There were pages of information about the family and references to other books which, in turn, gave us even more information about them.

We wondered how Christopher had come to leave home and settle in Dumfriesshire, and we still wondered whom he had married when he got there, but *at that time* we could not answer these questions.

We left Christopher in abeyance for a while and again concentrated on going further back with the Pearson family. We were most successful – considering that we were working in a period before the existence of the earliest church registers, and into the area I mentioned in the chapter on England and Wales – land records, tax rolls, feet of fines, pipe rolls, and so on. We eventually traced the family back to Wautier Pieressone, Count of Berwick, who was alive in 1296 and was mentioned in the Ragman's Roll as pledging allegiance to Edward I of England when he invaded Scotland.

Christopher was born at a farm called Bishopfield, in the parish of Allendale. He had two brothers and three sisters. One brother, William, died at the age of sixteen. The elder brother, Robert, inherited the farm from his father (also named Robert) in 1695. Christopher was twenty-six then and, presumably, looking after the family lead mines while his brother farmed. Both the sons were mentioned in the father's will:

To my eldest son, Robert Pearson, five hundred pounds, and to my second son, Christopher, two hundred and fifty pounds.

To my eldest son, Robert, one bedstead, one table, one iron pot, and all my oxen gear with plows and harrows.

To my sons, Robert and Christopher, all the rest of the gear belonging to the husbandry.

To my son Christopher one bedstead in the loft.

There were many other bequests to the daughters and the third son.

Christopher's brother married Catherine Fairless and died in 1753. The farm of Bishopfield was then bought by the Fairless family and today – over two hundred years later – it is still owned and occupied by the family. Since the Pearsons built the farm in 1609, on land which they had owned since 1480, it means that in a period of five hundred years only the two families of Pearson and Fairless have owned the property – quite a record!

We went to Northumberland and met the Fairless family and we have kept in touch with them over the years. This led to a quite extraordinary event which I'll tell you about a little later on.

In digging into the Pearson family history in Northumberland we discovered a very colourful character – a first cousin of Christopher (and his brother Robert) – called William, who was born in 1670, a year after Christopher. William had one sister, Mary, who married a Matthew Leadbitter.

In 1715 an army crossed the border from Scotland, marching on London in an attempt to put the Stuarts back on the throne – in particular James, The Old Pretender, father of Bonnie Prince Charlie. The Earl of Derwentwater, the greatest landowner in the north and a cousin of the Old Pretender, raised a force of several hundred men in Northumberland to join the invading army. William Pearson, also a cousin of the Earl, joined him in the rebellion and became a colonel in the rebel forces. He took part in the Battle of Preston, during which the rebels were defeated, and was taken prisoner and nearly hanged. He escaped from his guard and some months later was arrested near his cousin Robert's house at Bishop-field. The other leaders were all executed but Colonel Pearson was lucky. He was only fined, but it must have been a large sum because in that year he sold the Manor of Haltwhistle for £1100 and the family home at Hexham, the Spital, for £1325. This we found out, of course, from land records. He died six years later at the age of thirty-one.

We also found reference to an oil painting of him and thought how wonderful it would be if it was possible to trace it – if, by any chance, it still existed. We knew he had no children to inherit from him; and then we thought of his sister, Mary, who married Matthew Leadbitter. Could she have inherited the painting? If so, what had happened to the Lead-bitter family in the last two hundred and thirty years?

So, we then traced the Leadbitter family and found that the head of the family was Sir John Leadbitter, Clerk to the Privy Council in London. I wrote and asked him if, by chance, the portrait still existed. He replied and said, "Yes, my brother in Devonshire has it." We were thrilled, and off we went to Devon to see the portrait. It showed William Pearson with long, fairish hair, wearing an apricot-coloured velvet jacket, with lace at his neck and wrists. He was obviously a bold and resolute character and, strangely enough, bore a very great resemblance to my wife's father!

On the back of the portrait the following remarks were written by an uncle (born in 1835) of Sir John Leadbitter and his brother:

My father (born 1787) I am sorry to say does not know much about Colonel Pearson. Our late uncle Nicholas (born 1786) and Uncle Charlton were well up in all these matters. From his recollection he was present at the Battle of Preston, on the Jacobite side, and his title was taken from his association with Charles Stuart's forces. At the aforesaid battle he was taken prisoner and nearly hanged. He was renowned as a very brave, resolute, and determined man. He once started to fight a duel with swords with a man in a yard in London, and his antagonist bolted over a wall and disappeared – not liking the prospect.

That was the end of the Pearson story at that time, but ancestor-hunting never really stops – one is always looking for a few more bits of information. Over the years since then we have filled a few gaps:

1. From the sasine registers in Scotland we found that Chris-

topher Pearson's widow was Margaret Cunningham. So that finally told us who he had married (the sasines are transfers of land in Scotland – see Chapter Ten).

2. From an old history of lead-mining in Scotland we found

that the lead mines in Wanlockhead were leased in 1691 to a Matthew Wilson, of Allendale, Northumberland. The Wilsons were connected by marriage to the Pearsons and also owned a lead mine near by, so that was the reason young Christopher left home and became overseer in Wanlockhead – probably in the year when the mines were leased and when he would be twenty-two years old.

There was one more extraordinary happening in our search for the Pearson ancestors. A few years ago I went back to the ancestral homes of my wife and myself in England – to Bishopfield, in Northumberland, and to Bampton Hall, in Westmorland – to collect from each a stone to bring back home to Canada and cement into a wall at my house. This was just a small bit of nonsense to link the Old World with the New.

While I was at Bishopfield having lunch with the Fairless family, Mrs. Fairless said, "Last year, we took down the old barn at the back of the farm, and in the rafters, in the high V of the roof, we found a sliding panel and a secret hiding-place. In it were the remains of a straw mattress, a couple of water bottles, and a pistol. We cleaned the pistol up and sent it to the British Museum for identification. They told us it had markings on it which showed it had been issued to an army officer in the year 1715. Now, how on earth could that have got there?"

"I think I can hazard a very good guess," I replied. "Robert Pearson, who built this house, had a cousin William, who was a colonel in the rebel forces in 1715. We know he was taken prisoner at the Battle of Preston, escaped, and some months later was arrested near here. As he was an officer, he would be guarded by an officer. When he escaped he probably did so by hitting his guard over the head and taking off, with the pistol, for this part of the country, where he knew he could get food and shelter. His closest relative was his cousin Robert, who probably had the hiding-place built so William could hide whenever the search got too close for comfort. One day he was probably careless and got caught out in the open."

"I think you are absolutely right," said Mrs. Fairless, holding out the pistol, "so here it is – take it back to Canada and give it to your wife; the Pearsons have a better right to it than the Fairless family."

APPENDIX: THE MORMON RECORDS

The Genealogical Society of the Church of Jesus Christ of Latter-Day Saints (popularly known as the Mormons) possesses the greatest single source of genealogical information in the whole world, and no one starting off on an ancestor-hunt should do so without checking the records available in the library of this Society. It is not necessary to be a member of the Church, or even to approve of its teachings, to be able to use its records.

The Latter-Day Saints' interest in genealogy stems from their theological belief that family relationships and family associations are intended to be eternal, and not limited to a short period of mortality. Church members "sealed together" are not married only "until death do you part". It is believed the husband and wife and their children remain together throughout eternity as a family unit, with their ancestors and posterity.

Members of the Church collect genealogical data about their ancestors in order to perform "sealing" ceremonies in temples erected for the purpose. Before the sealings of families from generation to generation can be performed, the families must be properly identified. This is done by using the records of the Genealogical Society, which is located at 50 East North Temple Street, Salt Lake City, Utah 84150.

The Society is engaged in the most active and comprehensive genealogical programme ever known. Microfilming is the heart of the operation, and trained specialists are microfilming records each day in thirty-eight countries around the world. Documents such as parish registers, land grants, deeds, probate records, marriage bonds, and cemetery records are being microfilmed. More than 1,100,000 rolls of microfilm are in the library and several thousand new rolls are being added each month. There are over 200,000 printed volumes on the shelves (including 1,655 from Canada). Over three hundred new books are being added monthly.

There are records of over ten million families and sixty million names in the International Genealogical Index. A microfilm copy of the card catalogue, showing the holdings of the

Library, is available at all Church branch libraries. In Canada
the locations of these branches are:

Alberta: Edmonton, Calgary, Lethbridge, Cardston, Red Deer
British Columbia: Vancouver, Vernon, Cranbrook
Ontario: Toronto, Ottawa, Hamilton, London
Saskatchewan: Saskatoon

There are also a number of libraries in the United States
close to the United States–Canada border, and the addresses
of these can be obtained from the Genealogical Society. Microfilms can be ordered through any branch library and viewed at
that library.

In addition to the microfilms the Society has available a
large number of research papers containing genealogical
information from many different countries. These can be
ordered from the General Church Distribution Center, P.O.
Box 11627, Salt Lake City, Utah 84111.

If you are able to visit the Library in person (3,000 people do
every day) you will find four hundred microfilm viewers available, and all the printed volumes on open shelves for easy
access. The parish registers are indexed and printed in alphabetical order, so that a search for a particular individual can be
made very quickly.

However, remember that the extracts from the parish registers are not always accurate and the original registers should
be checked. Do not accept the Mormon records as the last
word.

The Genealogical Society has made sure that its records will
never be accidentally destroyed. In the Wasatch Range of the
Rockies is Granite Mountain. Under and in this mountain is
the Records Vault. There is three hundred feet of solid granite
above the office area, and seven hundred feet above the six
enormous storage rooms which contain the negative prints of
the microfilms.

The Society Library does not have a sufficient staff to do
research for people, but it will answer one or two specific questions. If more detailed information is required the Library will
mail you a list of accredited researchers. When asking for this
list be sure you specify the country in which you are interested.
You can then make your own financial arrangements with the
researcher you have selected.

BIBLIOGRAPHY

This is not intended to be a complete list of all possible books about genealogy. There is not enough room to give details of all the books written on the subject – after all, you must do some of the work yourself! This list includes some of the books I have found most useful over many years in tracing my own ancestors and those of my wife and of many people who have come to me for assistance. It does not include books written about individual families or small localities. Once you have found a particular area in which you are interested you should get in touch with the public library in the district, the local genealogical or historical society if one exists, or the local or national archives.

I have listed the Canadian books which will give you information about the early settlement of the various provinces – although there are very few of these (except for Quebec and the Acadian area).

Generally speaking, you will find the English-speaking countries have the greatest wealth of genealogical literature.

At the end of this section I give details of the national libraries of various countries – write to them for more details about the area of the foreign country in which you are interested.

4. CANADIAN CHURCH RECORDS

ANGLICAN

LEE, HERBERT. *An Historical Sketch of the First Fifty Years of the Church of England in the Province of New Brunswick, 1781-1833.* Saint John, 1880.

BAPTIST

BILL, I. E. *The Baptists of Saint John, New Brunswick, 1805-1891.*

———. *Fifty Years with the Baptists of the Maritime Provinces.* Saint John, 1880.

FITCH, E. R. *The Baptists of Canada.* Toronto, 1911.

GREENWOOD, W. R. *The Early Baptists of Cambridge Park, Nova Scotia.* 1941.

IVISON, STUART, and ROSSER, FRED. *The Baptists in Upper and Lower Canada Before 1820.* Toronto, 1956.

MENNO. *The Baptists of Nova Scotia, 1760-1860.* 1863.

SAUNDERS, E. M. *History of the Baptists of the Maritime Provinces, 1829-1916.* Halifax, 1902.

SHIELDS, T. T. *The Plot That Failed*. Toronto, 1937.

TARR, L. K. *This Dominion, His Dominion*. Willowdale, Ont., 1967.

WARREN, W. H. *A Century of Baptist History on Prince Edward Island*. 1920.

MENNONITE

EPP, FRANK. *Mennonites in Canada, 1786-1920*. Toronto, 1974.

———. *Mennonites in Canada, 1920-1940*. Toronto, 1982.

SCHAEFER, PAUL. *Woher? Wohin? Mennoniten*. 4 vols. Altona, Man., 1946. (The Mennonites in Russia and North America.)

METHODIST

LENCH, C. *The Story of Methodism in Bonavista, Newfoundland*. 1919.

5 to 8. CANADA – GENERAL

BOYER, CARL. *Ship Passenger Lists (U.S.)*. 3 vols. Newhall, California, 1978.

BRYCE, G. *The Scotsman in Western Canada*. Toronto, 1911.

CAMPBELL, W. *The Scotsman in Eastern Canada*. Toronto, 1911.

GELLNER, J. *The Czechs and the Slovaks in Canada*. Toronto, 1968.

GUILLET, EDWARD. *The Great Migration*. Toronto, 1963.

JONASSEN, E. *Icelandic Families*. Winnipeg, 1974.

*KAMINOW, J., and KAMINOW, M. *A List of Emigrants to America, 1718-1759*. New York, 1964.

KAYE, VLADIMIR. *Early Ukrainian Settlements in Canada, 1895-1900*. Toronto, 1964.

*LANCOUR, A. H. *A Bibliography of Ship's Passenger Lists, 1538-1825*. New York, 1963.

MORTON, A. S. *A History of the Canadian West to 1870-71*. Rev. ed. Toronto, 1973.

STANLEY, G. F. G. *The Birth of Western Canada*. Rev. ed. Toronto, 1960.

TEPPER, MICHAEL. *New World Immigrants*. 2 vols. Baltimore, 1979.

*WHYTE, D. *Dictionary of Scottish Emigrants to the U.S.A.* Edinburgh, 1972.

Directory of Canadian Records and Manuscript Repositories. Ottawa, 1977.

*NOTE: While these books refer to emigrants to the United States, many of the emigrants who landed at New York or Philadelphia or other east-coast ports continued on to Canada.

5. THE ATLANTIC PROVINCES

NEW BRUNSWICK

FELLOWES, ROBERT E. *Researching Your Ancestors in New Brunswick.* Fredericton, 1979.

HANNAY, JAMES. *History of New Brunswick.* Saint John, 1909.

MAXWELL, LILIAN. *An Outline of the History of Central New Brunswick.* Sackville, 1937.

TAYLOR, HUGH. *New Brunswick History: A Checklist of Secondary Sources.* Fredericton, 1975.

WRIGHT, ESTHER. *The Loyalists of New Brunswick.* Fredericton, 1955.

NEWFOUNDLAND

DEVINE, P. K. *Notable Events in the History of Newfoundland.* St. John's, 1900.

GLOVER, R. S. *Bristol and America: A History of the First Settlers, 1654-1685.* Bristol, 1931.

HARVEY, M. *A Short History of Newfoundland.* London, 1890.

MATTHEWS, K. *Who Was Who in the Fishing Industry, 1660-1840.* St. John's, 1971.

PROWSE, D. W. *A History of Newfoundland.* St. John's, 1971.

NOVA SCOTIA

BELL, WINTHROP, *The Foreign Protestants and the Settlement of Nova Scotia.* Toronto, 1961.

DUNN, CHARLES. *Highland Settler.* Toronto, 1953.

GILROY, MARION. *Loyalists and Land Settlement in Nova Scotia.* Halifax, 1937.

HALIBURTON, T. *History of Nova Scotia.* 1829. Reprint ed., Belleville, Ont., 1973.

PUNCH, TERRENCE. *Genealogical Research in Nova Scotia.* Halifax, 1978.

RAWLYK, GEORGE. *Nova Scotia and Massachusetts, 1630-1784.* Montreal, 1973.

STARK, JAMES. *The Loyalists of Massachusetts.* Boston, 1907.

PRINCE EDWARD ISLAND

CALLBECK, LORNE. *The Cradle of Confederation.* Fredericton, 1964.

CAMPBELL, DUNCAN. *History of Prince Edward Island.* Charlottetown, 1875.

CLARK, ANDREW. *Three Centuries and the Island.* Toronto, 1959.

GREENHILL, BASIL. *Westcountrymen in Prince Edward's Isle.* Toronto, 1967.

STEWART, JOHN. *Canada's Smallest Province.* Charlottetown, 1973.

WARBURTON, A. *A History of Prince Edward Island.* Saint John, 1923.

ACADIA

ARSENAULT, BONA. *Histoire et généalogie des Acadiens.* Québec, 1965.

BERNARD, ANTOINE. *Histoire de la survivance acadienne.* Montréal, 1935.

BLANCHARD, HENRI. *Histoire des Acadiens de l'Île du Prince-Edouard.* Moncton, 1927.

DOUGHTY, SIR ARTHUR. *The Acadian Exiles.* Toronto, 1920.

GAUDET, PLACIDE. *Acadian Genealogy and Notes.* Ottawa, 1906.

GRIFFITHS, NAOMI. *The Acadians: Creation of a People.* Toronto, 1973.

LAUVRIÈRE, ÉMILE. *La Tragédie d'un peuple.* Paris, 1924.

LEBLANC, EMERY. *Les Acadiens.* Montréal, 1963.

MARTIN, ERNEST. *Les Exilés acadiens en France au XVIII siècle et leur établissement au Poitou.* Paris, 1936.

RIEDER, MILTON. *The Acadiens in France, 1762-1776.* Metairie, La., 1967.

———. *The Crew and Passenger Lists of the Seven Acadian Expeditions of 1785.* Metairie, La., 1967. (Emigration from France to Louisiana.)

SAWTELL, W. O. "Acadia: The Pre-Loyalist Migration and the Philadelphia Plantation", *Pennsylvania Magazine*, 1927.

Inventaire général des sources documentaires sur les Acadiens. Moncton, 1975.

6. QUEBEC

DIONNE, N.-E. *Canadiens français: les origines des familles émigrées de France, d'Espagne, et de Suisse.* Québec, 1914.

ÉLOI-GÉRARD, FRÈRE. *Recueil de généalogies des comtés de Vauce-Dorchester-Frontenac.* 1948.

GINGRAS, RAYMOND. *Précis du généalogiste amateur.* Québec, 1973.

GRÉGOIRE, JEANNE. *À la recherche de nos ancêtres.* Montréal, 1957.

HUBBARD, B. F. *Stanstead County, Quebec.* Montreal, 1874.

JETTÉ, RENÉ. *Dictionnaire généalogique des familles du Québec.* Montréal, 1983.

LE BOEUF, J. A. *Complément au dictionnaire généalogique Tanguay.* 3 vols. Montréal, 1957-64.

MENNIE DE VARENNES, KATHLEEN. *Bibliographie annotée d'ouvrages généalogiques à la Bibliothèque de Parlement.* Ottawa, 1963.

MONTMESNIL, J. V. "Index des actes de mariage passés devant les notaires royaux du district de Montréal, 1674-1850." Ottawa, 1943.

(This is a typescript in the Archives Deschâtelets, Université Saint-Paul, 223 rue Main, Ottawa, Ontario K1S 1C4.)

POULIN, J.-P. *Premiers colons du début de la colonie, jusqu'en 1700.* Montréal, 1960.

ROY, ANTOINE. *Bibliographie de généalogies et histoires de famille.* Montréal, 1940.

_____. *Nos ancêtres au XVII siècle.* Québec, 1943.

ROY, PIERRE-GEORGES. *Inventaire des contrats de mariages du régime français conservés aux Archives Judiciaires de Québec.* 6 vols. Beauceville, 1937-8.

_____. *Inventaire des testaments, donations, et inventaires du régime français conservés aux Archives Judiciaires de Québec.* 3 vols. Beauceville, 1941.

ROY, ANTOINE, et ROY, PIERRE-GEORGES. *Inventaire des greffes des notaires du régime français.* 21 vols. Beauceville, 1943-64.

TANGUAY, CYPRIEN. *Dictionnaire généalogique des familles canadiennes.* 7 vols. Montréal, 1871-90.

Dictionnaire National des Canadiens Français, 1680-1760. Montréal, 1958.

List of Lands Granted by the Crown in Quebec. Ottawa, 1891.

7. ONTARIO

Canada-German Folklore. Pennsylvania Folklore Society of Ontario. Kitchener, 1978.

CHADWICK, E. M. *Ontarian Families.* Toronto, 1894. Reprint ed., 1970.

FIRTH, EDITH G. *The Town of York, 1793-1815.* 2 vols. Toronto, 1962-6.

KEFFER, MARION, et al. *Some Ontario References and Sources for the Family Historian.* Toronto, 1978.

LAJEUNESSE, E. J. *The Windsor Border Region.* Toronto, 1960.

REID, WILLIAM D. *The Loyalists in Ontario.* Lambertville, N.J., 1973.

RUBINCAM, M. *The Old United Empire Loyalists List.* Toronto, 1885. Reprint ed., 1969.

Records of the Court of Common Pleas of Upper Canada, 1789-1794. 1918.

Ontario's Heritage: A Guide to Archival Resources, Vol. 1 (Peterborough Region). Cheltenham, Ont., 1978.

County Marriage Registers of Ontario, 1858-1869. Vols. 1 to 6. Agincourt, Ont.

1: *Peel County.* 1979.
2: *Ontario County.* 1979.
3: *Prince Edward County.* 1979.

4: *Huron County.* 1980.
5: *York County.* 1981.
6: *Hastings County.* 1981.

8. THE WESTERN PROVINCES

ALBERTA

BLUE, JOHN. *Alberta Past and Present.* Chicago, 1924.

LIDDELL, K. *This Is Alberta.* Toronto, 1952.

MACGREGOR, J. C. *A History of Alberta.* Edmonton, 1972.

MACRAE, ARCHIBALD. *History of the Province of Alberta.* Calgary, 1912.

RICKER, M. B. *Alberta.* Toronto, 1949.

BRITISH COLUMBIA

BANCROFT, HUBERT. *History of British Columbia.* San Raphael, Cal., 1888. Reprint ed., 1967.

BEGG, A. *A History of British Columbia.* Toronto, 1894. Reprint ed., 1972.

GRIFFIN, HAROLD. *British Columbia: The People's Early Story.* Vancouver, 1958.

JOHNSON, P. M. *Canada's Pacific Province.* Toronto, 1966.

ORMSBY, MARGARET A. *British Columbia: A History.* Toronto, 1958.

PETHICK, DEREK. *British Columbia Recalled, 1741-1871.* Saanich, B.C., 1974.

MANITOBA

BRYCE, GEORGE. *A History of Manitoba.* Toronto, 1906.

HEALY, W. J. *Winnipeg's Early Days.* Winnipeg, 1927.

JACKSON, J. A. *The Centennial History of Manitoba.* Toronto, 1970.

MORTON, W. L. *Manitoba: The Birth of a Province.* Altona, Man., 1965.

————. *Manitoba: A History.* Toronto, 1957.

PATERSON, E. *Tales of Early Manitoba.* Winnipeg, 1970.

Henderson's Directory of Manitoba. Winnipeg, 1880.

Pioneers and Early Citizens of Manitoba. Winnipeg, 1971.

Pioneers and Prominent People of Manitoba. Winnipeg, 1925.

SASKATCHEWAN

BLACK, N. F. *History of Saskatchewan.* Regina, 1913.

FOWLER, CHARLES. *The Fowler Tree.* Regina, 1973.

HAWKES, J. *The Story of Saskatchewan.* Chicago, 1924.

REMPEL, D. D. *Family Chronicle.* Saskatoon, 1973. (Mennonite migration.)

WRIGHT, J. *Saskatchewan.* Toronto, 1955.

9. ENGLAND AND WALES

BARBER, HENRY. *Family Names.* Baltimore, 1968.

BARDSLEY, CHARLES. *English Ancestral Names.* Baltimore, 1968.

BARING-GOULD, S. *Family Names*. Baltimore, 1968.

BRIDGER, CHARLES. *An Index to Printed Pedigrees*. Baltimore, 1969.

CAMP, ANTHONY. *Tracing Your Ancestors*. London, 1971.

————. *Wills and Their Whereabouts*. London, 1974.

ELLIS, HENRY. *The Domesday Book*. Baltimore, 1968.

EWEN, CECIL. *Surnames of the British Isles*. Baltimore, 1968.

FAIRBAIRN, JAMES. *Crests of the Families of Britain*. London, 1905.

FOX-DAVIES, A. C. *Complete Guide to Heraldry*. London, 1969.

GIBSON, J. S. W. *Wills and Where to Find Them*. Chichester, 1974.

GUPPY, HENRY B. *Family Names in Great Britain*. Baltimore, 1968.

HAMILTON-EDWARDS, GERALD. *In Search of Ancestry*. Baltimore, 1974.

————. *In Search of Army Ancestry*. Chichester, 1977.

HARRIS, R. W. *England in the Eighteenth Century*. London, 1963.

HECTOR, L. C. *Handwriting of English Documents*. London, 1966.

KAMINOW, MARION. *Genealogical MSS in British Libraries*. Baltimore, 1967.

KITCHING, F., and KITCHING, S. *English Surnames in 1601 and 1602*. Baltimore, 1968.

MARSHALL, GEORGE W. *The Genealogist's Guide*. Baltimore, 1973.

PINE, L. G. *The Story of Surnames*. London, 1965.

REANEY, P. H. *British Surnames*. London, 1966.

RICHARDSON, J. *Local Historian's Encyclopedia*. New Barnet, 1974.

RYE, WALTER. *Records and Record Searching*. London, 1969.

SIMS, R. *Index to the Heralds' Visitations*. Baltimore, 1971.

————. *Pedigrees and Arms*. Baltimore, 1970.

SMITH, FRANK. *Genealogical Gazetteer (England)*. Baltimore, 1969.

UNETT, JOHN. *Making a Pedigree*. Baltimore, 1971.

WAGNER, SIR ANTHONY. *Heraldry in England*. London, 1946.

WHITMORE, J. *A Genealogical Guide*. London, 1953.

WILLIS, ARTHUR J. *Introducing Genealogy.* London, 1961.

Debrett's Peerage of England, Scotland, and Ireland. London, annual.

National Index of Parish Registers. London.
(This is a monumental work, sponsored by the Society of Genealogists, London, and when completed it will give the location of church registers throughout the United Kingdom.)

NOTE: The books listed above as published in Baltimore, Maryland, were reprinted by the Genealogical Publishing Company in the year shown. All were originally published in the United Kingdom and, in most cases, had been out of print for years.

Original Parish Registers in Record Offices and Libraries. Tawney House, Matlock, Derbyshire, 1974, 1976, 1978 (original issue and four supplements).

10. SCOTLAND

ADAM, FRANK. *Clans, Septs, and Regiments of the Scottish Highlands.* Edinburgh, 1908.

BLACK, G. F. *The Surnames of Scotland.* New York, 1965.

FERGUSON, JOAN. *Scottish Family Histories Held in Scottish Libraries.* Edinburgh, 1960.

————. *Scottish Newspapers in Scottish Libraries.* Edinburgh, 1965.

GRAHAM, H. G. *Social Life of Scotland in the Eighteenth Century.* London, 1937.

HAMILTON-EDWARDS, GERALD. *In Search of Scottish Ancestry.* Baltimore, 1972.

HEWISON, J. K. *The Covenanters.* Glasgow, 1908.

INNES, SIR THOMAS. *Scots Heraldry.* Baltimore, 1971.

————. *The Tartans of the Clans and Families of Scotland.* Edinburgh, 1964.

PLANT, MARJORIE. *Domestic Life of Scotland in the Eighteenth Century.* Edinburgh, 1952.

SMITH, FRANK. *Genealogical Gazetteer of Scotland.* Logan, 1971.

SMOUT, T. C. *A History of the Scottish People.* London, 1972.

Scottish Sources. National Index of Parish Registers, vol. 12. London, 1975.

Statistical Account of Scotland. 1790.

> (This remarkable set of volumes is of little value genealogically, but once you know the town or village in which your ancestors lived, it will tell you more about how they lived than any other book I know.)

STUART, MARGARET. *Scottish Family History.* Baltimore, 1978.

WHYTE, DONALD. *Introduction to Scottish Genealogical Research.* Edinburgh, 1979.

11. EIRE, NORTHERN IRELAND, THE CHANNEL ISLANDS, AND THE ISLE OF MAN

BERRY, H. F. *Registers of Wills, Dublin, 1475-1483.* Dublin, 1898.

BOLTON, CHARLES. *Scots-Irish Pioneers in Ulster and America.* 1967.

BREFFNEY, BRIAN DE. *Bibliography of Irish Family History.* Dublin, 1973.

CLARE, WALLACE. *Irish Wills.* Baltimore, 1972.

CRISP, F. A., and HOWARD, JOSEPH. *Visitation of Ireland.* Baltimore, 1973.

EUSTACE, B. *Irish Quaker Records.* Dublin, 1957.
———. *Registry of Deeds* (Wills). Dublin, 1956.

FALLEY, MARGARET. *Ancestral Research.* Evanston, Ill., 1961.

FARRAR, HENRY. *Irish Marriages (Index), 1771-1812.* Baltimore, 1972.

GARDNER; HARLAND; AND SMITH. *Genealogical Atlas of Ireland.* Salt Lake City, 1964.

HACKETT, D., and EARLY, C. M. *Passenger Lists from Ireland.* Baltimore, 1972.

HARRISON, J. *The Scot in Ulster.* London, 1888.

HERALDIC ARTISTS LTD. *How to Trace Your Ancestors in Ireland.* Dublin, 1978.

HILL, G. *The Plantation of Ulster.* London, 1877.

MACLYSAGHT, E. *Irish Families, Their Names, Arms, and Origins.* New York, 1970.

———. *Surnames of Ireland.* Dublin, 1973.

MARSHALL, W. F. *Ulster Sails West.* Baltimore, 1979.

O'HART, JOHN. *Irish Pedigrees.* Baltimore, 1976.

PENDER, SEAMAS. *Guide to Irish Genealogical Collections.* Dublin, 1935.

PHILLIMORE, W., and THRIFT, G. *Indexes to Irish Wills, 1536-1857.* Baltimore, 1970.

ULSTER HISTORICAL FOUNDATION. *County Down Gravestone Inscriptions* Vols. I XVI. Belfast, 1975-1980.

———. *County Antrim Gravestone Inscriptions.* Vols. I and II. Belfast, 1980.

VICKERS, A. *Index to the Prerogative Wills of Ireland, 1536-1810.* Baltimore, 1967.

WOULFE, P. *Irish Names and Surnames.* Baltimore, 1969.

ISLE OF MAN

FELTHAM AND WRIGHT. *Monumental Inscriptions in the Isle of Man.* London, 1868.

MOORE, A. W. *Manx Names.* London, 1903.

CHANNEL ISLANDS

BALLEINE, G. R. *A Biographical Dictionary of Jersey.* London, 1948.

PAYNE, J. B. *An Armorial of Jersey.* London, 1859.

TURK, M. G. *The Quiet Adventurers in Canada.* Detroit, 1979.

12. THE UNITED STATES

BAILEY, F. *Early Massachusetts Marriages Prior to 1800.* Boston, 1897.

BANKS, C. E. *English Ancestry of the Pilgrim Fathers.* Reprint. Baltimore, 1980.

BARDSLEY, C. W. *Dictionary of English and Welsh Surnames.* Reprint. Baltimore, 1980.

BLEGEN, T. *Norwegian Migration to America.* 1931.

BOLTON, ETHEL. *Immigrants to New England, 1700-1775.* Salem, Mass., 1931.

BOWEN, RICHARD. *Massachusetts Record.* Rehoboth, Mass., 1957.

BROMWELL, H. *Old Maryland Families.* 1916.

BROWNING, C. *Welsh Settlement of Pennsylvania.* 1912.

FILBY, P. W., and MEYER, M. K. *Passenger and Immigration Lists Index.* Detroit, 1980.

FORD, HENRY. *The Scotch-Irish in America.* Princeton, 1915.

GLENN, THOMAS. *Welsh Founders of Pennsylvania.* Baltimore, 1970.

HOCKER, E. W. *Genealogical Data Relating to German Settlers in Pennsylvania, 1743-1800.* Baltimore, 1980.

KNITTLE, W. A. *Early 18th Century Palatine Emigration.* Baltimore, 1979.

LANCOUR, A. H. *Passenger Lists of Ships Coming to North America, 1607-1825.* New York, 1946.

LOUHI, EVERT. *The Delaware Finns.* New York, 1925.

PETERSON, STEWART. *Bibliography of County Histories of the 3,111 Counties in the 48 States.* New York, 1946.

SARGENT, W. M. *Maine Wills, 1640-1760.* Portland, Me., 1887.

STAUDT, R. W. *Palatine Church Visitations, 1609.* Baltimore, 1979.

STEVENSON, NOEL. *Search and Research.* Salt Lake City, 1959.
(Buy or borrow this book — it is an excellent source of information about United States records in the various states.)

TEPPER, M. *Emigrants to Pennsylvania, 1641-1819.* Baltimore, 1978.

Guide to Genealogical Records in the National Archives. Washington, 1964.

Handbook of American Genealogy. Washington, 1975.

NOTE: There are many useful books available in the United States for those with ancestors from that country. In many cases the books provide a great deal of information, right down to the township and village level. The books listed are just a representative sample. I suggest you write to three genealogical publishers for their latest list of books:

Gale Research Co.,
Book Tower,
Detroit, Mich. 48226.

Genealogical Publishing Co., Inc.,
111 Water Street,
Baltimore, Maryland 21202.

Goodspeed's Book Shop, Inc.,
18 Beacon Street,
Boston, Massachusetts 02108.

They both have early and out-of-print books as well as modern reprints of the most popular of these.

The National Genealogical Society, Washington, has many publications of value to the ancestor-hunter.

13 to 16. EUROPE AND OTHER COUNTRIES

GERMANY

HENNING AND RIBBE. *Handbuch des Genealogie*. Neustadt, 1972.

HOVEL, R, *Mitgliederverzeichnis 1974 der DAGV.* Stuttgart, 1974.

HUNGARY

KEMPELEN, BELA. *Magyar forangu csaladok*. Budapest, 1931.

ICELAND

THORGEISSON, OLAFUR. *Almanach Fyrir*. Reykjavik, 1895.

NETHERLANDS

VAN RESANDT, W. *Searching for Your Ancestors in the Netherlands*. The Hague, 1973.

———. *Wenken en Adressen voor Genealogisch Onderzoek in het Buitenland*. The Hague, 1973.

SOUTH AFRICA

DE VILLIERS, C. G. *Geslagsregisters van die ou Kaapse Families*. Cape Town, 1966.

HOGE, J. *Personalia of the Germans at the Cape*. Cape Town, 1946.

LOMBARD, R. T. J. *Genealogical Research in South Africa*. Published by the Human Sciences Research Council. Pretoria, 1979.

MALHERBE, D. F. *Stamregister van die Suid-Afrikaanse Volk (Family Register of the South African Nation)*. Stellenbosch, 1966.

PAMA, C. *Heraldry of South African Families*. Cape Town, 1965.

ROSENTHAL, ERIC. *South African Surnames*. Cape Town, 1965.

SWEDEN

FURTENBACH, BORJE. *Slaktforskning for alla*. Stockholm, 1971.

HILDEBRAND, BENGT. *Hand bok i slakt-och personforskning*. Stockholm, 1961.

JOHANSSEN, CARL-ERIK. *Cradled in Sweden.* Salt Lake City, 1972.

SWITZERLAND

Familiennamen-Buch des Schweiz. Zurich, 1968.

17. JEWISH RECORDS

BELKIN, SIMON. *Through Narrow Gates.* Montreal, 1966. (Jewish immigration to Canada, 1840-1940.)

CHIEL, A. *The Jews in Manitoba.* Toronto, 1975.

FEINGOLD, H. L. *Zion in America.* Boston, 1979.

FISHMAN, PHYLLIS. *The Jews of the United States.* New York, 1973.

GOTTESMAN, A. *Who's Who in Canadian Jewry.* Montreal, 1965.

HART, ARTHUR D. *The Jew in Canada.* Toronto, 1926.

HOWE, IRVING. *World of Our Fathers.* New York, 1976.

HYAMSON, ALBERT M. *The Sephardim of England.* London, 1951.

KAGANOFF, BENZION. *A Dictionary of Jewish Names.* 1977.

KEMPELEN, BELA. *Magyarorszagi zsido es zsido eredetu csaladok. (Jewish Families and Families of Jewish Origin).* Budapest, 1937.

KRANZLER, DAVID. *My Jewish Roots.* New York, 1979.

ROSENSTEIN, NEIL. *The Unbroken Chain.* New York, 1976.

ROTH, CECIL. *A History of the Jews in England.* London, 1951.

ROTTENBERG, DAN. *Finding Our Fathers.* New York, 1977.

STEARNS. *Genealogies of Early American Jewish Families.*

STERN, MALCOLM H. *Americans of Jewish Descent.* Cincinnati, 1960.

———. *First American Jewish Families.* New York, 1978.

Bevis Marks Records: Sephardic Marriage Registers, 1837-1901. London, 1973.
(Fewer than one-third of the Jews at present in England are of British descent.)

Genealogical Research. (Volume 2 of this work, published by the American Society of Genealogists, contains a chapter on Jewish migrations and lists several sources of information.)

Jews in American Life. (Published by the American Jewish Committee, this work contains a section on "Tracing Your Jewish Ancestors".)

FOREIGN LIBRARIES

ENGLAND

Guildhall Library, King Street, London EC2.
Society of Genealogists, 37 Harrington Gardens, London SW7 4JX.
British Library, London.

WALES

The National Library of Wales, Aberystwyth.

SCOTLAND

The Scottish Genealogy Society, 21 Howard Place, Edinburgh.
The National Library of Scotland, George IV Bridge, Edinburgh.
The Scottish Central Library, Lawnmarket, Edinburgh.
The Mitchell Library, North Street, Glasgow.

NORTHERN IRELAND

The Central Library, Royal Avenue, Belfast.

EIRE

The Genealogical Office, Dublin Castle.
The Trinity College Library, Dublin.
The National Library, Dublin.

UNITED STATES

The Library of Congress
(State Libraries are shown in Chapter 12).

AUSTRALIA

Commonwealth National Library, Canberra.

AUSTRIA

Österreichische Nationalbibliothek, Vienna.

BULGARIA

Vassil Kolarov, Boulevard Tolbukhin, Sofia.

FRANCE

Direction de Bibliothèques de France, 55 rue St. Dominique, Paris.

GREECE

National Library, Athens.

HUNGARY

Magyar Orszagos Levéltar Konyvtara, Budapest.

ICELAND

Landsbokasafn Islands, Reykjavik.

IRAN

National Library of Iran, Tehran.

ITALY

Biblioteca Nazionale Centrale, Rome.

KOREA

Historical Society of Korea, 134 Sinchon-dong, Serdaemun-gu, Seoul.

LUXEMBOURG

Bibliothèque Nationale, Luxembourg.

MEXICO

Biblioteca Nacional, Mexico City.

NETHERLANDS

Centraal Bureau voor Genealogie, Nassaulaan 18, The Hague.

NORWAY

Universitetsbiblioteket, Oslo.

POLAND

Biblioteka Narodowa, Warsaw.

PORTUGAL

Biblioteca Nacional, Lisbon.

SPAIN

Biblioteca Nacional, Madrid.

SWITZERLAND

Bibliothèque Nationale Suisse, Berne.

SYRIA

Al Maktabah Al Zahiriah, Damascus.

TUNISIA

Bibliothèque Nationale de Tunisie, Tunis.

TURKEY

Milli Kutuphane, Ankara.

U.S.S.R.

State Historical Library, Moscow.

YUGOSLAVIA

Narodna Biblioteka, Belgrade.

INDEX

Jersey, 177, 178
Jewish records, 263-5
Jordan, 255-6

Latvia, 230
Lebanon, 256
Liechtenstein, 237
Lithuania, 230
Louisiana Church
   Registers (Acadian),
   79
Lutheran Church,
   29-30
Luxembourg, 237-8

McMaster Divinity
   College, Hamilton,
   27-8
Malta, 238-9
Manitoba, 117-20
Maritime Baptist
   Historical
   Collection, 28
Mennonite Church,
   30-2, 104
Mennonite
   Genealogical
   Institute, 32
Mennonite Library
   and Archives, 32
Methodist Church, 19,
   41, 104
Mormon Church, 141
Mormon Church
   Records, 84, 283-4

Netherlands, 239-43
New Brunswick, 47-58
New Register House,
   Scotland, 157
New Zealand, 256-8
Newfoundland, 58-61

Northern Ireland,
   172-7
Norway, 215-19
Nova Scotia, 62-70

Ontario, 95-109
Ontario Genealogical
   Society, 97

Pakistan, 258-9
Poland, 243-4
Portugal, 244-5
Presbyterian Church,
   19, 32-3, 41-2, 104
Prince Edward Island,
   70-6
Provincial Archives.
   *See under each
   province*
Public Archives of
   Canada, 4-7
Public Record Office,
   England and Wales,
   134-5
Public Record Office,
   Ulster, 175-6

Quakers (Society of
   Friends), 40-1
Québec, 81-94
Quebec genealogical
   societies, 85

Regnal Years, U.K.,
   126-7
Roman Catholic
   Church, 33-40

St Catherine's House
   (General Register
   Office), 129
Saskatchewan, 120-4

Saskatchewan
   Genealogical
   Society, 122
Scandinavia, 211-23
Scotland, 156-71
Scottish Record
   Office, 164
Society of Friends
   (Quakers), 40-1
Society of
   Genealogists, U.K.,
   151-3
Somerset House. *See*
   St. Catherine's
   House
South Africa, 259-62
Spain, 245-6
Sweden, 220-3
Switzerland, 246-9

Telephone directories,
   86, 97
Tithes, 144
Tunkers, The, 30

Ukrainian Catholics,
   35
Ulster. *See* Northern
   Ireland
Ulster Historical
   Foundation, 177
United Church, 19,
   41-2, 104
United Empire
   Loyalists, 97-8
United Presbyterian
   Church, 104
United States, 181-202

Wales, 129-55